Woman

THE GLORY OF MAN

KRISTEN M. DUGAS

WOMAN THE GLORY OF MAN by Kristen M. Dugas
www.womanthegloryofman.com

Published by Paradise Creative Group
12801 Commerce Lakes Dr. #26
Fort Myers, FL 33913
www.paradisecreativegroup.com

Unless otherwise noted, Scripture quotations in this book are
taken from the New American Standard Bible ®, Copyright
© 1960, 1962 ,1963, 1968, 1971, 1972, 1973, 1975, 1977,
1995 by The Lockman Foundation. Used by permission.

Scripture verses marked NIV are taken from the Holy Bible,
New International Version. Copyright © 1973, 1978, 1984,
International Bible Society. Used by permission.

Scripture verses marked NKJV are taken from the New King
James Version. Copyright © 1979, 1980, 1982 by Thomas
Nelson, Inc. Used by permission. All rights reserved.

Scripture verses marked KJV-NIV are taken from the Greek portion
of the Interlinear KJV-NIV Parallel New Testament In Greek And
English. Copyright © 1975 by The Zondervan Corporation.

Scripture verses surrounded by ** are translations of the
author. Scripture verses at the end of each chapter are
translations of the author. Scripture verses in the Scripture
Translations chapter are translations of the author.

Library of Congress Control Number: 2021901388
International Standard Book Number: 978-0-578-83692-8
Printed in the United States of America.

Contents

Preface

When I was in my late twenties, I took a class at McLean Bible Church in McLean, Virginia. The class was for one day and was titled "How to Share Your Faith with Others." I don't remember much about the dialogue, except for one thing. As the instructor was teaching, he suddenly started telling us that the word for "submit" in the Bible was a Greek military term and meant to arrange troops in a military fashion under their leader. He then went on to say that the Bible uses this word when it says that wives are to submit to their husbands. I thought to myself, "Why did he bring this up? What does this have to do with sharing your faith with others?" As I was thinking this, a woman who seemed to be approximately ten years older than me spoke up and said, "I don't believe that, I'm sorry, I just don't believe that." She said it with such sternness that it silenced the instructor and left a silent awkwardness in the room. I remember thinking, "I agree with you." And I wanted very badly to agree with her right there in that room. But the only thing that prevented me was the fact that the Bible says that wives are to submit to their husbands in everything. I knew that I couldn't speak up if I couldn't defend what I said. I needed to be able to say why.

Years later, in about my mid-thirties, I participated in a week-long Jews for Jesus campaign. I had previously been a financial supporter of Jews for Jesus, but now I wanted to go out on the street to tell Jews and Gentiles about Christ. One of the memories that stuck with me during the campaign was a discussion that I had with one of the participants. I don't remember what started it, but he said that although he believed a woman could go out on the street to teach men, he adamantly believed that women could not teach men in a church setting. I thought this was ludicrous thinking, but again, I could not disprove his statements because the Bible does say that women cannot teach men.

It was examples like these that happened throughout my life that prompted me to search the Scriptures and understand what God's truth really was. I knew that to defend myself and other women that I couldn't just say, "I disagree with you," but that I had to back up my beliefs with sound doctrine. I certainly did not agree with complementarians, but I also did not agree with a lot of what egalitarians said either. So, I began searching for answers to my questions, praying to God and seeking His counsel, always asking Him to show me the truth. I knew that I would have the truth only when every contradiction to Scripture disappeared.

I estimate that I have spent more than eleven thousand hours doing research for this book, which includes reading books and online commentaries, studying Scripture, comparing Scripture with Scripture, and studying the Greek. Over the course of eight years, in constant prayer and study, I wrote and rewrote, checked and cross-checked my findings, until every inconsistency and discrepancy vanished in the passages I present in this book. I want to acknowledge and thank the men and women who had previously gone before me who searched and studied the Scriptures and imparted their knowledge to me through their writings. They were instrumental in helping me understand that Bible translations are full of errors on passages having to do with women, in both the Old and New Testaments.

Introduction

Within the church today, there are differing opinions on the roles of women. These opposing views are due to specific passages of Scripture that appear to limit women. But is it any coincidence that the passages regarding women consistently seem to be hard to understand? And why is it that they contradict so much of Scripture? Indeed, the passages regarding women all have the same problem. They are incoherent, nonsensical, and inconsistent with Scripture, yet they are justified repeatedly by many with their own biased opinions and faulty interpretations of Scripture.

But the truth of the matter is that many of the passages regarding women are disgraceful mistranslations. Yet, translator after translator continues to print and reprint these distortions in our Bibles. People interpret these passages a million times over trying to make sense of them, but the reason they do not make sense is that there is no truth in them. Unequivocally, they are lies. The translators have distorted God's Word to fit their own traditional way of thinking, and this is why the passages regarding women contradict Scripture throughout. And no matter how many times we try to reinterpret the passages about women, they will always be confusing and will always contradict Scripture until they are correctly translated from God's Word.

There is no doubt that men have woven a web of lies throughout Scripture regarding God's beloved daughters. But thankfully, God has safeguarded His Word from the manipulations of men. He has preserved for us a great abundance of evidence so that we may know the truth.

The Woman Who Stood Alone

There is a story in the Bible about a woman. And this woman was a sinner—for she was caught in adultery, in the very act. She was brought alone to the center of the court. The self-righteous ones had set her there. Jesus was there teaching the many who had gathered. There was a hush among the crowd. The woman stood alone. She looked down at the ground, ashamed before the crowd. Her heart was racing. She was trembling. The crowd looked on to see what would happen. The self-righteous ones had encircled her. The men had stones in hand. They were ready to stone her to her very death. But where was the man? Did they let him go free? For he was nowhere to be found. His sin did not matter to the men, for it was only the sin of the woman that they focused on. They called out to Jesus. Their haughty arrogance filled the air. "Moses commanded us to stone such women," they chanted. But Jesus stooped down and with His finger wrote on the ground. What did our Lord write, we wonder? But the men persisted. They wanted an answer. Would Jesus break the Law of Moses they hoped? Then came His words, the words that struck them to the very core. "He who is without sin among you, let him be the first to throw a stone at her." One by one, the men left. No one could condemn her. Her accusers could not call her to account. Jesus had brought their sin to the forefront. Their own sin was staring them in the face. They left. All of them—they left. They did not leave because of a sudden sense of pity. Nor did they feel empathy for this woman. The reason they did not stone her was that they could not stone her—for they too were sinners. These men did not grasp their own sin until that very moment. But the reality that they too were sinners had suddenly set in. The men were gone. The woman was left alone with the One who had redeemed her. He spoke in a gentle and loving voice, "Woman, where are they? Did no one condemn you?" "No one, Lord," she said. "Then neither do I condemn you," Jesus said.

Today it is not the scribes and Pharisees who accuse, but nonetheless, it is the self-righteous ones—and they come in the name of Christ! They stand in our pulpits. They attend our churches. They are on Christian radio. They are armed with pen and paper. And they too have stones in hand. Among them are murderers, rapists, adulterers, fornicators, coveters, child abusers, drug users, liars, cheaters, thieves, haters, slanderers, and porn users. They are all sinners, yet they surround the women. But who are they? They are our very own brothers in Christ. They point, accuse, and blame, yet they ignore their own sin. They let themselves go free. They confidently assert that their shameful sins have been freely forgiven by the blood of Christ—for they all may teach God's Word no matter how wretched their sin. "But a woman, she may not teach," they chant. She is never truly forgiven—forever to be cursed. She must be silent. The sin of Eve remains on her.

But there is good news for women! Just as Jesus did not condemn the woman who stood alone, neither does He condemn His daughters. He has fully forgiven us. He has redeemed us. Through His blood, He has set us free. Christ's love for us is immense. It is immeasurable, limitless, and infinite. The Lord gives the command—the women who proclaim the good tidings are a great host. Daughters of the Most High God, go out for Christ. Do not fear, for He is with you. Stand up for Christ. Stand firm for Him, and do not be afraid. Tell others of the hope that is in you. Do not listen to the lies of men. Teach all in the name of Christ. Teach men in the name of Christ. Speak from the pulpit, speak on the street corner; speak at home, or abroad to all who will listen. Ladies, follow the calling God has placed on your heart and let he who is without sin cast the first stone.

1

WHO SINNED FIRST—ADAM OR EVE?

Who sinned first, Adam or Eve? If you ask people in the church today, you will find that most people believe that Eve sinned first. And they believe this for two reasons. First, it was Eve who ate of the fruit first. And secondly, it is universally taught that Eve sinned first but that Adam only incurred the blame because he was the "head." Now, Scripture does tell us that Eve ate the fruit first. However, the teaching that Eve sinned first but that Adam only incurred the blame because he was the "head" is found nowhere in Scripture. Therefore, in this chapter, we will examine what Scripture has to say on this most crucial question. Whether it is Eve or Adam, let us accept the clear Word of God.

So, who sinned first, Adam or Eve?

To answer this question, we need to turn to Scripture.

[12]"Therefore, just as through one man sin entered into the world, and death through sin, and so death spread to all men, because all sinned—[13]for until the Law sin was in the world, but sin is not imputed when there is no law. [14]Nevertheless death reigned from Adam until Moses, even over those who had not sinned in the likeness of the offense of Adam, who is a type of Him who was to come" (Rom. 5:12–14).

[18]"So then as through one transgression there resulted condemnation to all men, even so through one act of righteousness there resulted justification of life to all men. [19]For as through the one man's disobedience the many were made sinners, even so through the obedience of the One the many will be made righteous" (Rom. 5:18–19).

[20]"But now Christ has been raised from the dead, the first fruits of those who are asleep. [21]For since by a man *came* death, by a man also *came* the resurrection of the dead. [22]For as in Adam all die, so also in Christ all will be made alive" (1 Cor. 15:20–22).

Furthermore, in Genesis 3:17, God says to Adam, [17]"...Cursed is the ground because of you...." The word that is translated as "ground" in verse seventeen is "adama" in Hebrew and means "earth, the entire surface of the place where humans dwell."[1]

In the previous passages, there is no mistaking that the person in view is Adam because he is mentioned specifically by name. Accordingly, from the previous passages of Scripture, we can see that sin entered into the world through one man, Adam. And if sin entered into the world through Adam, this means that sin was not in the world before Adam sinned. Therefore, it is evident through plain Scripture that Adam sinned first, not Eve. Furthermore, this Scripture states that it was because of Adam's transgression that condemnation resulted to "all" people. This would include Eve. Condemnation resulted to Eve because of Adam's transgression. This Scripture also states that because of Adam's disobedience, the "many" were made sinners. This would include Eve. Eve was made a sinner because of the disobedience of her husband. Moreover, it is stated that as a result of Adam's sin, the earth is cursed and death has spread to all people. It is because of Adam that we die.

So nowhere in the previous passages of Scripture does it say that sin entered into the world through Eve. Nowhere in these passages does it say that because of Eve's transgression, that condemnation resulted to all people. Nor does it say that because of her disobedience that her husband or anyone else was made a sinner. Nor does it say that the earth is cursed because of her or that all people die because of her. Furthermore, nowhere in the previous passages of Scripture does it say that sin entered into the world through "two" people. Nor does it say that because of "two" transgressions, that condemnation resulted to all people. Nor does it say that because of "two" people's disobedience, the many were made sinners. Nor does it say that the earth is cursed because of Adam and Eve. Nor does it say that we die because of Adam and Eve. Again, the Bible clearly states that sin entered into the world through "one" man, Adam. Because of "one" transgression, condemnation resulted to all people. Because of "one" man's disobedience, the many were made sinners. The earth is cursed because of Adam only. And we all die because of Adam only.

So it was Adam, and Adam alone, who caused "the Fall." Adam was not made a sinner because of the disobedience of his wife, as is widely taught. But instead, Eve was made a sinner because of the disobedience of her husband. This is what Scripture clearly teaches. Therefore, it should not be taught that Eve sinned first because to do so is to completely twist what Scripture says on the matter. The teaching that Eve sinned first but that Adam only incurred the blame because he was the "head" is a false doctrine as it is not found in the previous passages or anywhere in Scripture. Therefore, since the Bible is abundantly clear that sin entered into the world through Adam, I suggest that we actually take Scripture at its word and try to understand then just how it was that sin entered into the world through Adam. And this is what we will now do. In the following segment, we will journey to see exactly how sin entered into the world through Adam, how his disobedience caused Eve to become a sinner, and will unravel the lies that have been taught for centuries.

The Bible states that God formed Adam from the dust of the ground and then put him in the Garden of Eden to cultivate it and keep it. And as He put Adam there, He commanded the man, saying, [16]"...From any tree of the garden you may eat freely; [17]but from the tree of the knowledge of good and evil you shall not eat, for in the day that you eat from it you will surely die" (Gen. 2:16–17). However, when God formed Eve and brought her to the man, the Bible does not give any reference that He had told her about the forbidden fruit. It appears that she heard about the command from Adam because of the way that God questions each of them after they ate. To Adam, He said, [11]"...Have you eaten from the tree of which I commanded you not to eat?" (Gen. 3:11). But to Eve, He said, [13]"...What is this you have done?..." (Gen. 3:13).

Since the evidence in Scripture shows us that Adam gave the command to Eve, we now need to see whether Adam gave the command to Eve correctly, or whether he gave it to her incorrectly. Let us take a look. In Genesis 3:2–3, when Eve replies to the questioning of Satan, she says, [2]"...From the fruit of the trees of the garden we may eat; [3]but from the fruit of the tree which is in the middle of the garden, God has said, 'You shall not eat from it or touch it, or you will die.'" Now, in beginning here, I would like to say that it is clear from Scripture that Adam and Eve were

3

in view of the tree when Satan tempted them. Therefore, the fact that Eve referred to the tree of the knowledge of good and evil (KGE) as "the tree which is in the middle of the garden" when she was standing directly in front of it shows us unequivocally that Eve did not know which tree was the tree of the KGE. If she did know, then she would have pointed to the tree and stated something like, "From the fruit of the trees of the garden we may eat; but from the fruit of this tree, the tree of the knowledge of good and evil, God has said, 'You shall not eat from it or touch it, or you will die.'" It is illogical to think that Eve would give a non-specific answer while directly in front of the tree, all the while knowing that it was the tree of the KGE. Even if Eve had forgotten the name of the tree, she still could have pointed to it because of her proximity to the tree. Clearly, her answer is indicative of someone who does not know which tree is the tree of the KGE. Therefore, it is clear that Eve is not bungling the command of God in Genesis 3:2–3, as is commonly taught, but rather, that she is repeating the command of God "verbatim" the way she received it from Adam. Adam neither gave her the name of the tree nor did he previously take her to the tree so that she could identify its fruit.

I also want to add that the fact that Eve did not recognize the tree shows us that Adam and Eve were not created with an innate knowledge of which tree was the tree of the KGE. They had to be taught, just as we have to be taught, which is an apple tree or an orange tree. Therefore, it is clear that God told Adam not to eat from the tree of the KGE while standing directly in front of it and pointing to it. Otherwise, Adam would have had to guess which of the many vast trees was the tree of the KGE because, if we notice, God said nothing about "the tree which is in the middle of the garden" when he spoke to Adam. This was Adam's analogy when giving it to Eve. Therefore, it is clear that God had taken Adam to the tree, which is why he knew it was the tree in the middle of the garden.

Furthermore, it is obvious why Adam did not give Eve the name of the tree, and that is, they were not in view of the tree when he told her about the command. In his mind, giving her the name would not have done any good until she was at the tree and could associate its name with its fruit. Therefore, since he was not close enough to point to the exact tree, he stated its location instead. However, as we will see a little later, giving her the name would have helped.

4

It is easy to see why Adam did not give Eve the name of the tree. However, we must now ask the question, "Why did Adam add the words 'or touch it' to God's command?" Well, if we study Genesis 2:16–17, we will find that God did not give Adam a reason as to why he could not eat from the tree or a reason why he would die. He only told him that he could not eat from the tree of the knowledge of good and evil, or he would die in the day that he ate from it. Therefore, not knowing that God was speaking of spiritual death, I believe that Adam naturally assumed that the fruit was poisonous and therefore thought that God was warning him that he would die if he ate it. It was not until Satan spoke to Eve in Genesis 3:5 that Adam understood the reason he was not supposed to eat of it—he would be like God. Therefore, I believe that Adam had added the words "or touch it" to God's command as an extra precaution when he gave it to Eve because he wanted to make sure that nothing harmful would be absorbed through her skin. Furthermore, the fact that it was Adam who added the words "or touch it" to God's command also explains why he did not correct Eve when she replied to the questioning of Satan. There would not have been a need for Adam to correct her since she replied exactly as he had told her.

To confirm that it was Adam who gave the command to Eve incorrectly, I would like to bring attention to what Paul says in 1 Timothy 2:14. And that is, [14]"And *it was* not Adam *who* was deceived, but the woman being deceived, fell into transgression." Now, we know that when Paul says that Adam was not deceived and that Eve was deceived, he is speaking about the incident that happened in the Garden of Eden. Furthermore, we can see that Paul is making a distinction between Adam and Eve as to why he was not deceived, and she was deceived. Therefore, we need to ask the question, "What is Paul referring to when he says that Adam was not deceived and that Eve was deceived?" Every clue in Genesis points to Adam giving the command to Eve incorrectly, which would naturally be the reason that Adam was not deceived and that Eve was deceived. But because men do not want to acknowledge what is apparent, and insist that Adam gave the command to Eve correctly, we then have to assert one of the following about 1 Timothy 2:14:

1) When Paul says that Adam was not deceived and that Eve was deceived, he is speaking in reference to the words of Satan in Genesis 3:4. Adam was not deceived into thinking that he would not die, and Eve was deceived into thinking that she would not die.

2) When Paul says that Adam was not deceived and that Eve was deceived, he is speaking in reference to the command regarding the tree. Adam was not deceived in regard to the tree because he remembered the information that God had given him, and Eve was deceived in regard to the tree because she could not remember the information that Adam had given her.

Now let us look at the first scenario.

If Paul is speaking in reference to the words of Satan in 1 Timothy 2:14, and he is saying that Adam was not deceived into thinking that he would not die and Eve was deceived into thinking that she would not die, then we could put Adam in the category of a complete idiot to knowingly eat from a fruit that would cause him death that very day. Remember, Adam had no knowledge that God was speaking of spiritual death, which would eventually lead to physical death. He thought that physical death would occur that very day. Therefore, he would not be able to be like God. Furthermore, for this scenario to be true, we would also have to believe that Adam knew that his wife, whom he loved, would also die that very day and that no benefit of any sort would be passed onto future generations since they did not have children. It is silly for anyone to argue for this scenario because no one in their right mind would take ten million dollars if they had to drink poison first because if they did, they would not be able to benefit from the money. And if no one today would do this, then it is clear that Adam would not have either.

Now let us look at the second scenario.

If Paul is speaking in reference to the command regarding the tree, and he is saying that Adam was not deceived because he could remember the information that God had given him and Eve was deceived because she could not remember the information that Adam had given her, then we could put Eve in the category of a complete idiot. Indeed, for this scenario to be true, we would have to believe that Eve, after previously being taken to the tree to view its fruit, could not recall which tree was the tree of the KGE. This is even more absurd when we consider the fact that there were only two trees in the middle of the garden (Gen. 2:9). It would mean that Eve could not differentiate between the two trees in the middle of the garden that were clearly separated out from the rest of the trees. However, it would be a total stretch to think that Eve did not cement this one tree in her mind, as it was the only tree that would cause them to die.

So, two completely ridiculous scenarios are what we have to deal with if Adam gave Eve God's command correctly. The scenarios are so ridiculous, in fact, that it would be nearly impossible today to find any man or woman to replicate them. But men would rather think of this passage in terms of sheer lunacy rather than acknowledge that it was Adam who gave Eve God's command incorrectly. Nevertheless, if we want to be honest with this passage and look at it in a logical fashion, the only plausible scenario is that Adam gave Eve misinformation about God's command, which caused her to be deceived. Therefore, in 1 Timothy 2:14, when Paul's says that Adam was not deceived and that Eve was deceived, he is not speaking in reference to Satan's words, but rather, he is speaking directly in relation to the information that each of them had about the command regarding the tree. Clearly, Adam was deceived in reference to Satan's words; else, he would not have eaten, nor let his wife eat, from the fruit.

I also want to say one more thing in relation to the previously stated comments before I move on. Men inappropriately apply to Eve what they should apply to Adam. Men say that Eve was given the command correctly (by Adam), and she knew which tree was forbidden. They then say that she willfully ate with full knowledge because she was deceived by Satan's words into thinking that she would not die because she wanted to be like God. However, this is exactly what happened with Adam. Adam was given the command correctly (by God), and he knew which tree was forbidden. Indeed, Adam willfully ate with full knowledge because he was deceived by Satan's words into thinking that he would not die because he wanted to be like God. Therefore, with this analogy, there is no distinction between Adam and Eve as to why she was deceived, and he was not deceived.

Since the evidence in Scripture clearly shows us that Adam gave Eve misinformation about God's command, we will now take a look at how this misinformation affected Eve and why she was not able to decipher the truth. In beginning here, I would like to say that it is evident that the misinformation given Eve is the reason that Satan addressed her in the garden instead of Adam. Satan knew that she had been given incorrect information about God's command and was easy prey, which brings me to another point. I do not believe that Satan was an actual snake, but that the term "serpent" was used of him metaphorically to describe that he lay-in-wait for his prey and was cunning and crafty in nature. In Revelation 12:7–9, we can also see that Satan is called a "dragon"; this too is used of him metaphorically. Furthermore, Scripture tells us that Satan walked the earth and stood upright (Job 1:7; Zech. 3:1). This would not be possible if he was an actual snake slithering around on his belly. Therefore, I believe that Satan looked human in appearance and appeared as a man to Adam and Eve in the garden. However, he had the characteristics of a serpent. Satan knew that Eve had been given misinformation about God's command and took full advantage of it. He lay-in-wait at the forbidden tree, and when Adam and Eve came near, he went in for the strike to the injured prey, Eve, before Adam had time to make clear to her the tree that God had forbidden.

We can also see evidence by the questioning of Satan to Eve in Genesis 3:1 that his misleading question would not have worked with Adam, the one who knew exactly which tree was forbidden by God. If Satan had asked Adam the same question, Adam would have pointed to the tree of the KGE and told Satan that they could eat from any tree of the garden except this tree. For Adam's heart at this point had not yet turned to sin, and he would have answered correctly. Eve, on the other hand, did not know which tree was the tree of the KGE, which is why she stated they could not eat or touch the fruit from "the tree which is in the middle of the garden." Furthermore, the fact that Eve did not defer to Adam at the questioning of Satan, or turn to him at any point for guidance, also shows us that Eve did not know that Adam knew which tree was the tree of the KGE. She did not know that God had taken him to the tree but thought that they were both to be on the look-out for the poisonous tree together. So the line of questioning that Satan used, along with the way that Eve responded to him, confirms that he went after Eve because she was easy prey.

Since it is clear that Satan went after Eve because of the misinformation given to her about the tree, we must now ask the question, "How did Satan deceive Eve by his craftiness?" (2 Cor. 11:3). It is commonly believed that Satan swayed Eve to eat the deadly fruit just by the mere words he stated to her in Genesis 3:4–5. However, merely telling a person that the fruit will not kill them does not require much craftiness. Furthermore, no one in their right mind would be swayed to eat something that was thought to be deadly by mere words alone, especially those of a complete stranger. What they would need is for someone to eat the fruit first so that they would know unequivocally that the fruit was safe. However, in Eve's case, she only needed to see someone touch the fruit. This is why when the Bible says, in verse six, that Eve "saw" that the tree was good for food, I believe that this means she "physically saw" that the tree was good for food, not that she realized the tree was good for food. And the only way that she would have been able to physically see that the tree was good for food was if Satan touched its fruit and remained alive. So I believe that this is how Satan deceived Eve by his craftiness. I believe that he picked the fruit off the tree in order to show her that she would not die from touching it, which also showed her that it would be safe to eat. For I believe that Eve had full trust and confidence in her husband and had no reason to doubt or distrust the information that he had given her. She did not know that Adam had added the words "or touch it" to God's command but fully believed that they were part of God's command. And when she "saw" that Satan touched the fruit and did not die, she then knew from the evidence before her that "this tree" was safe to eat from which, in turn, also showed her that the other tree in the middle of the garden, the tree of life, was the one that was forbidden by God. For Scripture tells us that it was only after Eve "saw" that the tree was good for food that she took from its fruit and ate.

I also want to say to those who may be skeptical of whether Satan actually touched the fruit, since the Bible does not specifically mention it, that if Satan did not touch the fruit, then the addition of the words "or touch it" to God's command by Adam would have had no bearing what-so-ever on why Eve was deceived. They would have been a harmless and incon-sequential addition. Therefore, only the subtractions to God's Word, the unnamed, unspecified tree, would have been the problem. However, as I stated before, the only logical scenario to Paul's words in 1 Timothy 2:14 is that Adam gave Eve misinformation about God's command, which caused her to be deceived. Therefore, I believe that both Adam's taking away from God's Word and his addition to God's Word had an impact on why Eve was not able to decipher the truth. Furthermore, the very nature of Satan is evil. He opposes God and any and all righteousness. Therefore, he wanted to ensnare Eve into eating the fruit because he wanted her to transgress God's command. So, do you think then that Satan would not have taken full advantage of the misinformation that was given to Eve? Do you think that he would have let the opportunity to touch the fruit slip him by? Or do you think perhaps, that Satan missed out on the chance

9

to touch the fruit because he was just not quite smart enough to figure out how touching the fruit would affect her ability to attain the truth? Certainly, Satan was smart enough, which is why he took full advantage of the misinformation given to Eve. He wanted her to transgress God's command and did everything in his power to make that happen. Indeed, he touched the fruit.

Another point that I would like to bring up is that I believe that Adam and Eve perceived the words of Satan differently, in Genesis 3:4–5, due to the fact that they each had different information about the tree. Therefore, I would like to take a little time here to relate how I believe each of them perceived Satan's words, starting with Adam. Now we know that Adam knew unequivocally that the tree in front of them was the tree of the KGE. Therefore, when Satan uttered the words, [4]"…You surely will not die! [5]For God knows that in the day you eat from it your eyes will be opened, and you will be like God, knowing good and evil," there is no mistaking how Adam perceived Satan's words. Adam had to have taken Satan's words to mean that God had lied to him and had only told him that he would die because He didn't want him to eat the fruit and therefore be like, or equal, to Him. In other words, Satan made it sound as if it was a jealousy thing on God's part. However, because Eve did not know which tree was the tree of the KGE, thinking in terms of a jealousy thing would not have crossed her mind. Therefore, when Satan uttered those words, I believe that Eve took his words to mean that God had given them this fruit because eating it would allow them to gain the needed wisdom to discern between good and evil, as He did. This analogy seems to be the case because of what the Bible says in verse six. Verse six says, [6]"When the woman saw that the tree was good for food, and that it was a delight to the eyes, and that the tree was desirable to make one wise, she took from its fruit and ate…." This analogy would also explain why Eve then gave to her husband, who was with her. She also would have wanted Adam to gain this wisdom from the fruit that she thought God wanted them to eat. So Adam ate knowing full well that the tree in front of them was the forbidden tree because he wanted to be equal to God. Eve, on the other hand, ate because she was deceived into thinking that the tree in front of them was not the forbidden tree, but rather, a good tree that God had put there to make them wise.

Furthermore, the fact that Adam did not give Eve the name of the tree was by no means a small omission. Indeed, if Adam had given Eve the name of the tree, she would have realized that this was the tree of the KGE due to the fact that Satan used the name of the tree in his reply back to her. Not only would his reply have clued her in to the fact that this was the tree, but it also would have caused her to distrust his words altogether because she would have thought that he was trying to poison them.

It is clear that Adam's incorrect teaching had a profound impact on why Eve was not able to decipher the truth. However, I will say that Adam's incorrect teaching was not the only reason Eve was deceived. Another reason that Eve was deceived is that Adam exercised his own jurisdiction, or authority, apart from God. Indeed, it was actually Adam's incorrect teaching in conjunction with the fact that he exercised his own jurisdiction apart from God that caused Eve to fall into transgression. Let me explain.

Earlier I had stated that Adam initially remained silent when Eve replied to the questioning of Satan. His silence would have been natural since Eve replied with the same information that he had given her. However, when Adam found out that the reason he could not eat from the tree was that he would be like God, he continued to remain quiet. This time, however, his silence was due to the fact that his heart had turned to sin, and as a result, his silence had now turned into disobedience. He purposefully remained quiet and did not set the record straight with Eve because he wanted to eat the fruit. But what he should have done at this point was told Eve that he had added the words "or touch it" to God's command out of concern for her safety, and he also should have told her that this was indeed the forbidden tree that they were standing at, including its name. But he did not because he now had a premeditative intent to disobey God and eat of the fruit. So, in reality, it was Adam's incorrect teaching in conjunction with the fact that he exercised his own jurisdiction apart from God that caused Eve to fall into transgression. Adam could have corrected the misinformation he had given her, but because of his pride in wanting to be like God, he chose not to.

The foregoing scenario is what I believe played out in the garden. Eve was not seeking in any way to eat from the fruit of the forbidden tree. It was because of the incorrect information that Adam had given to her about God's command, and his refusal to correct it, that she was deceived by the craftiness of Satan. So it is clear that Eve unknowingly transgressed. Adam, on the other hand, sinned with full premeditation. He was not deceived by Satan because he had the truth of God's command and knew

11

which tree was forbidden. When God confronted them, Adam tried to blame the woman. But God, in His infinite wisdom, knew that the heart and mind of Adam were premeditative and tied to sin. God knew that Adam's sin preceded Eve's because he had eaten the fruit in his heart before Eve physically ate of the fruit. And indeed, He correctly charged Adam as the one who brought sin into the world. So it is vital for us to understand that sin entered into the world because of Adam's premeditative intent to disobey God. It was Adam's premeditative intent that caused "the Fall" from God's grace. It is also vital for us to understand that Adam had brought sin into the world before Eve ever took a bite of the fruit and that it was his disobedience that caused her to become a sinner. We must understand that sin did not enter into the world through Eve. Nor did sin enter into the world through Adam and Eve. It was through "one" man that sin entered into the world. Indeed, it was Adam who sinned first. This is what Scripture clearly teaches.

2

GENESIS 3:16

Many mistranslations of Scripture have come from the false teaching and belief that Eve sinned first. These mistranslations are why it is imperative to understand that it was actually Adam who sinned first. When Scripture states that sin entered into the world through one man Adam, we can trust this information with full confidence and know that sin did enter into the world through Adam. The first mistranslation of Scripture that is based on the claim that Eve sinned first is Genesis 3:16. In this chapter, we will go over verse sixteen in depth because this is the foundational passage upon which all other mistranslations have been built. The correct foundation must be laid on this passage so that we can expose the lies that have been placed in Scripture.

In Genesis 3:16, we can see the supposed punishment to Eve by God. However, this is not a punishment but is actually a warning to Eve of what is to come. But the reason this passage is translated as a punishment is that men can then justify their claim that the man is to rule over his wife as part of her punishment for Eve bringing sin into the world. For it would not make sense that the man would get to rule over his wife if Adam was the one who brought sin into the world. Hence, by this mistranslation, they can show that Eve sinned first and that because of it, the husband is to rule over his wife. However, because we do know from plain Scripture that sin entered into the world through Adam, we can be certain by the character of God that He would not reward Adam for bringing sin into the world by authorizing him to rule over his wife, and that the current translation is a "misfit all around."[1]

The question is, "How did verse sixteen get so mistranslated?" This question is answered for us by a woman named Katharine C. Bushnell. In her book, "God's Word to Women," she explains in great detail the error with which this verse is translated. I will only briefly summarize her findings because her work is very in-depth, but I encourage you to read her book for yourselves so that you can see in greater detail why this verse is mistranslated. It is also essential to know that Ms. Bushnell was a scholar in both the Hebrew and Greek languages. She went home to be with the Lord in 1946.[2]

According to Katharine Bushnell, the original Hebrew had completely different looking letters than the Hebrew of today. In addition, the original Hebrew had only consonants; it did not have vowels. Furthermore, there was no separation between words or verses, nor was there any distinction between small and capital letters, nor was there punctuation. Now the reason that the original Hebrew started to be changed or updated was that it was becoming a dead language due to the Babylonian captivity. So to make the original Hebrew easier for ordinary people to read, the Jewish scribes added a system of vowel-letters and vowel-signs to the original Hebrew. However, if the vowel-letters or vowels-signs were not placed correctly, then a sentence could be easily manipulated to read as something else. With this in mind and due to the fact that the given rendering of Genesis 3:16 is a misfit with the rest of the text and with Scripture as a whole, Ms. Bushnell looked at the Hebrew in its original form, without the vowel-letters and vowel-signs, to determine if what was translated was correct. And she believes by her study of the original Hebrew that the given translation is incorrect and that the actual translation is quite different. It is also important to note that the addition of vowel-letters and vowel-signs were most likely made by Jewish scribes who held women in utter contempt. We must remember that God inspired the original Scriptures. God did not inspire the additions and changes to His Word by the Jewish scribes.[3]

In addition to the manipulations of the vowel-letters and vowel-signs, Ms. Bushnell also found mistranslations that have occurred to Genesis 3:16 that are of more recent invention. She found that some words had mysteriously taken on a different meaning than they had in the original Hebrew. For example, Ms. Bushnell has done extensive research to ascertain the true meaning of the Hebrew word "teshuqa." "Teshuqa" is rendered as "desire" in the NASB and most modern translations. But as Ms. Bushnell

14

discovered, the true meaning of "teshuqa" is "turning" or "will turn." And she discovered this by gathering all of the early translations of Scripture such as the Septuagint Greek, Syriac Peshitto, Samaritan, Old Latin, Sahidic, Bohairic, Aethiopic, and Arabic, to see how this word was rendered. And all of the early translations of Scripture, which were not made under rabbinical influence, render the word "teshuqa" as "turning" or "will turn" in Genesis 3:16 with the single exception of the Arabic, which renders the word "teshuqa" as "direction."[4]

(Note: The word "teshuqa" is found a total of three times in the Old Testament, with the other two verses being Genesis 4:7 and Song of Solomon 7:10. Ms. Bushnell found that the word "teshuqa" was rendered as "turning" or "will turn" in these verses as well, with the exception of the Arabic, which renders the word "teshuqa" as "moderation" in Genesis 4:7, and the Samaritan which renders the word "teshuqa" as "lacking" in Song of Solomon 7:10. Also, two renderings are unknown.)[5]

Therefore, with the manipulations and mistranslations of the scribes, coupled with the more recent mistranslations of men, the current translation of Genesis 3:16 that we have in our Bibles today is nothing more than a falsification of God's inerrant Word. Therefore, according to Katharine Bushnell, the following is the correct translation of Genesis 3:16:

> [16]"To the woman He said, 'A snare hath increased thy sorrow and thy sighing. In sorrow thou shalt bring forth children. Thou art turning away to thy husband, and he will rule over thee.'"[6]

Now that we have the correct rendering of Genesis 3:16, I would like to comment on each part. First, I would like to point out that God is not pronouncing a curse upon Eve. Instead, God is informing Eve that a snare has increased her sorrow and her sighing. And it is obvious that the snare He is speaking of is Satan.[7] It is also important to note that the phrase "sorrow and sighing" is used in Isaiah 35:10 and Isaiah 51:11. In these verses, Isaiah writes that one day the ransomed of the LORD will find "gladness and joy"; their "sorrow and sighing" will flee away. So again, in the first sentence, God is informing Eve that Satan has increased her sorrow (sadness) and her sighing (frustration), which started with his trickery in getting her to eat from the tree. Moving along, we can also see that God is further informing Eve that these sorrows would continue throughout her life in two main ways. First, God warns Eve that she will now bring forth children in sorrow. What was to be a mutually agreed upon and joyful event would now be one filled with rape, complications in childbirth, and the like. And secondly, God warns Eve that when she turns to her husband, he will now rule over her.[8] For God knew that Satan would also influence Adam to rule over his wife. The one-flesh relationship that God had designed would be replaced with a hierarchal relationship, a relationship born out of evil.

I also want to say that men have placed a most abhorrent lie in our Bibles by switching Satan into God. By this lie, Scripture shows God pronouncing direct physical punishment on Eve via pain in childbirth, versus remote physical punishment on Adam via the earth being cursed. It also shows us that God is decreeing that the husband is to rule over his wife. As a result, one can only conclude that it was Eve who brought sin into the world. Therefore, it is this lie mixed in with the truth of God's Word (that sin entered into the world through Adam) that has caused a false doctrine to be created—of Eve being the first to sin but of Adam only incurring the blame because he was the "head." Indeed, this lie has laid a false foundation upon which many more mistranslations of Scripture have been built.

Now that we have seen that it is actually Satan who brings destruction upon Eve, we must ask, "Why does Satan single Eve out for harm? Why is he not also seen as bringing evil upon Adam?" The reason that Satan singles Eve out for harm is that Satan has a vendetta against Eve. He wants retaliation against her. But why would Satan have a vendetta against Eve? Well, if we read Scripture, we will find that Adam did not name Satan as the cause of his transgression. He completely sheltered Satan (Gen. 3:12). Eve, on the other hand, named Satan as the one who deceived her. She called him to account before the righteous Judge (Gen. 3:13). And as a result of her accusal of him, Satan was given a sentence by the righteous Judge (Gen. 3:14).[9]

If we study the judgment that God gives to Satan, we can see that God cursed him more than all the cattle and all the wild animals because he deceived Eve. In essence, God was making him lower than animals. Now, this part of Satan's punishment is to be taken literally. Satan was cursed more than all the cattle and all the wild animals because he deceived the woman. However, I would also like to point out that the next part of Satan's punishment is metaphoric in nature. When God tells Satan, [14]"...on your belly you will go and dust you will eat all the days of your

16

life…" we know that this cannot be taken literally because Satan is seen to walk the earth (Job 1:7; 2:2). Satan is also seen standing at the right hand of Joshua in order to accuse him (Zech. 3:1). Therefore, I believe that God uses a metaphor here so that Satan can picture just exactly how low he is. And the picture is he will be on his belly. Therefore, he will be prone, or prostrate, with his face to the ground. And his face will be so low to the ground that he will be eating dust. Furthermore, he will be this way forever—all the days of his life. So because Eve called Satan to account before God, Satan was forever cursed and made low by God. This low status, again, is why he has a vendetta against her. Satan hates his lowly place. He wants to be supreme over all creation, not lower than it. And since he can't be supreme, he wants to get back at her. As a result, he would aim his blows to her as a woman and a mother. He would also influence Adam to rule over her. Since he was made lower than all life forms because of her, he wanted to influence Adam to subjugate her in return. He wanted to return like for like.

Furthermore, this vendetta has, likewise, been carried out upon Eve's daughters. This is because women are a constant reminder to Satan that he has forever been made lower than all life forms because of Eve, a woman. So, the woman being a reminder is why he has, throughout the centuries, inflicted his blows on women in childbearing. It is also why he has influenced men to rule over women and husbands to rule over their wives. He is still seeking retaliation against her. His hatred of her has never waned. And whenever we as women are being attacked by Satan in this way, we can know that it is because of a righteous decision (a decision to turn in the perpetrator) that a godly woman made thousands of years before.

I would like to comment further on the fact that the Bible shows Eve to be a godly woman and that it does not show the same for Adam. If we read further God's words to Satan, we can see that after God cursed Satan because he deceived Eve, God then also put enmity between Satan and the woman and between his seed and her seed (Gen. 3:15). Now it is essential to understand here that Satan did not have any biological children. Therefore, his seed is representative of those who are unrighteous. Eve's seed, by contrast, is representative of those who are righteous. So for God to contrast Eve and her seed from Satan and his seed clearly shows us that God knew that Eve had a repentant heart and that she chose to stand on the side of righteousness. For if we revisit the way that Eve responded to God

17

after she and Adam ate, we can again see that Eve rightly named Satan as the reason as to why she ate. By her accusal of Satan, she separated herself from him and aligned herself to the side of God. Adam, on the other hand, completely sheltered Satan and named Eve (whom he had given misinformation to) as the direct cause, and God (who is righteous) as the remote cause, as to why he ate. Adam showed no repentance before God, and as a result, he aligned himself to the side of Satan. So, because Eve's response indicated that she desired to be separated from Satan, God put enmity between them to show that they would not be allies in any way. Furthermore, if we keep reading Genesis 3:15, we will find that God then pronounces that (one of) her seed, the righteous Messiah, will one day conquer Satan. Therefore, as a result of Genesis 3:15, we can see that Eve was constituted the progenitor of Jesus Christ, and of all believers, because of her repentance and faithfulness to God.[10]

We have seen thus far, that Eve called Satan to account before God, that God cursed Satan more than all the wild animals because he deceived Eve, and that God warned Eve that Satan would carry out his vengeance against her. Now I would like to point out that in Genesis 3:17–19, God curses the earth because of Adam and tells him that he will endure certain sorrows because of it.[11] For God had explicitly told Adam not to eat from the tree of the knowledge of good and evil, and he willfully chose to disobey Him. Now the reason I point this out is that God warns Eve that she will endure certain "sorrows" due to the revengefulness of Satan; however, God warns Adam that he will endure certain "sorrows" due to his own sin since the earth is cursed because of him. He has no one to blame but himself. I would also like to add that women will not only feel the effects of the retaliation of Satan, but they also will feel the effects of the earth being cursed, as do men, for the very reason that they live upon the earth. In essence, women feel the effects of the retaliation of Satan due to the righteous decision of Eve to call Satan to account, and women feel the effects of the earth being cursed due to the willful disobedience of Adam toward God.

I also want to say one more thing about the words God states to Adam in verse seventeen, the words, [17]"...Because you have listened to the voice of your wife...." And that is, many have taken these words to mean that Eve persuaded Adam to eat the fruit and that she was at fault. However, it certainly does not mean this. If we remember, Adam blamed Eve when God confronted him as to why he ate. Therefore, God states these words because He is responding to Adam in a way that both includes and addresses the excuse that Adam gave Him. Indeed, we can see from God's reply to Adam that God is telling him that his excuse isn't valid because He had directly told him not to eat from the tree of the KGE.

> Adam's excuse: [12]"…The woman whom You gave *to be* with me, she gave me from the tree, and I ate" (Gen. 3:12).

> God's reply: [17]"…Because you have listened to the voice of your wife, and have eaten from the tree about which I commanded you, saying, 'You shall not eat from it'; Cursed is the ground because of you…" (Gen. 3:17).

Eve certainly distinguished herself from Adam that day. She showed herself to be faithful before God, while Adam did not. And her faithfulness, I believe, is the reason for what we see next, in Genesis 3:20. In verse twenty, we can see that Adam called his wife's name Eve because she was the mother of all the living. And I believe that Adam called his wife's name Eve because God gave her the honorable name of Eve.[12] The Bible states in Genesis 5:2 that God named both the man and the woman "adam" (rendered as "Man" in the NASB) in the day when they were created. But on this day, the woman became known as Eve. She distinguished herself from Adam because of her repentance, faithfulness, and trust in God, and God credited it to her as righteousness. As a result, she was the first person to gain eternal life after the fall.[13] And this is why God renamed her Eve. She was now the mother of all the (spiritually) living.[14]

Now, some have claimed that Adam was the one who named Eve. However, I do not believe this claim to be valid because, first of all, if Adam gave her the name of Eve, then he would have been taking it upon himself to rename what God had already named (Gen. 5:2). Secondly, Adam was an unrepentant unbeliever. Therefore, I do not believe that he would have had the insight, wisdom, or understanding to give Eve such a name since her name had special meaning. Nor do I believe that God gave him divine revelation since he was an unbeliever. And thirdly, the third chapter of Genesis seems to be written in the order of occurrence. And immediately after Adam called his wife's name Eve, we are told from Scripture that God made garments of skin for Adam and his wife, and He sent Adam out of the garden. Now, these two events would have most likely occurred very soon after the fall. Therefore, they are indicative that

Eve was renamed on the same day of the fall, shortly after she was told that the Messiah would be from her seed. Furthermore, God is the One who had distinguished "Eve and her seed" from "Satan and his seed," not Adam. Thus, it was God who established her as the progenitor of all believers, which would correspond to her being the "mother of all the living."[15] So again, I believe that Adam called his wife's name Eve because that was the name God had given to her because of her repentance, faithfulness, and trust in Him.

I also want to say that Eve was not sent out of the garden as is routinely taught. The Bible is abundantly clear that only the man was sent out (Gen. 3:22–24), the one who was taken from the ground (Gen. 3:23). And he was sent out for the reason that God did not want him to stretch out his hand and take from the tree of life, and eat, and live forever (Gen. 3:22–24). Now it should be a little obvious here why God did not want Adam to reach out his hand and eat from the tree of life. He was an unrepentant unbeliever. And just as the "tree of the knowledge of good and evil" meant "spiritual death," so also the "tree of life" meant "spiritual life." Therefore, God did not want him to eat of the fruit because now that sin was in the world, spiritual life could only come from repentance before God and believing in the One to come that God spoke of in verse fifteen. Now, it is evident that the mother of all the living, Eve, was not sent out of the garden because she had the right to the tree of life (Rev. 22:14); for she had already gained eternal life because of her repentance and faithfulness to God and her belief in the coming One.[16] But the reason that most people have assumed that Eve was sent out of the garden is that she is seen in the next verse (Gen. 4:1) as having (sexual) relations with Adam. But she had relations with Adam because she "turned" to be with him as God predicted she would (Gen. 3:16). Or as the Arabic translation puts it, she went in the "direction" of her husband.[17] Therefore, it is clear that Eve did not harbor any ill will against her husband for the incorrect information he had given her. She forgave him and voluntarily "turned" to be with him when he was sent out of the garden by God.

Since we are on the topic of the fact that Eve turned to be with her husband, meaning she followed Adam out of the garden, I would like to bring up one thing regarding Katharine Bushnell's translation of Genesis 3:16. As one can see, Ms. Bushnell translated the word "teshuqa" as "turning away" in verse sixteen rather than as "turning." But the reason Ms. Bushnell has done so is that the Septuagint Greek, the translation that was deemed to be most accurate of the early renderings, rendered the word "teshuqa" as "apostrophe" in both Genesis 3:16 and Genesis 4:7, and as "epistrophe" in Song of Solomon 7:10. The Greek word "apostrophe" means "turning away," while the Greek word "epistrophe" means "turning to."[18] Therefore, because the Septuagint Greek translated the word "teshuqa" as "turning away" in Genesis 3:16, Ms. Bushnell did as well and stated that the teaching, then, is that God was speaking warningly to Eve at this time (not to leave the garden) because He was telling her that she was inclining to turn away from Himself to her husband and that if she did so, her husband would rule over her. Ms. Bushnell also stated that because Eve did follow Adam out of the garden, she was the first to forsake her heavenly kindred for her husband by reversing God's marriage law (Gen. 2:24). She then said that if Eve had remained steadfast with God, Adam might, through the double influence of God and Eve, have returned (in repentance) to God in the garden.[19] I, however, disagree with this analogy and believe that we are seeing a biased translation of the Septuagint here to show disobedience on Eve's part. Indeed, if God was warning Eve not to leave the garden because He wanted her to be separated from her husband until he repented, why would He not also say the same to believers in 1 Corinthians 7:12–16? Indeed, it is clear from Scripture that God wants believers to stay with their unbelieving spouse (if the unbelieving spouse consents to live with them, which Adam did because he had relations with her) for the reason that they may save them. For God does not tell believers to stay away from difficult situations, but sends them out into the darkened world so that they can be a witness to others. Furthermore, Adam could have turned to God in repentance from anywhere outside the garden, and God would have listened. Therefore, it was not his location that was important, but his heart. Thus, I believe that Eve left the garden to be steadfast with God. For Eve knew that, although Adam was an unbeliever, it was still God's will that they be together as husband and wife so that she could be a godly influence on him. And we know from Scripture that Eve was a godly influence on Adam because, in Genesis 4:1 and Genesis 4:25, Eve is seen giving God the glory (undoubtedly in front of Adam) for the children He had blessed her with. So, because I believe that God was not referring to Eve turning away from Him in disobedience, and was merely referring to her following Adam out of the garden, I would simply translate the last sentence of Genesis 3:16 as, "You will turn to your husband, and he will rule over you."[20]

21

(Note: Even though the Septuagint Greek is considered to be the most accurate of the early renderings, it is not without its mistranslations. As Ms. Bushnell pointed out, the technical term used in Exodus 38:8 and 1 Samuel 2:22 is "serving women." However, the Septuagint Greek translators altered this term to "fasting women" in Exodus 38:8 and dropped it entirely in 1 Samuel 2:22 to erase any trace that woman originally had her place in the regular Tabernacle services, either as priestess or Levite.)[21]

Still, the question remains, "Did Adam ever repent?" The Bible does not say. However, I believe a possible indication that Adam repented was the fact that Adam agreed with Eve in giving their newborn son the name of Seth (Gen. 4:25; 5:3). I believe that after Cain killed Abel, a horrific family tragedy, Adam realized that he was an ungodly influence on his son Cain and that he needed to turn his life over to God.

In ending this chapter, I would like to say that through the corruption of Genesis 3:16, men have painted a picture of Eve that is far from the truth. Not only have they portrayed her as an ungodly woman and the one who caused "the Fall," but they have also portrayed her as causing her husband to sin. But Eve was indeed a very godly woman. And in my opinion, she is one of the godliest examples of women that we have in all of Scripture. For on that day many years ago, Eve was not seeking in any way to eat from the fruit of the forbidden tree. She ate only because she had misinformation about God's Word and was deceived. And when God confronted her, she did not return the blame to her husband, or bring forth the blame to God, but immediately repented before God and called Satan to account. By her repentance, she aligned herself to the side of God so that God distinguished her and her seed from the evil one and his seed. And she held dear in her heart the words God declared about the One who was to come who would bruise Satan's head. Furthermore, because Eve chose to stand on the side of righteousness, God bestowed upon her great honor. He renamed her Eve and pronounced her the mother of all the living. Indeed, it was Eve who, by God, was constituted the progenitor of Jesus Christ, and of all believers, because of her repentance and faithfulness to God. Moreover, Eve did not harbor any ill will or bitterness toward her husband for the misinformation that he had given her or for his undeserved blame of her. But instead, she forgave him and turned to be with him, all the while knowing that their relationship would be different. And finally, Eve gave God the glory for the children He had blessed her with. Truly, she placed her faith and trust in Him all the days of her life.

3

1 CORINTHIANS 11:3-16

Through the centuries, men have sought to disallow women from both translating and teaching Scripture. And for the most part, they have succeeded. As a result, men have been mistranslating and misinterpreting Scripture to read as though women are subject to men and are not fit for use in certain service to God. For it is not by coincidence that most passages regarding women are hard to understand. Nor is it by coincidence that they contradict so much of Scripture. And women need to wake up to this fact. With that being said, this passage is not difficult in the least when it is understood correctly. In fact, Paul makes a very coherent and ingenious argument as to why women should not be covered. But again, the reason why this passage is difficult to understand in its present form is that the translators mistranslate several parts of the text, which includes adding words that are not in the original Greek, to skew the passage in the way that they want it to read. Furthermore, they fail to identify one crucial element. As a result, this passage is confusing, incoherent, and contradictory to other parts of Scripture.

Now to understand this passage the correct way, we must recognize that it consists of three parts. And they are as follows:

1) Verse 3 — Paul's model.

2) Verses 4–6 — Paul quotes the words of a faction of men from Corinth who wrote him.

3) Verses 7–16 — Paul's rebuttal, where he refers back to his model.

I would like to start explaining this passage with the second part because this is the crucial element that the translators fail to identify. Furthermore, it is the key to understanding this passage correctly. Indeed, verses 4–6 are not Paul's words, but rather, they are the words of a faction of men from Corinth who wrote him (1 Cor. 11:19).

(Note: The original Greek was written in all majuscule [capital] letters, had no spacing between words or sentences, and had no punctuation of any kind.[1] Therefore, one has to determine by context whether a portion of Scripture is quoted.)

Before I begin showing just how I know that verses 4–6 are quoted, I would like to say that many scholars themselves believe that Paul quotes in his first letter to the Corinthians in response to those who wrote him. For instance, the translators of the NIV believe that Paul is quoting in 1 Corinthians 6:12 because they put a portion of the sentence in quotation marks. First Corinthians 6:12, NIV says, [12]*'Everything is permissible for me'*—but not everything is beneficial. *'Everything is permissible for me'*—but I will not be mastered by anything." Also, 1 Corinthians 10:23, NIV [23]*'Everything is permissible'*—but not everything is beneficial. *'Everything is permissible'*—but not everything is constructive." (Note: The Greek word translated as "permissible" is "exesti," which means "it is legal, it is proper, it is permitted.")[2]

Now, I agree with the translators of the NIV that the words in quotations in these verses are not Paul's words but rather the words of some from Corinth who wrote him. Indeed, Paul would not make the argument that all things were now permissible or lawful for us. If he did, then he would be saying that what was sinful for us before is now acceptable with God. What I believe, then, is that Paul is responding to people who were making the argument that all things were permissible for them since they were saved by grace through Jesus Christ. I believe that certain people were trying to take advantage of the grace and freedom that Christ had given to them as believers. However, Paul, in his refutation of this, tells them that not all things would be beneficial for them if they did take advantage of His grace and that not all things would be constructive for them. Furthermore, Paul tells them that they should have the same mentality as he does, of not being mastered by sinful desires of the flesh (1 Cor. 6:12, NIV).

If one would like to claim that Paul does not quote in his first letter to the Corinthians and that the words "everything is permissible for me" are Paul's words, then this would be true for women as well. All things would be permissible, legal, and proper for women. Why, then, would Paul even make the argument that women should have their heads covered? Wouldn't it be proper for women to be uncovered if all things were permissible, legal, and proper for them? Or better yet, why would Paul make any argument at all if all things were permissible, legal, and proper for us? Furthermore, how could that which is permissible and proper for us in God's sight, not be beneficial for us? Or maybe Paul just meant that "some" things were permissible for us even though he said that "all" things were permissible. Does one see how not understanding Scripture the right way turns Scripture into a bunch of contradictions and gibberish? This is why it is imperative to understand when Paul is quoting. And it is abundantly clear that Paul quotes, in order to refute, in his first letter to the Corinthians.

There are actually six clues in Scripture that alert us to the fact that verses 4–6 are quoted. I will mention only two now. The other four I will mention when we come to them in this passage.

The first clue that verses 4–6 are quoted is verses 4–6 themselves, coupled with the words of Paul in his second letter to the Corinthians. I will go over verses 4–6 first and will use the Greek portion of the Interlinear KJV-NIV Parallel New Testament in Greek and English because it has the correct translation of 1 Corinthians 11:4–6 according to the Greek. It says:

> 4"Every man praying or prophesying down over [his] head having [anything] shames the head of him. 5But every woman praying or prophesying unveiled with the (her) head shames the head of her; for one it is and the same thing with the woman having been shaved. 6For if is not veiled a woman, also let her be shorn; but if shameful for a woman to be shorn or to be shaved, let her be veiled."

The reason why the Interlinear KJV-NIV Parallel New Testament in Greek and English has the correct translation is that they do not add the word "head" four additional times in these verses, as many other translations do. And more importantly, they correctly translate the Greek word "katakalypto" as "veiled"; "kata" meaning "down over" (KJV-NIV) and "kalypto" meaning "to cover [as in to cover over or conceal], veil, or hide."[3] The question is, "Why should the words 'akatakalyptos/katakalyp-to' be translated as 'unveiled/veiled' instead of 'uncovered/cover'?" It is because the word "kalypto" never refers to a partial covering. It always refers to a complete covering. And when we look closely at the wording of verse five, it speaks of the woman's head, not her hair. This would mean that the person or persons making this argument wanted a woman to completely cover over her head, which would include her face since her face is part of her head. This is why the translation of "unveiled/ veiled" is the correct translation. The translation of "veiled" gives the reader the correct understanding that the woman's face was included in what was intended because a veil would cover the whole of a woman's head, including her face. The translation of "cover" makes it sound as if only her hair was to be covered. But indeed, the person or persons making this argument wanted a complete covering over of a woman's head while praying and prophesying.

Now we will look at the words of Paul in his second letter to the Corinthians. He writes:

> [16]"…but whenever a person turns to the Lord, the veil is taken away. [17]Now the Lord is the Spirit, and where the Spirit of the Lord is, *there* is liberty. [18]But we all, with unveiled face, beholding as in a mirror the glory of the Lord, are being transformed into the same image from glory to glory, just as from the Lord, the Spirit" (2 Cor. 3:16–18).

Here, in Paul's second or follow-up letter to the Corinthians, we can see that Paul wants ALL believers, both men and women, to go with an unveiled face. This is because whenever one turns to the Lord, the veil is taken away. For believers understand what unbelievers do not. Unbelievers' hearts are hardened. Therefore, a veil lies over their heart (2 Cor. 3:14–15). But when one turns to the Lord, the veil is taken away. Therefore, being unveiled shows that we are followers of Christ. Consequently, Paul wants all believers to go with an unveiled face so that they can behold as in a mirror the glory of the Lord. Therefore, it is abundantly clear from these words that Paul is quoting in verses 4–6 of his first letter. For Paul would not say in one letter that women should be veiled and then in another letter say that women should be unveiled. Otherwise, Paul would be completely contradicting himself from letter to letter. Indeed, Paul, in his first letter, is responding to the men who made the argument that women should be veiled, and Paul, in his second letter, is reminding those in Corinth that they should all be unveiled. Certainly, women cannot behold as in a mirror the glory of the Lord if they are covered up.

The second clue that verses 4–6 are quoted is Jesus' own words. Jesus said in Matthew 5:14–15:

> [14]"You are the light of the world. A city set on a hill cannot be hidden; [15]nor does *anyone* light a lamp and put it under a basket, but on the lampstand, and it gives light to all who are in the house."

In this passage, Jesus tells believers that they are the light of the world. And here, He is speaking figuratively to show that believers are a light because they speak God's truths. It is also abundantly clear that Jesus does not want believers to be hidden or covered up. This is why He uses the example of a city set on a hill that cannot be hidden. We are that city; we cannot be hidden. It is also why He uses the example of a lamp not being covered. We are that lamp; we should not be covered. We should also note that in the first example, a city set on a hill cannot be hidden because it is seen by all who pass by. But in the second example, only the occupants in the house can see the light. Therefore, Jesus is making the point that believers are to be a light not only when they are in public view, but also in every house that they enter. This would include God's house. Indeed, it is believers who prophesy and speak God's truths. Therefore, no believer should be covered up in God's house, especially when they prophesy.

I also want to say that Paul is always faithful to Christ's teachings. Therefore, there is no doubt that this specific teaching of Christ is the reason why Paul makes the case against women being covered up to the men at Corinth. Paul knows that Christian women are the light of the world, just as Christian men are. And women cannot shine forth for God if they are covered up, even partially covered up. Indeed, the lamp is not to be covered, nor is it to be partially covered. Women are to behold, as in a mirror, the glory of the Lord. They are to reflect His bright, radiant light. So, by understanding the teachings of Christ (Matt. 5:14–15), and by comparing Scripture (1 Cor. 11:4–6) with Scripture (2 Cor. 3:16–18), we can indeed be confident that verses 4–6 are quoted.

So again, the following argument was sent to Paul in a letter from some of the men in Corinth.

> *[4] *"Every man who has anything down over his head while praying or prophesying disgraces his head. [5]But every woman who has her head unveiled while praying or prophesying disgraces her head, for it is one and the same thing as having been shaved. [6]For if a woman is not veiled, let her also have her hair cut off; but if it is disgraceful for a woman to have her hair cut off or to be shaved, let her be veiled."**

(Note: This translation closely resembles the original Greek; however, it has been put in the English word order.)

Paul has read their argument and begins to lay out in detail the reason why women should not be veiled. He, therefore, starts with his "model" and writes, [3]"But I want you to understand that Christ is the head of every man, and the man is the head of a woman, and God is the head of Christ." Now, in looking at Paul's model, there are three things that I need to explain, which are critical in gaining the correct understanding of this passage.

1) The reason why Paul uses the word "andros," meaning "man," at the beginning of his model (Christ is the head of every "man"), instead of the word "anthropos," meaning "human being,"[4] is because it is "men" who wrote him and he directs both his model and rebuttal (vv. 7–16) to the men.

2) The reason why Paul gives his model using the word "head" in a FIGURATIVE way is that the men who wrote him based their argument on a LITERAL understanding of the word "head" (vv. 4–5). Therefore, Paul wants them to understand "head" in a figurative sense so that he can refer back to his model when he gives his rebuttal to explain exactly why women are not to be veiled.

3) "Head" used figuratively in Greek, in Paul's time, meant "source/origin/first/beginning." It did not mean "leader/ruler/chief/authority" as it does here in America. (See fifth chapter "Head—Source or Leader?")

Since the first explanation needs no further exposition, I would first like to draw attention to the second explanation. Men who teach on this passage maintain that Paul is saying, in verse five, that every woman who has her head uncovered while praying or prophesying disgraces her figurative head, the man (husband). However, it is evident by the context of verses 4–6 that the person or persons who coined these words are speaking of a woman disgracing her own literal head, not her figurative head. This is because they deem that for every woman who has her head unveiled while praying or prophesying, *5"...it is one and the same thing as having been shaved."* And indeed, a woman is the one who feels disgrace and humiliation if her head is shaved, not her husband. Furthermore, if verse five were referring to a woman's figurative head, the man, then verse six would also be referring to her figurative head due to the words *5"...it is one and the same thing as having been shaved."* Therefore, verse six would say, *6"...but if it is disgraceful **to the man** for a woman to have her hair cut off or to be shaved, let her be veiled."* Indeed, if it were her husband who was disgraced because she did not cover her head while praying or prophesying, then it would also be her husband who would be disgraced by her having her hair cut off. However, verse six is clear that it is the woman who is disgraced by having her hair cut off. Therefore, it is also the woman who is disgraced by praying and prophesying unveiled. Thus, the following shows the correct and incorrect way to understand verses 4–6.

Correct:

4"Every man who has anything down over his head (L) while praying or prophesying disgraces his head (L). 5But every woman who has her head (L) unveiled while praying or prophesying disgraces her head (L), for it is one and the same thing as having been shaved. 6For if a woman is not veiled, let her also have her hair cut off; but if it is disgraceful for a woman to have her hair cut off or to be shaved, let her be veiled."

Incorrect:

4"Every man who has anything down over his head (L) while praying or prophesying disgraces his head (F). 5But every woman who has her head (L) unveiled while praying or prophesying disgraces her head (F), for it is one and the same thing as having been shaved. 6For if a woman is not veiled, let her also have her hair cut off; but if it is disgraceful for a woman to have her hair cut off or to be shaved, let her be veiled."

In looking at the third explanation, we should also note that the Strongest NIV Exhaustive Concordance lists one of the definitions of the Greek word "kephale" or "head" as "the point of origin."[5] The Strongest NIV Exhaustive Concordance also lists some of the definitions of the Hebrew word "rosh" or "head" to be "source/origin/first/beginning."[6] Furthermore, although it is not our most common way of understanding the word "head," we in America even understand "head" to be "the source or beginning of a river or a stream" or "the source of a flowing body of water."

Now that we understand the figurative meaning of the word "head" as Paul meant it to be understood let us once again look at Paul's model (v. 3). Remember, Paul is directing his model to the men at Corinth, who wrote him. He states:

[3]"But I want you to understand that Christ is the head [source] of every man…"

> [16]"For by Him [Christ] all things were created, *both* in the heavens and on earth, visible and invisible, whether thrones or dominions or rulers or authorities—all things have been created through Him and for Him" (Col. 1:16).

> [3]"All things came into being through Him [Christ], and apart from Him nothing came into being that has come into being" (John 1:3).

"…and the man is the head [source] of a woman…"

> [22]"The LORD God fashioned into a woman the rib which He had taken from the man…" (Gen. 2:22).

> (Note: The word translated as "rib" is "sela" in Hebrew and literally means "side."[7] Therefore, God took both flesh and bone from the side of the man to form the woman. See Genesis 2:23.)

"…and God [the Father] is the head [source] of Christ [incarnate]."

30

[14]"And the Word became flesh, and dwelt among us, and we saw His glory, glory as of the only begotten from the Father..." (John 1:14).

[4]"But when the fullness of the time came, God sent forth His Son, born of a woman, born under the Law..." (Gal. 4:4).

[18]"I am He who testifies about Myself, and the Father who sent Me testifies about Me" (John 8:18).

Next, as previously stated, Paul then quotes the men's very own words in his argument back to them (vv. 4–6). Paul repeats their words not only so that they will understand which argument it is of theirs he is referencing (as Paul responds to other arguments in 1 Corinthians), but also because he will agree with them on one point—well, sort of. Subsequently, Paul starts his rebuttal to the men in verse seven and states, [7]"For a man ought not to have his head covered, since he is the image and glory of God...." So, here in verse seven, Paul agrees with the men that a man ought not to have his head covered. (Remember, in verse four of their argument, the men had stated that every man who has anything down over his head while praying and prophesying disgraces his head.) The only difference is the men were talking about their own "literal" heads, while Paul, in his rebuttal, is referring to his model with the "figurative" meaning of head. Consequently, Paul is saying that a man ought not to cover (veil) his head, Jesus Christ, because He is the image and glory of God. Indeed, it is Jesus Christ, and **NOT** a man, who is the image and glory of God. Therefore, verse seven should be rendered as, [7]"For a man indeed ought not to veil his head, since He is the image and glory of God...."

Also, for those who are unsure of whether Paul is referring to a man's "literal" or "figurative" head in verse seven, I would like to take some time here so that we can examine Scripture for ourselves to see whether it is Christ or a human man who is the image and glory of God.

[4]"...the god of this world has blinded the minds of the unbelieving so that they might not see the light of the gospel of the glory of Christ, who is the image of God" (2 Cor. 4:4).

[15]"He is the [visible] image of the invisible God, the firstborn of all creation" (Col. 1:15).

31

[14]"And the Word became flesh, and dwelt among us, and we saw His glory, glory as of the only begotten from the Father..." (John 1:14).

[3]"And He is the radiance of His glory and the exact representation of His nature..." (Heb. 1:3).

[5]"Have this attitude in yourselves which was also in Christ Jesus, [6]who, although He existed in the form of God..." (Phil. 2:5–6).

[5]"Then the glory [Christ] of the LORD will be revealed and all flesh will see it [Him] together..." (Isa. 40:5).

[23]"And the city has no need of the sun or of the moon to shine on it, for the glory of God has illumined it, and its lamp is the Lamb" (Rev. 21:23).

These verses clearly say that it is Jesus Christ who is the image and glory of God and are only some of the verses in the Bible which state this. Furthermore, if Paul were referring to a man being the image ("eikon" in Greek) of God in 1 Corinthians 11:7, then why does Paul say in 2 Corinthians 3:18, NIV, that when we reflect the Lord's glory, we are **being** transformed into the likeness [image/eikon] of the Lord? Also, why does Paul say in Romans 8:29 that, [29]"For those whom He foreknew, He also predestined to **become** conformed to the image [eikon] of His Son..."? And why does Paul say in 1 Corinthians 15:49 that, [49]"Just as we **have** borne the image [eikon] of the earthy, we **will** also bear the image [eikon] of the heavenly"? Furthermore, if a man were already the glory of God, then why does Hebrews 2:10, NIV say, [10]"In **bringing** many sons to glory, it was fitting that God, for whom and through whom everything exists, should make the author of their salvation perfect through suffering"? (Note: The word translated as "sons" is "huious" in Greek and means children of either gender.[8] God brings His daughters to glory as well.)

Again, I ask, if 1 Corinthians 11:7 were talking about a man, why then would a man need to be transformed into the Lord's image, or need to be brought to glory, as the previous verses say if he was already the image and glory of God? The reason, once again, is that verse seven is talking about Jesus Christ and not a man. In fact, the Bible never refers to a man as being the image of God, nor does it refer to him as being the glory of God. However, the Bible does say that a man and a woman are both equally

32

created in the image of God. Genesis 1:26–27 states, [26]"Then God said, 'Let Us make man [humankind] in Our image, according to Our likeness; and let them rule over the fish of the sea and over the birds of the sky and over the cattle and over all the earth, and over every creeping thing that creeps on the earth.' [27]God created man [humankind] in His own image, in the image of God He created him, male and female He created them." So Scripture tells us that a man is created "in" the image of God. However, it is another thing altogether to say that a man "is" the image of God. Jesus Christ is the Word made flesh. Thus, it is Jesus Christ, who is the image of the invisible God. Therefore, Jesus Christ **IS** the image of God, and male and female are created **IN** God's image. Truly, it is Jesus Christ, and Jesus Christ alone, who is the image and glory of God.

Now back to verse seven. As we have seen, Paul has told the men from Corinth that a man indeed ought not to veil his head (Christ) since He is the image and glory of God. The question is, "Why would Paul make such an argument?" Why would Paul tell the men that they ought not to veil their head, Christ? Were the men trying to veil Christ? Indeed, no! However, the men were trying to veil women. Therefore, the reason that Paul makes this argument is that he is using Christ as an example, as a correlation, as to why women should not be veiled. For Paul then says in verse seven, [7]"…but the woman is the glory of man." So what Paul is actually saying is, [7]"For a man indeed ought not to veil his head, *Jesus Christ*, since He is the image and glory of God, but the woman is the glory of man *so she ought not to be veiled either*." Now I would like to take a moment here to say that verse seven is the third clue that alerts us to the fact that verses 4–6 are quoted. Indeed, since Paul is using Jesus Christ as a correlation as to why women should not be veiled, he absolutely would not have previously made the case for a woman to be veiled. Therefore, it is absolutely essential to understand that Jesus Christ is the image and glory of God because this will lay a completely different foundation for this passage than the one that is laid when men claim that they are the image and glory of God. So again, Paul is making the correlation that a man ought not to veil Christ since He is the image and glory of God, and the man ought not to veil the woman because she is his glory. Also, notice that Paul does not say that a woman is the image of a man. This is because a woman is not the image of a man. A woman is created in the image of God. Therefore, Paul makes no such statement in his argument.

The next question is, "What does Paul mean when he says that the woman is the 'glory' of man since he is obviously speaking in figurative terms?" I believe that Paul is using the word "glory" in regard to light. In other words, Paul is saying that the woman is a lamp or a light that helps the man see; that she is a source of spiritual illumination and strength. This is why she is not to be covered up. For light makes what is invisible to the eye visible. A lamp gives light to all who are in the house (Matt. 5:15). Hence, just as Christ, who being the glory of God, is the lamp that illumines the New Jerusalem (Rev. 21:23), so also the woman, being the glory of man, is a lamp that helps to illumine his path. Indeed, a woman, through her wisdom, understanding, prudence, insight, and discernment, is a light unto a man. Unfortunately, most people do not understand that a woman was created as a source of spiritual illumination and strength for the man. This is because the woman, through many mistranslations and misinterpretations of Scripture, has instead been portrayed as a menial helper to the man, incapable of spiritual insight and easily deceived. However, this could not be further from the truth. Therefore, before we move on in this passage, I would like to take the time here to clear up some of these mistranslations and misinterpretations of Scripture.

In the Bible, we can see that God said, [18]"...It is not good for the man to be alone; I will make him a **helper suitable** ['ezer kenegdo' in Hebrew] for him" (Gen. 2:18). Now in reading this verse, most people assume that the reason the man was not good alone was that he was lonely. However, as we can see, God did not make a companion for Adam. God made him a "helper," an "ezer."[9] Therefore, since God made Adam an "ezer," it reveals to us one very important thing. Something was lacking on Adam's part. Now, one may ask, "How do we know from the word 'ezer' that something was lacking on Adam's part?" Well, we know this because the word "ezer" is always used to describe the one who comes to the aid of someone who is in need. It describes the one who has the strength or power to help. In fact, the word "ezer" has a combination of two roots: one means "to rescue, to save"; the other means "to be strong."[10] Furthermore, of the twenty-one times that the word "ezer" is used in the Bible, sixteen of those times, it refers to God as our helper. The NIV even translates the word "ezer" as "strength" in Psalm 89:19. Hence, since we know that a woman was not created as a physical strength for the man, she was created as a spiritual strength. The woman was taken from the man's own flesh and bone to fill what was lacking on his part. The man needed a helper, someone wiser than himself.

The second word, "kenegdo" (translated as "suitable"), also confirms that the woman was created because of her wisdom. The word "kenegdo" comes from two words in Hebrew—"ke" and "neged." "Ke" means "marker of comparison," meaning one "similar, as, or like," and "neged" means "in front of."[11] Consequently, by these words, we can see that God made for man, the woman, one "like" him, to be "in front of" him. Now, what is meant by the woman being "in front of" the man? Well, as we have seen, the woman is the "glory" of man. She is a source of spiritual illumination and strength; a lamp, or a light that helps the man see. And just as we would not cover up a light, so also, we would not hold a light behind us. Indeed, a light is held "in front of" a person to help guide the way.

(Note: The word "neged" is also translated as "before" and "opposite"; however, the words "before" and "opposite" mean "in front of." See the following examples.)

> NASB—[13]"Now it came about when Joshua was by Jericho, that he lifted up his eyes and looked, and behold, a man was standing **opposite** [neged] him…" (Josh. 5:13).

> NIV—[13]"Now when Joshua was near Jericho, he looked up and saw a man standing **in front of** [neged] him…" (Josh. 5:13).

> NIV—[11]"…when all Israel comes to appear before the LORD your God at the place he will choose, you shall read this law **before** [neged] them in their hearing" (Deut. 31:11).

> NASB—[11]"…when all Israel comes to appear before the LORD your God at the place which He will choose, you shall read this law **in front of** [neged] all Israel in their hearing" (Deut. 31:11).

(Also note: Out of the 151 times that the word "neged" appears in Scripture, it is translated as "suitable" only twice, when used of the woman. However, if one looks in a concordance, the word "suitable" would not make sense in any of the other 149 passages. See the following for several examples.)

[13]"Now it came about when Joshua was by Jericho, that he lifted up his eyes and looked, and behold, a man was standing **suitable** him…" (Josh. 5:13).

[11]"…when all Israel comes to appear before the LORD your God at the place which He will choose, you shall read this law **suitable** all Israel in their hearing" (Deut. 31:11).

[2]"When they set out from Rephidim, they came to the wilderness of Sinai and camped in the wilderness; and there Israel camped **suitable** the mountain" (Exod. 19:2).

(Note: The NASB translates "neged" as "in front of" in Exodus 19:2.)

[23]"After them Benjamin and Hasshub carried out repairs **suitable** their house…" (Neh. 3:23).

(Note: The NASB translates "neged" as "in front of" in Nehemiah 3:23.)

It is clear from Scripture that God not only created the woman similar to the man, but He also created her as a strength to help the man; to be in front of him. Therefore, I would translate Genesis 2:18 as, [18]"Then the LORD God said, 'It is not good for the man to be alone. I will make him a strong helper, one like him, to be in front of him.'"

Furthermore, the fact that God commanded the man to "cling" ("dabaq" in Hebrew) to his wife (Gen. 2:24) is further proof that the woman was created as a strength for the man. However, most people do not understand this analogy because the word "dabaq" is most often mistranslated as either "joined" or "united." However, Scripture does not state that a man is to be "joined" or "united" to his wife. It clearly states that the man is to "cling" to his wife; that he is to "hold fast" to her. For if one was in a dark forest, would they not cling or hold fast to their light? Furthermore, we must understand that the whole reason the man is commanded to cling to his wife is that she was taken out of man (Gen. 2:23–24). And she was taken out of man because he needed an "ezer" (Gen. 2:18–22). Therefore, Scripture is clear in showing us that the man is to cling to his wife because she is his "ezer."

36

The following are examples of the word "dabaq" as translated in Scripture.

[20]"You shall fear the LORD your God; you shall serve Him and **cling** [dabaq] to Him, and you shall swear by His name" (Deut. 10:20).

[22]"For if you are careful to keep all this commandment which I am commanding you to do, to love the LORD your God, to walk in all His ways and **hold fast** [dabaq] to Him..." (Deut. 11:22).

[5]"Only be very careful to observe the commandment and the law which Moses the servant of the LORD commanded you, to love the LORD your God and walk in all His ways and keep His commandments and **hold fast** [dabaq] to Him and serve Him with all your heart and with all your soul" (Josh. 22:5).

[6]"For he **clung** [dabaq] to the LORD; he did not depart from following Him, but kept His commandments, which the LORD had commanded Moses" (2 Kings 18:6).

[8]"My soul **clings** [dabaq] to You; Your right hand upholds me" (Ps. 63:8).

Still, another misinterpretation of Scripture comes from those who insist that Adam was somehow over Eve because he named all of the animals. However, Adam naming all of the animals was not part of some special privilege that he had, but was simply the process that God was using to find him a helper. This is evident by Genesis 2:20, which states, [20]"The man gave names to all the cattle, and to the birds of the sky, and to every beast of the field, but for Adam there was not found a helper suitable for him." In fact, the whole portion of Scripture which tells about God bringing the animals to Adam to see what he would call them is surrounded at the beginning and the end by the statements, [18]"...I will make him a helper suitable for him" (Gen. 2:18) and [20]"...but for Adam there was not found a helper suitable for him" (Gen. 2:20). Furthermore, it is clear that after Adam named all of the animals and was unable to find a helper, God immediately caused a deep sleep to come upon him in which He took Adam's own flesh and bone to fashion from him the woman (Gen. 2:20–22). So, these examples are just a few of the many mistranslations and misinterpretations of Scripture that cloud the fact that man was insufficient on his own and that the woman was created to fill what was lacking on his part.

In getting back to the passage at hand, we have seen in verse seven that Paul has made the correlation that a man ought not to cover (veil) Christ because He is the image and glory of God, and a man ought not to cover (veil) the woman because she is the glory of man. Subsequently, in verses 8–9, Paul then goes on to give the reason as to **WHY** a woman is a man's glory. He states, [8]"For man does not originate from woman, but woman from man; [9]for indeed, man was not created for the woman's sake, but woman for the man's sake." And indeed, these words of Paul go back to what I had explained previously (that the woman was created to fill what was lacking on the man's part), because again, Paul has just stated the reason as to why a woman is a man's glory. Oddly enough, though, many people seem to think that Paul has just stated the reason why a woman is inferior to a man; that she (contrary to Genesis 2:18–24) was created solely to perform the mundane tasks that the "all-sufficient" man desires. However, would it make sense for Paul to state that a woman is the glory of man and then, immediately afterward, state the reason as to why she is inferior? No! It would only make sense that Paul, after stating that a woman is a man's glory, would then state the reason as to why a woman is a man's glory. Therefore, Paul is saying that the woman is the glory of man because she originated from man. Indeed, the man was not created because of a deficiency on the woman's part, but rather, the woman was created because of a deficiency on the man's part. She was created for his sake, for it is he who needed an "ezer kenegdo." So again, in verses 8–9, Paul is stating the reason why a woman is a man's glory. Indeed, a woman was created with the needed wisdom, understanding, prudence, insight, and discernment to help illumine his path.

> [7]"…but the **woman is the glory of man**. [8]For man does not originate from woman, but woman from man; [9]for indeed man was not created for the woman's sake, but woman for the man's sake."

Then, in verse ten, Paul (supposedly) states, [10]"Therefore the woman ought to have *a symbol of* authority on her head…." However, if we were to translate this verse accurately, and according to the Greek, it would instead read as, [10]"For this reason, the woman ought to have authority over her head…." Now, the latter is the correct rendering for three reasons. First, when the Greek word "dia" is used in conjunction with the

Greek word "houtos," it means "for this reason."[12] Secondly, the words *"a symbol of"* are not in the original Greek. And thirdly, when the word "exousia," meaning "authority, power, the right to control or govern," is used in conjunction with the word "epi," meaning "on, over," it always refers to having "authority over" something or someone.[13] (See Matthew 9:6; Mark 2:10; Luke 5:24; Revelation 2:26; 6:8; 11:6; 13:7; 16:9; 20:6.) Therefore, again, verse ten should be rendered as, [10]"For this reason, the woman ought to have authority over her head...."

Now, one may ask, "Is Paul referring to a woman's literal or figurative head in verse ten?" Is Paul saying that because the woman was created for the man's sake, the woman ought to have authority over her own head? Or is he saying that because the woman was created for the man's sake, the woman ought to have authority over her head, the man? It is evident by the context that Paul is referring to a woman's figurative head. Paul is saying that since the woman was created for the man's sake, since she was created because of a deficiency on his part, the woman ought to have authority over her head, or source, the man. And the reason Paul says this, I believe, is because he is addressing the pride of these men. For I believe that Paul well understood that these men made their argument (for women to be veiled) under the guise that if a woman was unveiled, it was the same as a woman's head being shaved but that the real reason was one of dominance. Men had always given themselves prominence for the reason that they were the source of a woman. They claimed, as men do today, that they were to be in authority over women because a man was created first and a woman came from him. Therefore, having women veiled was a sign of their subordination. However, because Paul is aware of their underlying reason for wanting women to be veiled, he makes the following argument. It was the woman who was created for the man's sake; she was created because of a deficiency on his part. For this reason, she ought to have authority over the source from which she came.

> [7]"...but the woman is the glory of man. [8]For man does not originate from woman, but woman from man; [9]for indeed man was not created for the woman's sake, but woman for the man's sake. *[10]For this reason the woman ought to have authority over her head...."*
> (Paul's model: [3]"...and the man is the head of a woman....")

(Note: The fact that Paul says that the woman ought to have "authority over" her head, when he is speaking in reference to the man, in itself proves that the word "head," used figuratively in Greek, means "source/origin" rather than "leader/ruler." For it would not make sense for Paul to say that the woman ought to have authority over her "leader." It does, however, make sense for him to say that the woman ought to have authority over her "source" since she was created for his sake.)

Some may still argue that verse ten means that a woman is to have authority over her "own" head. However, there is no basis for this, because first of all, a literal meaning of head does not fit in with the context, including verses 11–12, which we will go over shortly. And secondly, in Paul's whole rebuttal (vv. 7–16), Paul uses the word "head" only twice, once in verse seven, when referring to Christ, and here in verse ten. Therefore, would Paul refer back to his model in verse seven with the figurative meaning of head, but then in verse ten, use the word head in a literal manner without indicating that he was not referring back to his model? No! Paul has given his model for a reason and lays out a very clear rebuttal. He gives absolutely no indication that he would now be talking about the woman's literal head. He does not use the common Greek word "idios," meaning "one's own,"[14] before the word head to indicate that he was now talking about the woman's own or literal head. And he does not do this because he is talking about the woman's figurative head, the man. Indeed, Paul is referring back to his model in verse ten, just as he did in verse seven.

As we have seen, Paul has just finished telling the men that the woman was created for the man's sake and that for this reason, the woman ought to have authority over the man. Then Paul adds a perplexing little statement—[10]"…because of the angels" [dia tous angelous]. The woman ought to have authority over the man because of the angels? This statement seems a bit odd because no place in Scripture states anything of the sort. But I believe this misfit has to do with the fact that the word "angelous" was left in its untranslated form (angels) when it should have been translated as "messengers." (Note: The Young's Literal Translation Bible renders this portion of verse ten as, [10]"…because of the messengers.") This is because the Greek word "angelous" actually means "messengers" and can also refer to human messengers (Luke 7:24, 27; 9:52; James 2:25) or a manifestation of God Himself (Acts 7:30–32, 35, 38). Therefore, the context must determine who the "messenger" is.

40

The next question is, "Which messengers is Paul speaking about?" Is he speaking about the angelic messengers that serve God? Is he speaking of human messengers? Or is he speaking of God (Elohim)? The first two options do not make sense with the text. A woman would not have authority over the man because of angelic or human messengers. However, a woman can have authority over the man if it is from God. Therefore, I believe it is the last option; that "angelous" is a reference to "Elohim." (Note: Elohim means God; plural of majesty. Elohim is plural in form but singular in meaning.)[15] For it is Elohim who saw that it was not good for the man to be alone (Gen. 2:18). It is Elohim who stated (gave us His message) that the man needed a strong helper, one like him, to be in front of him (Gen. 2:18). It is Elohim who created the woman for the man's sake (Gen. 2:20–22). And it is Elohim who stated (gave us His message) that a man shall leave his father and mother to cling to his wife (Gen. 2:24).

(Note: The definite article in Greek often has the force of a possessive pronoun.[16] Therefore, this portion of verse ten should be rendered as, [10]"…because of our Messengers." Also, just as the word Elohim is plural in form but singular in meaning, so also the word Messengers is plural in form but singular in meaning.)

Furthermore, I would like to show evidence that the word "angelous" is sometimes used in Scripture to refer to "Elohim." Read carefully the following two passages.

> [4]"What is man that You take thought of him, and the son of man that You care for him? [5]Yet You have made him a little lower than God [Elohim] and You crown him with glory and majesty! [6]You make him to rule over the works of Your hands; You have put all things under his feet" (Ps. 8:4–6).

> [6]"But one has testified somewhere, saying, 'WHAT IS MAN, THAT YOU REMEMBER HIM? OR THE SON OF MAN, THAT YOU ARE CONCERNED ABOUT HIM? [7]YOU HAVE MADE HIM FOR A LITTLE WHILE LOWER THAN THE ANGELS [angelous]; YOU HAVE CROWNED HIM WITH GLORY AND HONOR, AND HAVE APPOINTED HIM OVER THE WORKS OF YOUR HANDS; [8]YOU HAVE PUT ALL THINGS IN SUBJECTION UNDER HIS FEET'" (Heb. 2:6–8).

41

(Note: It is clear by reading these passages that the author of Hebrews is directly quoting the prophecy of King David. Unfortunately, though, there are some discrepancies between the two passages because of inconsistent translation. Also, the highlighted/underlined letters should be capitalized as King David and the author of Hebrews are referring to Christ. More will be said about this in my sixth chapter, "Hypotasso, Part I.")

In looking at the preceding passages, we can see that the author of Hebrews has used the Greek word "angelous" when quoting the Hebrew word for God—"Elohim." Therefore, I must ask, "Did the author of Hebrews accidentally misquote the inspired words of King David? Or, did the author of Hebrews purposefully change the inspired words of King David?" No! Clearly, the author of Hebrews is also saying that Christ was made for a little while lower than God, just like the author of Psalms. Clearly, "angelous/messengers" here is a reference to "Elohim." Indeed, Christ was not made lower than "angels" as is commonly taught due to the mistranslations in Hebrews 2:7, 9, for Christ created angels (Col. 1:15–16). Instead, Christ was made for a little while (while here on earth) lower than God (Elohim), the plurality of majesty. Philippians 2:5–8 confirms this. It says, [5]"Have this attitude in yourselves which was also in Christ Jesus, [6]who, although He existed in the form of God, did not regard **equality with God** a thing to be grasped, [7]but emptied Himself, taking the form of a bond-servant, *and* being made in the likeness of men. [8]Being found in appearance as a man, He humbled Himself by becoming obedient to the point of death, even death on a cross." So, just as the word "angelous" refers to God (Elohim; plural of majesty) in Hebrews 2:7, 9, I also believe that the word "angelous" refers to God (Elohim; plural of majesty) in 1 Corinthians 11:10. Furthermore, I believe the reason that Paul uses the word "messengers" when referencing God is that he is reminding the men that it is God who gave us His message at the beginning, which stated that the man needed a "strong helper, one like him, to be in front of him" and that the man is to "cling to" his wife.

So, to review, Paul has stated thus far, [7]"…but the woman is the glory of man. [8]For man does not originate from woman, but woman from man; [9]for indeed man was not created for the woman's sake, but woman for the man's sake. *[10]For this reason the woman ought to have authority over her head [the man], because of our Messengers [Elohim; plural of majesty]."*

42

Now that Paul has addressed the pride of these men, he then goes on to say in verses 11–12, [11]"However, in the Lord, neither is woman independent of man, nor is man independent of woman. [12]For as the woman originates from the man, so also the man *has his birth* through the woman; and all things originate from God." (Note: The words *"has his birth"* are not in the original Greek. For the Greek, KJV-NIV, literally reads as, [11]"Nevertheless, neither woman without man nor man without woman, in [the] Lord; [12]for as the woman of the man, so also the man through the woman; but all things of God.")

So here, Paul makes the point that, in the Lord, neither is woman without man nor is man without woman. And the reason Paul says this is because he understands that God has purposefully designed the relation between men and women to be one of mutual dependence, both in creation and in life. For God does not want either gender to have a sense of haughtiness or self-adulation. God does not want either gender to boast. Hence, this again is the reason why Paul first states, in verse ten, that the woman "ought" to have authority over the man. Again, he is addressing the pride of the men who wrote him. He is addressing their unfounded attitude of superiority over women since it was the woman who was created for the man's sake. Nevertheless, Paul used the word "ought" because he knows that God did not give the woman actual authority over the man because neither is the woman without the man. For again, Paul understands that God has designed the relation between men and women to be one of mutual dependence so that neither one can boast. And what is more, Paul then makes the point that all things are of God. For neither a man nor a woman has anything to do with the creation process, for God alone is the creator of all. Consequently, it is God who has the authority over us, not man over woman or woman over man. Thus, Paul is making the point that men and women should give God the glory and that neither one should boast. Indeed, no one is to boast in themselves, for all things come from God.

(Note: Throughout these verses, we can see that Paul is talking about origination. Therefore, a literal meaning of the word "head" would not make sense in verse ten because it would not fit in with the passage as a whole. As a result, it again is easy to see that the word "head," used figuratively in Greek, means "source/origin.")

[7]"…but the woman is the glory of man. [8]For man does not originate from woman, but woman from man; [9]for indeed man was not created for the woman's sake, but woman for the man's sake. *[10]For this reason, the woman ought to have authority over her head [or source, the man], because of our Messengers [Elohim; plural of majesty].* [11]However, in the Lord, neither is woman independent of man, nor is man independent of woman. [12]For as the woman originates from the man, *so also the man through the woman;* and all things originate from God."

Next, we come to verse thirteen. It says, [13]"Judge for yourselves: Is it proper for a woman to pray to God *with her head* uncovered?" However, the Greek literally reads as, [13]"Among you yourselves judge proper **it is** for a woman unveiled to God to pray." As a result, verse thirteen should be rendered as, [13]"Judge for yourselves that **it is** proper for a woman to pray to God unveiled." For indeed, Paul is not asking a question (is it), but rather, he is making a statement (it is).[17] The Greek word "estin" means "he is, she is, it is." Hence, the translators have incorrectly made this verse into a question. For as we have seen, Paul has just given his rebuttal to the men as to why a woman should not be veiled while she prays or prophesies. He now wants the men to judge (determine the correctness of this matter) for themselves that it is proper for a woman to pray to God unveiled. Now, perhaps the translators have put this sentence into question format because to do otherwise would make it incredibly obvious that verses 4–6 were not words original to Paul. For indeed, verse thirteen, correctly translated, contradicts verses 5–6 outright. As a result, this is the fourth reason why we know unequivocally that verses 4–6 are quoted. Again, when this verse is translated correctly, we can see that Paul plainly states that it is proper for a woman to pray to God unveiled. As a result, Paul would not have made the argument that every woman who has her head unveiled while praying or prophesying disgraces her head.

(Note: It is evident that the reason Paul omitted the word "prophesy" in verse thirteen was that he was stressing to the men the fact that women pray to God throughout the day, not just while in church. Consequently, by this omission, Paul is saying to the men that just as it is proper for a woman to pray to God unveiled outside of the church, so also it is proper for her to pray to God unveiled inside of the church.)

44

I want to point out one more thing concerning the translation of verse thirteen by the NASB translators. Notice the words *"with her head"* are in italics. This is because these words are not in the original Greek. And this is important to note because Paul has intentionally left the word "head" out in this statement. But one may ask, "Why has Paul done this?" Well, he has purposefully left the word "head" out because he is now talking about the woman's literal head. And his use of the word "head" in his rebuttal only corresponds to his model with the figurative meaning of head. Thus, Paul leaves the word "head" out so that he will not confuse the people to whom he is writing. This omission is further proof that Paul is talking about a woman's figurative head, the man, in verse ten.

Now we come to verses 14–15. In these verses, we can see, once again, that the translators have made this sentence into a question. But again, it should remain a statement. The translators have translated a disjunctive particle near the beginning of verse fourteen as "does" in order to make it a question. However, this disjunctive particle actually means "or, than, and, either."[18] It does not mean "does." In fact, out of its 341 uses in the New Testament, it is translated as "does" only one time, right here in 1 Corinthians 11:14. Therefore, below I will first translate the sentence as the NASB has rendered with the disjunctive particle translated as "does." Then I will translate it with its most common meaning "or" so that we can see how the mistranslation of this disjunctive particle changes the meaning of the sentence.

> [14]"Does not even nature itself teach you that if a man has long hair, it is a dishonor to him, [15]but if a woman has long hair, it is a glory to her?"

> [14]"Or not even nature itself teaches you that if a man has long hair, it is a dishonor to him, [15]but if a woman has long hair, it is a glory to her."

The first sentence (put into rhetorical question format) is saying that nature teaches us that if a man has long hair, it is a dishonor to him, but if a woman has long hair, it is a glory to her. And the second sentence is saying the very opposite, that nature does not teach us this. And nature does not teach us this, as Paul says, because a man's and a woman's hair "by nature" is the same. For both men's and women's hair grows at the same rate, feels the same, and looks the same, as human hair is

45

indistinguishable to the human eye to tell which sex it came from if it is not attached to the person. Moreover, both men and women can grow their hair long or can cut their hair with scissors or a razor. Indeed, a man's and a woman's hair "by nature" is the same. So by the translators taking the liberty of making Paul's statement into a question, they have made an argument that is the complete opposite of what Paul was actually saying. For cultural practices, not nature, determine whether long or short hair is honoring or dishonoring to a man or a woman.

Furthermore, if Paul were saying that long hair was a dishonor to a man, then what about Samson? Did not the angel (Messenger) of the LORD appear to the mother of Samson and say to her, [3]"…Behold now, you are barren and have borne no *children*, but you shall conceive and give birth to a son. [4]Now therefore, be careful not to drink wine or strong drink, nor eat any unclean thing. [5]For behold, you shall conceive and give birth to a son, and **no razor shall come upon his head,** for the boy shall be a Nazirite to God from the womb…"? (Judg. 13:3–5). So, did the angel (Messenger) of the LORD tell Samson's mother to have Samson grow long hair as a dishonor to him? And did not God's blessing of strength upon Samson disappear when he disobeyed God, and his hair was shaved? (Judg. 16:19–20). Also, what about Samuel? Does not Hannah pray to God to give her a son, and in return, she would give him to the LORD all the days of his life, and that in obedience to God no razor would ever come on his head? (1 Sam. 1:11). So if Paul here is saying that it is a dishonor for a man to have long hair because nature teaches us this, then hasn't God gone against his own teaching of nature by wanting both Samson and Samuel to have long hair? Hasn't God created nature? Certainly, if God did not want men to have long hair, then He would have disallowed it through "nature" just as He has disallowed women from growing mustaches or beards through "nature." So, since nature does not teach us that if a man has long hair, it is a dishonor to him, it is therefore not disgraceful for a man to grow long hair. Likewise, since nature does not teach us that if a woman has long hair, it is a glory to her, it is therefore not disgraceful for a woman to cut her hair.

Paul then goes on to say in verse fifteen, [15]"…For her hair is given to her for a covering." However, verse fifteen should be rendered as, [15]"…because the long hair has been given **instead of** a covering." (Note: The word translated as "for," in verse fifteen, is "anti" in Greek and means "in exchange for, in place of, or instead of."[19] Also, the pronoun "aute"

46

[translated as "to her"] is "omitted by Papyrus 46, D, F, G, and also by the majority of later Greek manuscripts."[20] Therefore, since the majority of ancient Greek manuscripts do not contain the word "aute," it confirms to us that the words "to her" were not words original to Paul. For it would be absurd to think that the scribes would have overlooked this word in one of the most scrutinized passages of the Bible. Indeed, it is much more probable that this word was added to some manuscripts by scribes because of their own bias.)

So what Paul is saying here is that nature does not teach us that if a man has long hair, it is a dishonor to him, but if a woman has long hair, it is a glory to her because the long hair has been given (to us all) instead of a covering. In other words, Paul is telling the men that their argument has no basis. He is telling them that God did not give a man long hair as a dishonor to him, since the men had made the argument that every man who has *anything* ("anything" would include hair) down over his head while praying or prophesying disgraces his head. Nor did God give a woman long hair for vain beauty purposes, as many women have unmanageable hair, e.g., flat, limp, frizzy. Instead, Paul explains, God gave long hair to men and women for protection from the sun and protection from the cold so that they would not have to wear a covering every time they stepped outdoors. So again, what Paul is actually saying in verses 14–15 is this, [14]"Not even nature itself teaches you that if a man has long hair, it is a dishonor to him, [15]but if a woman has long hair, it is a glory to her because the long hair has been given [to us all] instead of a covering."

Before I move on, I would like to say that verses 14–15 are the fifth reason why we know undeniably that verses 4–6 are quoted. For indeed, verses 14–15 contradict verses 4–6 outright. (See the following.)

> **Argument:** *[4]"Every man who has anything down over his head while praying or prophesying disgraces his head."*

> **Refutation:** *[14]"Not even nature itself teaches you that if a man has long hair, it is a dishonor to him, [15]…because the long hair has been given instead of a covering."*

(Note: In Jewish culture, men wore their hair either long or short. See 2 Samuel 14:25–26. Therefore, it is highly probable that some of the men who wrote Paul had long hair. Also, when the men coined verse four, it is apparent that they were thinking of a man disgracing his head in relation to a veil, not long hair. However, because the men made the argument of women disgracing their head in relation to hair, Paul makes a similar argument for them. In addition, the fact that Paul is speaking of a man, and not Christ, in verse fourteen shows us that the person or persons who coined verse four are speaking of a man disgracing his own literal head, not his figurative head.)

> **Argument:** *[5] *"But every woman who has her head unveiled while praying or prophesying disgraces her head, for it is one and the same thing as having been shaved. [6]For if a woman is not veiled, let her also have her hair cut off; but if it is disgraceful for a woman to have her hair cut off or to be shaved, let her be veiled."**

> **Refutation:** *[14]"Not even nature itself teaches you that...[15]if a woman has long hair, it is a glory to her because the long hair has been given instead of a covering."**

And finally, in verse sixteen, Paul says, [16]"But if one is inclined to be contentious, we have no other practice, nor have the churches of God." However, verse sixteen should be translated as [16]"But if one is inclined to be contentious, we have no **such** practice, nor have the churches of God." (Note: The Greek word "toiauten" means "such," not "other."[21] Also, the only practice that is mentioned in this passage is in verse six—[6]"... let her be veiled.") As a result, Paul is making clear to the men that if any of them are inclined to be quarrelsome about this subject, then they should plainly know that they have no such practice of requiring women to veil their heads, nor have the churches, or people, of God. Hence, since Paul has stated that the people of God have no such practice, we know unequivocally that verses 4–6 are not Paul's words. Indeed, verse sixteen is the sixth reason why we know that verses 4–6 are quoted.

Within this passage, Paul ingeniously answers both the underlying argument of these men, which was one of dominance, and the stated argument of these men, which was one of shorn or shaven hair. The real argument (which was not stated), he answers with his model (v. 3) and verses 7–13, and the argument of guise (vv. 4–6), he answers in verses 14–16. He intertwines both answers with such perfection and flawlessness that we cannot help but see the penmanship of God and the love He has for His daughters. This passage clearly shows us that although the world may treat women with disdain and inequity, the God of the universe does not. Certainly, one would think that Christian men would be different, but even they, through their lies, have made Galatians 3:28 ring hollow. But truly, there is neither male nor female in Christ.

In ending this chapter, I would like to say that the teachings of Paul in this passage are in perfect harmony with the teachings of Christ and with Scripture as a whole. Nowhere does Paul contradict God's Word but holds fast to it every step of the way. It is unfortunate, then, that men since Paul have shown themselves to be dishonest and untrustworthy with God's Word in this passage. Through their mistranslations and misinterpretations of Scripture, they have rendered this passage as nonsensical and have twisted the intended meaning 180 degrees. Indeed, their manipulations of Scripture have turned God's truth into lies. Furthermore, their foolish claim that they are the image and glory of God is a result of pride and is a prime example of men who do not understand either what they are saying or the matters about which they make confident assertions. Nevertheless, if men took the time to compare Scripture with Scripture, and put a little effort into trying to understand the truth of God's Word instead of trying to further their own agenda, they would be able to avoid the heresy that they teach. Certainly, there is no doubt that many men will hold on to the usual teaching of this passage as the presented rendering will not sit well with them. However, to do so, they must continue to claim that they are the image and glory of God. As we go along, we will again see the "wall of lies" tumble down in regard to women. And we must always remember that all of Scripture is in perfect harmony. God's Word will never contradict itself.

1 Corinthians 11:3–16

Paul's Model:

[3]"But I want you to understand that Christ is the head **(F)** of every man, and the man is the head **(F)** of a woman, and God is the head **(F)** of Christ."

Paul Quotes a Faction of Men from Corinth Who Wrote Him:

[4]"Every man who has anything down over his head (L) while praying or prophesying disgraces his head (L). [5]But every woman who has her head (L) unveiled while praying or prophesying disgraces her head (L), for it is one and the same thing as having been shaved. [6]For if a woman is not veiled, let her also have her hair cut off; but if it is disgraceful for a woman to have her hair cut off or to be shaved, let her be veiled."

Paul's Rebuttal and Reference Back to His Model:

[7]"For a man indeed ought not to veil his head **(F)**, since He is the image and glory of God, but the woman is the glory of man. [8]For man is not of woman, but woman of man; [9]for indeed, man was not created because of the woman, but woman because of the man. [10]For this reason, the woman ought to have authority over her head **(F)**, because of our Messengers. [11]However, in the Lord, neither is woman without man, nor is man without woman. [12]For as the woman is from the man, so also the man through the woman, and all things from God. [13]Judge for yourselves that it is proper for a woman to pray to God unveiled. [14]For not even nature itself teaches you that if a man has long hair, it is a dishonor to him, [15]but if a woman has long hair, it is a glory to her because the long hair has been given instead of a covering. [16]But if one is inclined to be contentious, we have no such practice, nor have the people of God."

(F) – Figurative (source/origin)

(L) – Literal

1 CORINTHIANS 11:3-16
[with added words]

Paul's Model:

[3]"But I want you to understand that Christ is the head [source] of every man, and the man is the head [source] of a woman, and God is the head [source] of Christ [incarnate]."

Paul Quotes a Faction of Men from Corinth Who Wrote Him:

[4]*"Every man who has anything down over his head while praying or prophesying disgraces his [own] head. [5]But every woman who has her head unveiled while praying or prophesying disgraces her [own] head, for it is one and the same thing as having been shaved. [6]For if a woman is not veiled, let her also have her hair cut off; but if it is disgraceful for a woman to have her hair cut off or to be shaved, let her be veiled."*

Paul's Rebuttal and Reference Back to His Model:

[7]"For a man indeed ought not to veil his head [Christ], since He is the image and glory of God, but the woman is the glory of man [so she ought not to be veiled either]. [8]For man is not of woman, but woman of man; [9]for indeed, man was not created because of the woman, but woman because of the man [because of his need for her]. [10]For this reason, the woman ought to have authority over her head [the man], because of our Messengers [Elohim; plural of majesty]. [11]However, in the Lord, [we do not rule over one another because] neither is woman without man, nor is man without woman. [12]For as the woman is from the man, so also the man through the woman, and all things from God [so give Him the glory and let neither one boast]. [13]Judge for yourselves that it is proper for a woman to pray to God unveiled. [14]For not even nature itself teaches you that if a man has long hair, it is a dishonor to him, [15]but if a woman has long hair, it is a glory to her because the long hair has been given [to us all] instead of a covering. [16]But if one is inclined to be contentious, we have no such practice [of requiring women to veil their heads], nor have the people of God."

1 CORINTHIANS 11:3-16

(Kephale – Head)

Correct:

Verse 3:   F   F   F

Verse 4:   L   L

Verse 5:   L   L

Verse 7:   F

Verse 10: F

Incorrect:

Verse 3:   F   F   F

Verse 4:   L   F

Verse 5:   L   F

Verse 7:   L

Verse 10: L

(F) – Figurative

(L) – Literal

4

1 Corinthians 14:34-35

In the previous chapter, we examined a passage of Scripture that was deemed to be one of the most difficult in the entire Bible. The passage was difficult, no doubt, because it was nonsensical and contradictory in nature. However, when we learned that several verses were a quote of a faction of men who wrote Paul, cohesion and understanding were brought to the passage as a whole and thus complete harmony to God's Word. There is no doubt then that 1 Corinthians 14:34-35 is also quoted. Indeed, verses 34-35 are not Paul's words[1] but rather the words of another faction of men from Corinth who wrote him. (See 1 Corinthians 11:17-19.) For it is clear that the words in these verses are opposed to everything Paul is saying in this passage. Let us take a look. Verses 34-35 state:

> [34]"The women are to keep silent in the churches; for they are not permitted to speak, but are to subject themselves, just as the Law also says. [35]If they desire to learn anything, let them ask their own husbands at home; for it is improper for a woman to speak in church."

Now let us take a look at the rest of 1 Corinthians 14. The following are key verses that Paul states to **ALL** believers in chapter fourteen.

> [1]"Pursue love, yet desire earnestly spiritual *gifts*, but especially that you may prophesy."

> [3]"But one who prophesies speaks to men for edification and exhortation and consolation."

[4]"One who speaks in a tongue edifies himself; but one who prophesies edifies the church."

[5]"Now I wish that you all spoke in tongues, but *even* more that you would prophesy...."

[12]"So also you, since you are zealous of spiritual *gifts*, seek to abound for the edification of the church."

[22]"So then tongues are for a sign, not to those who believe but to unbelievers; but prophecy *is for a sign*, not to unbelievers but to those who believe."

[26]"What is *the outcome* then, brethren? When you assemble, each one has a psalm, has a teaching, has a revelation, has a tongue, has an interpretation. Let all things be done for edification."

[29]"Let two or three prophets speak, and let the others pass judgment."

[31]"For you can all prophesy one by one, so that all may learn and all may be exhorted."

[39]"Therefore, my brethren, desire earnestly to prophesy, and do not forbid to speak in tongues."

We can clearly see that these are the words of Paul, both the main points (vv. 1–31) and the summation (v. 39). Therefore, verses 34–35 cannot be the words of Paul. For Paul's words and verses 34–35 are at the opposite ends of the spectrum. They are in complete opposition to one other. They are wholly and diametrically opposed. Therefore, there is no way for one to be true and also the other. For wouldn't it be an impossible feat for women to *speak* to both men and women for their edification and exhortation and consolation (v. 3) if they were not permitted to *speak* (v. 34)? And Paul would not tell women to desire earnestly spiritual gifts but especially that they may prophesy (v. 1) if they were to keep silent in the churches (v. 34). Paul would not tell women to seek to abound for the edification of the church (v. 12) if they were not permitted to speak (v. 34). Paul would not tell women that when they assembled with other believers, they could give a psalm, a teaching, a revelation, a tongue, or an interpretation (v. 26) if it was improper for them to speak in church (v. 35). Indeed, the possibility that both sets of instructions originated from Paul is nil, zip, zilch. Paul's words are reflective of God's Word, and verses 34–35 are in fierce opposition. As a result, verses 34–35 absolutely, positively, cannot be the words of Paul. Indeed, verses 34–35 are the words of a faction of men who wrote him. And if I surmise correctly, it is this faction of men who were causing the disorderly conduct that Paul speaks of in verse thirty-three. (Note: The word that is translated as "confusion" in verse thirty-three is "akatastasia" in Greek and means "disorder, rebellion, riot, revolution.")[2] Now I believe this to be the case because I do not believe that it is by mere coincidence that Paul's quote comes immediately after verse thirty-three. For I believe that these men had a major problem with the fact that women were equal heirs in the body of Christ and had full rights as daughters of God. They disliked the fact that women could read and quote Scripture, teach them, prophesy for their edification, exhortation, and consolation, speak in tongues and interpret tongues because they were used of their Jewish Law, which stated that it was a shame for a woman's voice to be heard among men.[3] So because they disliked this new way of things, they were causing "akatastasia" (v. 33). They were rebelling and rioting and trying to overthrow what was taking place. They were interrupting the women who were prophesying so that they could not speak (vv. 30–31).

It is also important to note that after Paul quotes these men, he immediately rebukes their attitude toward women by asking them two rhetorical questions. He first asks them, [36]"Was it from you that the word of God *first* went forth?" (Note: The word that is translated as "word" in verse thirty-six is "logos" in Greek and means spoken or written word or message.)[4] Now, Paul asks them this question because he knows the answer is a resounding "NO"! Indeed, Paul knows that no portion of Scripture originated through these men who were trying to silence women by their own traditions and rabbinical laws. At the same time, Paul knows that God's Holy Word did originate through women who prophesied. In fact, many people today do not understand this point that Paul is trying to make to these men. He is trying to get them to understand that God's Holy Word, the very Scripture that they will read and teach from on the Sabbath, and the very Scripture that they forbid women to read and teach from, did not originate through them, but through many holy men AND WOMEN whom God had chosen.

Therefore, let us now look at Scripture that has come forth to us through women. Turn to Luke 1:46–55. It says, [46]"And Mary said: 'My soul exalts the Lord, [47]and my spirit has rejoiced in God my Savior. [48]For He has had regard for the humble state of His bondslave; For behold, from this time on all generations will count me blessed. [49]For the Mighty One has done great things for me; and holy is His name. [50]AND HIS MERCY IS UPON GENERATION AFTER GENERATION TOWARD THOSE WHO FEAR HIM. [51]He has done mighty deeds with His arm; He has scattered *those who were* proud in the thoughts of their heart. [52]He has brought down rulers from *their* thrones, and has exalted those who were humble. [53]HE HAS FILLED THE HUNGRY WITH GOOD THINGS; And sent away the rich empty-handed. [54]He has given help to Israel His servant, in remembrance of His mercy, [55]as He spoke to our fathers, to Abraham and his descendants forever.'" So here, the Word of God has come forth to us through Mary. Now, please do not make the mistake of thinking it is Luke. Luke is writing down Mary's words, but they did not originate, or first go forth, through him. They originated to us through Mary by God, for it was Mary who was inspired by God to speak these words. Now Luke was inspired by God to write an account of things (Luke 1:1–4); nevertheless, much of what he has written down has not originated through him but from other men and women. Therefore, it is perplexing why we give more credit to the one who takes dictation than the one who gives the discourse. Furthermore, it was Mary who learned of Christ's birth through the angel Gabriel (Luke 1:26–38). No men were present at the time. No men were eyewitnesses. No men heard the voice of the angel. She was the only human ever to see or to hear the angel. We would not know about this part of Scripture if it were not for Mary.

Likewise, what about the resurrection of Christ? The women were the only ones to hear the angel's voices at the tomb (Matt. 28:5–7; Mark 16:5–7; Luke 24:4–7; John 20:12–13). None of the male disciples were present. Therefore, we have this testimony of the angels in God's Word because of the women. And Mary Magdalene was the very first one to see our risen Lord and to hear His voice (John 20:14–18). This testimony, too, we have first from a woman.

Also, do we not have the divinely inspired utterances of the prophetess Deborah? Did she not say to Barak, [6]"...Behold, the LORD, the God of Israel, has commanded, 'Go and march to Mount Tabor, and take with you ten thousand men from the sons of Naphtali and from the sons of Zebulun. [7]I will draw out to you Sisera, the commander of Jabin's army, with his chariots and his many *troops* to the river Kishon, and I will give him into your hand'"? (Judg. 4:6–7). And did not Deborah also say to Barak, after he showed himself to be weak in faith by not believing that God would speak through a woman (v. 8), ⁹..."I will surely go with you; nevertheless, the honor shall not be yours on the journey that you are about to take, for the LORD will sell Sisera into the hands of a woman"? (Judg. 4:9).

Also, what about Huldah? Did not King Josiah send Hilkiah the high priest, Ahikam the son of Shaphan, Achbor the son of Micaiah, Shaphan the scribe, and Asaiah the king's servant to inquire of the LORD concerning the words of the book of the Law which had been found? (2 Kings 22:12–13). And did not this high priest and the other men go to Huldah, the prophetess? (2 Kings 22:14). Did she not hear directly from God and speak to these men in 2 Kings 22:15–20 saying, ¹⁵ "...Thus says the LORD God of Israel..."? Are her words not recorded for us in both 2 Kings 22:15–20 and 2 Chronicles 34:23–28? From whom did these portions of Scripture originate? Did they originate from the unknown author of 2 Kings? Or did they originate from the possible author, Ezra, in 2 Chronicles? Did they originate through two different authors? Or did they originate to us through Huldah? Yes, this Word from God first came forth to us through the spoken words of Huldah. It was Huldah who heard God's voice. The very words of this woman not only taught the high priest, scribe, and other men in that day, but her very words still teach us today. Men are taught by her words; men teach by her words, yet men themselves, who have never heard God's voice as this woman had, still insist that a woman cannot teach.

Furthermore, what about Hannah's words? Are they not written down for us in 1 Samuel 2:1–10? From whom did they originate? Did they originate through Hannah or through the author of 1 Samuel? The author of 1 Samuel is unknown; however, they still originated through Hannah. It was she who first spoke these words, for it was Hannah who was inspired by God to speak these words.

In the Bible, do we not also have the words of wisdom of Abigail? (1 Sam. 25:24–31).

Do we not have the very words of the Queen of Sheba? (1 Kings 10:6–9; 2 Chron. 9:5–8).

What about the portion of Scripture recorded in Proverbs 31? In Proverbs 31:1 it says, [1]"The words of King Lemuel, the oracle which his mother taught him." Now the word that is translated as "oracle" is "massa" in Hebrew and also means a "prophetic utterance" or "prophecy."[5] So, who spoke by prophetic utterance, the king or his mother? Did King Lemuel say by God's Spirit, [2]"What, O my son? And what, O son of my womb?..." (Prov. 31:2). Did King Lemuel even have a womb? Or was it his mother who was inspired by God to speak these words? And did she not teach the king through her prophetic words? How many times have I heard men on Sunday morning, teach a sermon to God's people from the very words and wisdom of this woman, yet they themselves teach that a woman cannot teach. The ignorance of such men amazes me. They just don't get this simple rebuke of Paul's. They do not understand that it was through this woman that God's Word first came forth unto us. They act as if the words of women were not valid and did not count as Scripture until men wrote them down. But shall we apply this same reasoning to the words of Jesus? Shall we say that Jesus' words were not valid and did not count as Scripture until men wrote them down? Of course not! But men continually take for themselves the credit that is due to women for the words they have spoken. Not only did the men in Paul's day not get it, but men today do not get it. Because of their own hardheartedness toward women and lack of understanding of Scripture, they continually tell women that they cannot teach; yet, they themselves will teach from the very words of women in Scripture.

I would also like to say that it is ridiculous for one to say that prophesying is not teaching. For how could Paul say that all may *learn* by those who prophesy (v. 31) if prophesying is not teaching? For how can one *learn* if one is not taught? Furthermore, Paul spells out very clearly that prophesying is for the edification and exhortation and consolation of all believers (v. 3). And to "edify" is to "instruct in such a way as to improve, enlighten, or uplift morally, spiritually, or intellectually"; to "exhort" is to urge earnestly, by advice or warning, to do what is proper; and to "console" is to comfort those in distress.[6] Moreover, Paul's very own words, in verse nineteen, show us that prophesying is indeed teaching. For in verse nineteen, Paul states, when speaking of prophesying, that he desires to speak five words with his mind so that he can "instruct" others in the church. In addition, Paul makes clear, in verse six, that revelation is prophecy, and that knowledge is teaching. This means that something that is not previously known, revealed, or realized is prophecy, and something that is known, or is of knowledge, is teaching. As a result, prophecy must come first. (See 1 Corinthians 12:28.) For one cannot teach by way of knowledge if they do not have first, the prophecy revealed to them. Indeed, the one who prophesies teaches God's Word for the first time, either by hearing directly from God or by God speaking to their spirit, and the one who teaches, teaches from information given by the one who prophesied. Therefore, it is absurd to say that women can prophesy but not teach. Else, a woman could make known to others what was not previously known but then could not teach others what she had previously made known to them. (This is why prophecy was a greater gift than teaching—1 Corinthians 12:28, 31; 14:1, 3, 12.) And many men feel assured in their pride that no woman has actually written any portion of Scripture. However, there are many books of the Bible where the author is unknown, and many scholars think that Priscilla is the author of Hebrews. Certainly, a woman could have written God's Word since women were allowed to speak God's Word.

There is no denying the fact that God's Word first went forth through these very women and other women as well, women such as Sarah, Ruth, Naomi, Rahab, Esther, Miriam, King Solomon's lover, Elizabeth, Martha, and the woman at the well. It is also clear from Paul's question that no portion of Scripture first went forth through the self-righteous men whom he rebukes. So again, Paul knows the answer to his first question is a resounding "NO"! It was not from these men that the Word of God first went forth. Thus, Paul asks them a second question. For Paul knows that the answer to it is also a resounding "NO"! He then asks them, [36]"...Or has it come to you only?" For Paul wants to know if these men somehow thought that they were so superior that God gave His Word only to them and that the rest of us, and even Paul himself, did not know about it. But Paul indeed knows that these men were not the only ones to whom God gave His Word. Indeed, God gave His Word to ALL of us. As a result, we are all aware of its contents and cannot be deceived.

In verses 37–38, we should also note that Paul continues his rebuke and says, [37]"If anyone thinks he is a prophet or spiritual, let him recognize that the things which I write to you are the Lord's commandment. [38]But if anyone does not recognize *this*, he is not recognized." Therefore, Paul is making known to the men, and to all, that if they think themselves to be a prophet or a spiritual person, then they are to fully know that the things which he has written, in verses 1–33, are the Lord's commandment. But if they choose not to recognize this, then they themselves are not to be recognized. In other words, Paul is saying that believers are not to give credence to anyone who teaches that women cannot teach. Those men are to teach in an empty church.

And finally, we should note that Paul, in verses 39–40, sums up the things he has just written and says, [39]"Therefore, my brethren, desire earnestly to prophesy, and do not forbid to speak in tongues. [40]But all things must be done properly and in an orderly manner." Now, I would like to take a moment here to say that Paul's summation is extremely significant. When one sums up their words, they are giving, in brief form, a condensed statement of their main points that they previously had stated. And notice that a woman being silent is not part of it. For Paul sums up that both men and women should desire earnestly to prophesy and that no one should be forbidden to speak in tongues, but that all of these things should be done properly and in an orderly manner.

The following shows the different parts of 1 Corinthians 14:

Verses 1–33 – Paul's own view and the Lord's commandment.

Verses 34–35 – Paul quotes the faction of men from Corinth who wrote him.

Verses 36–38 – Paul gives a rebuke to the faction of men who wrote him.

Verses 39–40 – Paul sums up the things which he has written in verses 1–33.

In ending this chapter, I would like to say that it is shown in the Bible that the disciples sometimes could not grasp simple teachings of Jesus and of Scripture because of their hardheartedness (Mark 6:52; 8:14–21; 16:11; Luke 24:25–26; John 13:12–17). So it is the same here. For indeed, the reason that most men cannot grasp the concept that verses 34–35 are quoted is because of their hardheartedness, plain and simple. They do not believe because they refuse to believe. But the fact remains that the fourteenth chapter of 1 Corinthians is unambiguous. It is straightforward, completely clear in its message, and can only be misunderstood by the one who wants his own agenda instead of God's. For there is no escaping the fact that women, according to Joel (Joel 2:28–29), according to Peter (Acts 2:16–18), according to Paul (1 Cor. 14:1), according to GOD, may prophesy. It is also clear from God's Word that women may instruct, they may teach, they may give advice, they may warn, and they may comfort all members in the body of Christ, both men and women, for the building up of the body (1 Cor. 14:3, 26). Furthermore, there is no getting around the fact that prophesying is teaching. Any man who claims that prophesying is not teaching is himself teaching a different doctrine than what the Word of God teaches. And any man who teaches that a woman may not teach God's Word among God's people defames the Word of God. So, to any man today who is ignorant of God's Word, and believes that women should be silent and do not have the God-given right to teach His Word, I will ask you, "Was it from you that the Word of God first went forth? Or has it come to you only?"

1 Corinthians 14

Paul's View and the Lord's Commandment:

[1]"Pursue love, yet desire earnestly spiritual *gifts*, but especially that you may prophesy." [3]"But one who prophesies speaks to people for edification and exhortation and consolation." [4]"One who speaks in a tongue edifies themself; but one who prophesies edifies the church." [5]"Now I wish that you all spoke in tongues, but *even* more that you would prophesy...." [12]"So also you, since you are zealous of spiritual *gifts*, seek to abound for the edification of the church." [22]"So then tongues are for a sign, not to those who believe but to unbelievers; but prophecy *is for a sign*, not to unbelievers but to those who believe." [26]"What is *the outcome* then, brethren? When you assemble, each one has a psalm, has a teaching, has a revelation, has a tongue, has an interpretation. Let all things be done for edification." [29]"Let two or three prophets speak, and let the others pass judgment." [31]"For you can all prophesy one by one, so that all may learn and all may be exhorted."

Paul Quotes the Faction of Men from Corinth Who Wrote Him:

[34]"*The women are to keep silent among the people; for they are not permitted to speak, but are to be set as also the Law says. [35]If they desire to learn anything, let them ask their own husbands at home; for it is shameful for a woman to speak among the people.*"

Paul Rebukes the Men from Corinth:

[36]"Was it from you that the Word of God *first* went forth? Or has it come to you only? [37]If anyone thinks he is a prophet or spiritual, let him fully know that the things which I write to you are the Lord's commandment. [38]But if anyone does not recognize *this*, he is not recognized."

Paul Sums Up His Previously Stated Views,
Which Are Also the Lord's Commandment:

[39]"Therefore, my brethren, desire earnestly to prophesy, and do not forbid to speak in tongues. [40]But all things must be done properly and in an orderly manner."

5

HEAD—SOURCE OR LEADER?

There is a divide in the body of Christ as to whether the Greek word "kephale" (head), used figuratively, means "source/origin/first/beginning" or "leader/ruler/chief/authority." However, from looking at the context of passages in Scripture that use "kephale" figuratively, it is clear to me that its meaning is "source/origin/first/beginning." It is also important to note that the Strongest NIV Exhaustive Concordance lists one of the definitions of "kephale" as "the point of origin."[1] In this chapter, I will go over three passages of Scripture where the figurative meaning of "head" is used, so that we can see for ourselves whether the context better fits the definition of "s/o/f/b" or "l/r/c/a." I would like to begin with Colossians 1:15–18. It says:

> [15]"He is the image of the invisible God, the <u>firstborn</u> of all creation. [16]For by Him <u>all things were created</u>, *both* in the heavens and on earth, visible and invisible, whether thrones or dominions or rulers or authorities—all things have been <u>created</u> through Him and for Him. [17]He is <u>before</u> all things, and in Him all things hold together. [18]He is also <u>head</u> of the body, the church; and He is the <u>beginning</u>, the <u>firstborn</u> from the dead, so that He Himself will come to have <u>first place in everything</u>."

As you can see, I have underlined certain words in this passage because these words show the central theme of this passage. Therefore, I would like to go over each underlined word, starting in verse fifteen with the word "firstborn," so that we can fully understand this passage as Paul meant it to be understood. Now, to begin, the word "firstborn" was a prevalent word used in Paul's day. And without exception, it always referred to the child who was born "first" or to the oldest child. The firstborn child marked the "beginning" of one's family. The firstborn child came into the world "before" all of their siblings. The firstborn child was the "first" in chronological order and arrangement, from the firstborn to the youngest. Therefore, just as the firstborn child is the "first" of all their siblings in chronological order and arrangement, so too, Christ is the "first" of all creation in chronological order and arrangement. This is why Paul then says, in verses 16–17, that all things were created by Christ and that He is before all things. Indeed, if Christ created all things, then nothing could come before Him; He would be the "first" in chronological order and arrangement of all creation. So, Christ marked the beginning. He preceded creation. He was before creation. He is the Alpha. He is first. And this is what Paul meant when he said that Christ is the "firstborn" of all creation.

Now, many people try to apply the meaning of "supreme status" to the word "firstborn" in verse fifteen. However, in doing so, they are giving this word an atypical meaning and are using it in a way that was not used in Paul's day. When the word "firstborn" is used in Scripture, it never refers to the child with the "highest status." Again, it always refers to the child who was born "first." Even when the rights of the firstborn were given to a younger child, the younger child was still not referred to as the "firstborn." Likewise, when the firstborn child was stripped of their status and rights, they were still referred to as the "firstborn." (See 1 Chronicles 5:1–3.) Now, we know that Christ is of supreme status over all things, as is evident throughout Scripture, but again, that is not the idea that Paul is trying to communicate in this passage. Again, in this passage, Paul is trying to convey the thought that Christ is the "first" of all creation in chronological order and arrangement. Therefore, those who apply the meaning of "supreme status" to the word "firstborn" are misapplying the meaning of the word.

To confirm that I have applied the correct meaning to the word "firstborn" in verse fifteen, I would now like to go over the word "firstborn" in the other place that it is found in this passage, verse eighteen. Again, it says, [18]"...and He is the beginning, the firstborn from the dead, so that He Himself will come to have first place in everything." Now, when we look at the way that Paul uses the word "firstborn" in this verse, it is quite apparent that he is making the point that Christ is the "first" One to rise from the dead in chronological order and arrangement, especially since he uses it in conjunction with the word "beginning." Paul is not making the point that Christ is the "most supreme" One to rise from the dead (although true). In light of this, would Paul use the word "firstborn" two different ways in this passage? Indeed, he would not. Paul undoubtedly uses the word "firstborn," the same way in each verse. Furthermore, Paul had previously made the same argument, that Christ is the "first" to rise from the dead in chronological order and arrangement, in 1 Corinthians 15:20–23; however, in this passage, Paul referred to Christ as the "first fruits." And the "first fruits," in like manner, always referred to the "first" ripened produce of one's crops. Consequently, since Paul is using the word "firstborn" in verse eighteen to symbolize that Christ is the "first" to rise from the dead in chronological order and arrangement, we can assert with confidence that Paul is also using the word "firstborn" in verse fifteen to symbolize that Christ is the "first" of all creation in chronological order and arrangement. Indeed, Paul is bringing into view the fact that Christ is the "first" in chronological order and arrangement in everything.

Now that we have established the correct meaning of the word "firstborn," I would like to review this passage as a whole so that we can see the central theme of this passage and then properly conclude what Paul meant when he said that Christ is also "head" of the body, the church, in verse eighteen.

(Note: The highlighted words define the underlined words.)

> [15]"He is the image of the invisible God, the firstborn of all creation." (Christ is the "**first**" of all creation in chronological order and arrangement.)

> [16]"For by Him all things were created, *both* in the heavens and on earth, visible and invisible, whether thrones or dominions or rulers or authorities—all things have been created through Him and for Him." (Christ is the "**source**," the "**origin**" of all things.)

> [17]"He is before all things, and in Him all things hold together." (Christ is the "**beginning**" and the sustainer of all things.)

> [18]"He is also head of the body, the church; and He is the beginning, the firstborn from the dead, so that He Himself will come to have first place in everything." (Christ is the "**beginning**," the "**first**" in chronological order and arrangement to be raised from the dead, so

that He Himself will be "**first**" in chronological order and arrangement in everything.)

If we notice the highlighted words, we can see that the whole theme of this passage, from beginning to end, is that Christ is the "first," the "source," the "origin," the "beginning" of all things. Therefore, when Paul states in verse eighteen that Christ is also "head" of the body, the church, Paul is keeping with the central theme of this passage, and he is saying that Christ is the "source/origin/first/beginning" of the body, the church. Otherwise, his statement regarding the church lacks continuity with the rest of the passage. Therefore, it is clear by this passage that "head," used figuratively in Greek, means "source/origin/first/beginning." Truly, Christ is the first and the last, the Alpha and the Omega, the beginning and the end in everything.

The second passage that I would like to go over where the word "head" is used figuratively is Acts 4:11. It says, [11]"He is the STONE WHICH WAS REJECTED by you, THE BUILDERS, *but* WHICH BECAME THE CHIEF CORNER *stone*." (Note: The NASB translators have translated the word "kephale" as "chief" and have added the word "stone.") However, verse eleven should be translated as, [11]"He is the STONE WHICH WAS REJECTED by you, THE BUILDERS, *but* WHICH BECAME THE HEAD [FIRST] CORNER." In beginning this passage, I would like to say that when Peter speaks metaphorically of Christ, he is referencing the "cornerstone" of a building, not the "capstone," as the NIV has rendered. For it is written in Isaiah, [16]"...Behold, I am laying in Zion a stone, a tested stone, a costly **cornerstone *for* the foundation**, firmly placed" (Isa. 28:16). Hence, the question is, "What is the cornerstone of a building?" By definition, the cornerstone is the "first" stone set [laid at a corner] in the construction of a masonry foundation in which all other stones are set in reference to it, thus determining the position of the entire structure.[2] And as we can well see in this passage (Acts 4:1–12), the builders (the rulers and elders) rejected Christ because they wanted to lay their own foundation for what they deemed was righteous. However, Peter tells them that Christ, being the first to be raised from the dead by God, is the "first" stone laid in which all other stones (believers) are set in reference to Him, thus determining the position of the entire structure (the church). In other words, Peter is informing the rulers and elders that they are not the foundation for the church, but rather that Christ is the foundation for the church because there is salvation in no one else. As a result, a translation of "CORNERSTONE" or "FIRST CORNER" would be correct; however, the translation of "CHIEF CORNER *stone*" is incorrect because it gives a false impression that there are numerous cornerstones. But indeed, there is only "one" cornerstone set in each structure—and that's the "first" stone which is set. Therefore, "head" in this passage means "first."

To better understand the next passage, namely the metaphorical picture that Paul is painting for the saints at Colossae, we need to understand "head" (when it is defined as "source") in a twofold manner as they did. And a good way to do this is to picture a water tower. A water tower is an elevated tank used for water storage and for maintaining equalized pressure on a water system.[3] And the "source" of water that is kept at the elevated height is called the "head." (Note: This is where we get the term "head pressure." Head pressure is the same as discharge pressure/water pressure.) Furthermore, the head "supplies" (and maintains) all of the pipes and waterways that go to each home. So, the "head" is the **source** of the water, and the head **supplies** the water to each home. Similarly, we can also picture the head/body relationship of a person. The head of each person is the "source" from where the oxygen, water, and food come. And the head "supplies" oxygen, water, and food to the body so that it can grow and thrive.

The third and final passage that I would like to go over where the word "head" is used figuratively is Colossians 2:19. It says, [19]"...and not holding fast to the head, from whom the entire body, being supplied and held together by the joints and ligaments, grows with a growth which is from God." In this passage, we can see that the head (Christ) is supplying the body (the church) so that it can grow and thrive. In just the same way that the "head" of a water tower supplies all of the pipes and waterways that go to each home, and the "head" of a person supplies oxygen and nourishment to their own body, so also, Christ, being our "head," supplies each member of His body. He is our "source," and He "supplies" us. Therefore, "head" in this passage means "source."

HEAD—SOURCE/ORIGIN/ FIRST/BEGINNING

¹⁵"He is the image of the invisible God, the firstborn [first in chronological order and arrangement] of all creation. ¹⁶For by Him all things were created, *both* in the heavens and on earth, visible and invisible, whether thrones or dominions or rulers or authorities—all things have been created through Him and for Him. ¹⁷He is before all things, and in Him all things hold together. ¹⁸He is also head [source/origin/ first/beginning] of the body, the church; and He is the beginning, the firstborn [first in chronological order and arrangement] from the dead, so that He Himself will come to have first place in everything."

(Colossians 1:15–18)

¹¹"He is the STONE WHICH WAS REJECTED by you, THE BUILDERS, *but* WHICH BECAME THE HEAD [FIRST] CORNER."

(Acts 4:11)

¹⁹"…and not holding fast to the head [source], from whom the entire body, by means of the joints and ligaments being supplied and held together, grows with a growth which is from God."

(Colossians 2:19)

6

HYPOTASSO

(Part I)

For centuries now, it has been taught that wives are to submit to their husbands. It has also been taught that the husband is the servant leader of his wife. But Jesus never taught submission for wives, nor did He teach servant leadership for husbands. He simply taught servanthood for all. Now, Christ did not teach submission for wives because He taught that submission was to God—for no one can serve two masters. Indeed, if a woman submits to her husband in everything, then she submits to God in nothing. Likewise, Christ did not teach servant leadership for husbands because He taught that One is our leader, Christ—for no one can serve two masters. Indeed, if One is a wife's leader, and that leader is her husband, then Christ cannot be her leader. Therefore, it is clear from the teachings of Christ that the doctrine of submission (from one person to another) is a false doctrine. It is a teaching of man and not of God.

In both this chapter and the next, I will go over the word "hypotasso" in-depth in order to show how its true meaning harmonizes perfectly with God's Word. The typical translation of this word, as "submit" or "subject," should be suspect because many of the verses that contain it contradict God's Word. Hence, these contradictions are not to be ignored but are to be taken seriously as they are an indication of something more faulty than a misinterpretation. For God's Word will never contradict itself. God's Word is always in complete harmony.

Before I begin, I need to explain that the Greek to English dictionary and index in the Strongest NIV Exhaustive Concordance has the word "hypotasso," which is in verbal form, listed as being used a total of thirty-eight times in the New Testament. It also has the word "hypotage," the noun form of "hypotasso," listed as being used a total of four times.[1] I believe, however, that the word "hypotage" is a different word altogether from that of "hypotasso" and has a different meaning altogether. As a result, I believe that the word "hypotage" is actually used fourteen times in the Bible (four in noun form and ten in verbal form), and the word "hypotasso" is used twenty-eight times. Therefore, because I believe that both the words "hypotasso" and "hypotage" have different meanings from what the translators list them to be, I will go over all forty-two of their uses.

In addition, I need to explain briefly that Greek is a highly inflected language. This means that Greek words change form (the Greek spelling) in order to indicate the role that it plays in the sentence. As a result, the words "hypotasso" and "hypotage" will be used with different forms, as I will list the Greek beside the English in each passage that we go over. (Note: The English word(s) will appear in bold print.)

In this chapter, I will not go in chronological order of how these words appear in the Bible but would like to start with 1 Corinthians 15:27–28. The reason I would like to start here is because it is here that we will see concrete evidence of the true meaning of the word "hypotasso." I also want to go over 1 Corinthians 15:20–26 because of a mistranslation in verse twenty-four, so that we can get a full understanding of just exactly what Paul is trying to tell those in Corinth in verses 20–28. We will need to compare Scripture with Scripture to do this, so this will be the most involved and complex passage for me to explain.

In the fifteenth chapter of 1 Corinthians, the word "hypotasso" is used four times, and the word "hypotage" is used twice, and all six uses appear in verses 27–28. First Corinthians 15:27–28 reads as follows:

> [27]"For HE **HAS PUT** [hypetaxen] ALL THINGS **IN SUBJECTION** UNDER HIS FEET. But when He says, 'All things **are put in subjection** [hypotetaktai],' it is evident that He is excepted who **put** [hypotaxantos] all things **in subjection** to Him. [28]When all things **are subjected** [hypotage] to Him, then the Son Himself also **will be**

subjected [hypotagesetai] to the One who **subjected** [hypotaxanti] all things to Him, so that God may be all in all."

To understand this passage correctly, we first need to find out the correct meaning of the word "hypotasso." So, what does the word "hypotasso" mean? Well, we have a clue in the passage that we just read in verse twenty-seven. Notice, in verse twenty-seven, the NASB translators have put a portion in all capital letters; ²⁷"For HE HAS PUT ALL THINGS IN SUBJECTION UNDER HIS FEET." And they have put this portion in all capital letters to help the reader understand that Paul is quoting from the Old Testament. For Paul quotes King David in Psalm 8:6, who spoke by a prophetic utterance from the Holy Spirit. But notice the difference between each of these renderings.

⁶"…You have put all things under His feet" (Ps. 8:6).

²⁷"For HE HAS PUT ALL THINGS IN SUBJECTION UNDER HIS FEET…" (1 Cor. 15:27).

The question is, "Why would there be a difference between the two sentences if one author is directly quoting the other?" Did Paul decide to add to the prophecy of King David? Did he decide to give the prophecy his own little twist? No! Paul is not adding words or changing the inspired words of David. It is the NASB translators that are. For Paul is quoting the same words that the original author wrote in Psalms; the only difference is Paul is not speaking in Hebrew as David was. Paul instead puts his words into Greek because the people he is writing to speak and read Greek, not Hebrew. So, Paul carefully chooses words in Greek that most accurately represent what the author was saying in Hebrew. And since the Hebrew word "sit" (translated as "put" in Psalm 8:6) means "to place, to put, or to set,"² Paul chooses the word "hypotasso" in Greek, which also means "to place, to put, or to set." For if Paul chose a word in Greek that meant "to subject" when the original word that he is quoting from in Hebrew meant "to place, to put, or to set," then he would have been doing an injustice to God's Word by quoting Scripture with a different meaning. But I believe that Paul stayed true to the intended meaning, which is why he chose the word "hypotasso." I believe the word "hypotasso" in Greek has the same meaning as "sit" in Hebrew—"to place, to put, to set." I do not believe its meaning is "to subject." "Hypotasso" is a word of placement, **NOT** a word of subjection. When this is understood, then we come to the correct

73

rendering of [27]"For HE **HAS PUT** [hypetaxen] ALL THINGS UNDER HIS FEET" in verse twenty-seven of 1 Corinthians 15 just as we do in Psalm 8:6.

The subtle tweak given to this word may not seem like much at first, but it makes a huge difference in the accurate translation of Scripture, which we will see as we go along. For the translators err by always giving this word of placement a low placement; they make it into a word of subjection. However, a word of placement only indicates that something is being placed. One must read the context of the passage to see just where that placement is because things can be placed high as well as low. As a matter of fact, things can be placed in a wide variety of different ways, so the context is absolutely essential in finding out just how something is placed. So, in verse twenty-seven, it is the words "under His feet" that are denoting just how and where the placement is, not the word "hypotasso." The word "hypotasso" is only indicating that something is being placed. Indeed, it is the words "under His feet" that are denoting the subjection. So again, the context surrounding the word "hypotasso" is vitally important as it will always tell us how something is being placed.

Now that we understand that the word "hypotasso" is a word of placement, verse twenty-seven should be rendered as, [27]"For HE **HAS PLACED** [hypetaxen] ALL THINGS UNDER HIS FEET.' But when He says, 'All things **are placed** [hypotetaktai],' it is clear that it is apart from the One who **placed** [hypotaxantos] all things to Him."

Now we move to verse twenty-eight. Verse twenty-eight says, [28]"When all things **are subjected** [hypotage] to Him, then the Son Himself also **will be subjected** [hypotagesetai] to the One who **subjected** [hypotaxanti] all things to Him, so that God may be all in all." Here in verse twenty-eight, we have a most egregious mistranslation of the word "hypotage." For it is saying that Christ Himself also will be subjected. But is this correct? Will Christ be subjected? Are not the Father and Son One? Are they not always in total agreement with one another? What would be the reason for this subjection if they are One and always in total agreement? How long will it last? Will it be temporary or permanent? And why would God subject the One whom He has exalted to His right hand? Also, how would God be "all in all" by the subjection of Christ? And most of all, why would God subject our precious risen Lord, who suffered a barbaric, torturous, and

74

humiliating death in our place; on our behalf? Is this what will happen to our King, whose name is above all names?

I will tell you plainly that I do not believe that Christ will be subjected. As a matter of fact, this is the **ONLY** place in the entire Bible, both Old and New Testaments, where I could find that Christ, while in the heavenly presence of the Father, would be subjected, and I believe it is due to the mistranslation of this word. I believe that Christ will not be subjected, but rather that He will only be exalted, magnified, glorified, honored, and highly praised by the Father. This exaltation of Christ by the Father is seen throughout both the Old and New Testaments. This glorification of Christ is the treatment that is befitting our King.

In John 17:5, Jesus prayed, [5]"Now, Father, glorify Me together with Yourself, with the glory which I had with You before the world was." Now, this prayer of Jesus is essential for us to understand. Jesus shared the glory with His Father before the world was even in existence. And for all eternity past, there was not a time when Christ did not fully share this glory with the Father before the earth was formed. But then, for some amazing reason that is beyond my comprehension, Elohim said, *[26]"...Let Us make humankind in Our image..."* (Gen. 1:26). So He created humans in His own image, and He loved His beloved, but His beloved fell. Those whom He had created transgressed and grieved His heart. They were lost, so very lost. The evil one had captured His beloved. But God wanted them back. The Father and the Son were in total agreement on how to redeem their beloved. And because He loved them so, God sent His Son, His one and only Son who shared His glory, to save and redeem them. Thankfully, Christ was willing. He, for a time, gave up that glory which He had shared with His Father from eternity past. He gave up the glory that was His before the world was, the glory that was rightfully His. But He gave up that glory because He was on a mission; a mission to redeem the lost; a mission to redeem God's beloved. And He had to become like us in order to reach us. So Christ, who being in very nature God, was made for a little while lower than God, because He did not consider equality with God a thing to be grasped, but He willingly emptied Himself, taking the form of a bond-servant and being made in the likeness of humans, He was found in appearance as a man. He was brought forth from the womb by the One who sent Him, for Christ was born a defenseless baby. But the Father had His eye on Him, for He trusted the Father when upon His mother's breasts. He grew in wisdom, and the grace of God was upon Him. And finally, for the sake of His beloved, He humbled Himself by becoming obedient to the point of death, even death on a cross.

But thankfully, the story doesn't end here. Christ has risen. He has been exalted to the right hand of the Father. He has been raised from the lower status that He willingly took when He was sent to save us when He was made for a little while lower than God. He has accomplished the will of the Father and has redeemed His beloved. And now that He has completed God's redemption for us and was resurrected, He once again shares that same equality and glory with God that was His before the foundation of the earth was laid. He has been exalted to the right hand of God and is thus equal with Him once again. The Father has only the highest praise for the Son. He has not denied His prayer (John 17:5). The Father has glorified Christ together with Himself. He has crowned Him with glory and honor. And one day, God will make it known to all that Christ is King of kings and Lord of lords, and there will be no one who will not see His glory. The Father will **NOT** subject Christ, for it is His will that Christ only be exalted. The following verses confirm this exaltation of Christ.

> [13]"Behold, My servant will prosper, He will be high and lifted up and greatly exalted" (Isa. 52:13).

> [13]"...One like a Son of Man was coming, and He came up to the Ancient of Days and was presented before Him. [14]And to Him was given dominion, glory ..." (Dan. 7:13–14).

> [32]"This Jesus God raised up again, to which we are all witnesses. [33]Therefore having been exalted to the right hand of God..." (Acts 2:32–33).

> [13]"The God of Abraham, Isaac and Jacob, the God of our fathers, has glorified His servant Jesus..." (Acts 3:13).

> [31]"He is the one whom God exalted to His right hand as a Prince and a Savior..." (Acts 5:31).

> [20]"...which He brought about in Christ, when He raised Him from the dead and seated Him at His right hand in the heavenly *places*, [21]far above all rule and authority and power and dominion..." (Eph. 1:20–21).

[9]"For this reason also, God highly exalted Him, and bestowed on Him the name which is above every name..." (Phil. 2:9).

[8]"But of the Son *He says*, 'YOUR THRONE, O GOD, IS FOREVER AND EVER...'" (Heb. 1:8).

So, I cannot see any hint of the subjection of Christ by the Father anywhere in the Bible, with the single exception of this mistranslated verse in 1 Corinthians 15. And as I said before, I believe this error comes from the improper translation of the word "hypotage." But what does "hypotage" mean? I believe, from doing a word study, that the true meaning of "hypotage," with its different forms, is will, willed, appointed by the will of, willing, willingness, etc. Further proof that this is the correct meaning will be reinforced in "Hypotasso (Part II)" in showing how it is used in each passage. But for now, in verse twenty-eight, I believe that Paul is saying that Christ Himself also will be "willed," or more appropriately, "appointed by the will" of the Father, **NOT** subjected by the Father. And this will happen right after the Father has willed all things to Christ. Therefore, I believe verse twenty-eight should be rendered as, [28]"But as soon as all things **are willed** [hypotage] to Him, then also the Son Himself **will be appointed by the will** [hypotagesetai] of the One who **placed** [hypotaxanti] all things to Him, so that God may be all in all."

And putting both verses together, 1 Corinthians 15:27–28 should be translated as:

> [27]"'For HE **HAS PLACED** [hypetaxen] ALL THINGS UNDER HIS FEET.' But when He says, 'All things **are placed** [hypotetaktai],' it is clear that it is apart from the One who **placed** [hypotaxantos] all things to Him. [28]But as soon as all things **are willed** [hypotage] to Him, then also the Son Himself **will be appointed by the will** [hypotagesetai] of the One who **placed** [hypotaxanti] all things to Him, so that God may be all in all."

Also, as I mentioned previously, there is another mistranslation in 1 Corinthians 15:24. Verses 20–26 read as, [20]"But now Christ has been raised from the dead, the first fruits of those who are asleep. [21]For since by a man *came* death, by a man also *came* the resurrection of the dead. [22]For as in Adam all die, so also in Christ all will be made alive. [23]But each in his own order: Christ, the first fruits, after that those who are Christ's at His coming, [24]then *comes* the end, when He hands over the kingdom to the God and Father, when He has abolished all rule and all authority and power. [25]For He must reign until He has put all His enemies under His feet. [26]The last enemy that will be abolished is death."

Now, because of the mistranslation in verse twenty-four, it is very difficult to tell whether parts of this passage are talking about the Father or Christ, because both the Father and Christ are in view in verse twenty-four. For example, it says, [23]"...Christ, the first fruits, after that those who are Christ's at His coming, [24]then *comes* the end, when He [Christ] hands over the kingdom to the God and Father, when He [the Father or Christ?] has abolished all rule and all authority and power. [25]For He [the Father or Christ?] must reign until He has put all His enemies under His feet." However, we know from Psalm 110:1 that Paul has to be speaking of the Father in verses 24–25 because Psalm 110:1 says, [1]"The LORD [Father] says to my Lord [Christ]: 'Sit at My right hand until I make Your enemies a footstool for Your feet.'" However, this doesn't make sense because, in verse twenty-four, Christ is the One who hands over the kingdom to the Father. And if Christ hands over the kingdom to the Father, then wouldn't it be Christ who is reigning until He abolishes all rule and authority and power? But the reason this passage is confusing is because the translators have translated the Greek definite article "τω" as "to the" when they should have translated it as "the." For what Paul is actually saying is, [24]"...then comes the end, when He hands over the kingdom, the God and Father, as soon as He abolishes all rule and all authority and power...." Indeed, Paul is not saying that Christ will hand over the kingdom "to" the God and Father; instead, he is saying that the One who hands over the kingdom "is" the God and Father. And the reason that Paul has to specifically state "the God and Father" here is that up until now, in verses 20–23, he has only been talking about Christ, so Paul now has to clarify that he is now talking about the God and Father. If he left out the words "the God and Father," his readers would have thought he was still talking about Christ. So the text is actually saying that it is the God and Father who will hand over the kingdom to Christ after He (the Father) has abolished all rule and all authority and power. Therefore, verses 20–26 should be translated as, [20]"But now Christ has been raised from the dead, the first fruits of those who are asleep. [21]For since by a man *came* death, by a man also *came* the resurrection of the dead. [22]For as in Adam all die, so also in Christ all will be made alive. [23]But each in his own order: Christ, the first fruits, after that those who are Christ's at His coming, [24]then *comes* the end, when

He hands over the kingdom, the God and Father, when He [Father] has abolished all rule and all authority and power. ²⁵For He [Father] must reign until He has put all His [Christ's] enemies under His [Christ's] feet. ²⁶The last enemy that will be abolished is death."

Also, something that is important to note before we go on is that the word that is translated as "kingdom" in verse twenty-four is "basileia" in Greek. This word means "kingdom," but it also means "kingship" and "royal rule."[3] Therefore, the Father is not only handing over the "kingdom" to Christ but also the "kingship" and the "royal rule." For verse twenty-five does say that God the Father must "**reign until**." And the word that is translated as "reign" is "basileuo" in Greek and means "to reign as a king."[4] Also, the word that is translated as "until" is "achri" in Greek and means "until, up to, as far as, as long as."[5] So the Father will reign right up to the time when He has put all Christ's enemies under Christ's feet; then He will hand over the kingdom, the kingship, the royal (or sovereign rule) to Christ.

Therefore, I would translate verses 20–28 as follows:

> ²⁰"But now Christ has been raised from the dead, the first fruits of those who are asleep. ²¹For since by a man *came* death, by a man also *came* the resurrection of the dead. ²²For as in Adam all die, so also in Christ all will be made alive. ²³But each in his own order: Christ, the first fruits, after that those who are Christ's at His coming, ²⁴then *comes* the end, when the God and Father hands over the sovereign rule, as soon as He abolishes all rule and all authority and power. ²⁵For He must reign until He has put all His enemies under His feet. ²⁶The last enemy that will be abolished is death. ²⁷'For HE HAS PLACED ALL THINGS UNDER HIS FEET.' But when He says, 'All things are placed,' it is clear that it is apart from the One who placed all things to Him. ²⁸But as soon as all things are willed to Him, then also the Son Himself will be appointed by the will of the One who placed all things to Him, so that God may be all in all."

Now, to be certain of whether or not this is the correct translation, we need to look at the prophecy of King David. For the whole reason that Paul was quoting King David in verse twenty-seven was that he was explaining David's prophecy in greater detail to those in Corinth about what would happen when the end comes. In David's prophecy, will we see Christ handing over the sovereign rule to God, or will we see God handing over the sovereign rule to Christ? Will we see the subjection of Christ after all things have been placed under His feet, or will we see Christ being appointed by the will of God after all things have been placed under His feet? The prophecy given through King David is as follows:

> *[4]"What is man that You take thought of him, and the Son of Man that You care for Him? [5]Yet You have made Him for a little while lower than God, and You crown Him with glory and majesty! [6]You make Him to rule over the works of Your hands; You have put all things under His feet" (Ps. 8:4–6).*

Here, in David's prophecy, we can clearly see that after God the Father has put all things under Christ's feet, then the Father will make Christ to rule over the works of His hands. (Notice the "past tense" in the last part of verse six and the "present tense" in the first part of verse six.) Indeed, God the Father is handing over the sovereign rule (and kingdom, the works of His hands) to Christ. So we have complete harmony between David's prophecy and Paul's detailed explanation of what will happen when the end comes. For just as David's prophecy says that God will make Christ to rule over the works of His hands after He puts all things under Christ's feet, so also Paul explains that Christ will be appointed by the will of the Father after the Father puts all things under His feet. Also, it is vital to note that there is not even the slightest hint anywhere in the prophecy of King David that Christ will be subjected, which shows us that Paul is not saying that Christ will be subjected. For God's will is that Christ only be exalted. Furthermore, when Paul says that God will be "all in all" in verse twenty-eight, he means that God will first put all things **UNDER** Christ's feet, and then God will appoint Christ **OVER** the works of His hands. Indeed, this is the way that God will be "all in all."

Also, you may have noticed that I made several changes in the above translation of Psalm 8:4–6 from that of the NASB. For one, I have capitalized the words that are referring to Christ. In this passage, the first part of Psalm 8:4 is talking about a human man. It says, [4]"What is man that You take thought of him...." And the Hebrew word for man here is "enos." "Enos" refers to mortal humankind with an emphasis on frailty.[6] However, verse four then switches to speaking of Christ. For it continues and says, [4]"...and the Son of Man that You care for Him?" And the Hebrew word for man here is not "enos" but rather "adam." "Adam" also refers to

80

humankind but also often assumes messianic significance and can refer to the Messiah.[7] So the first part of verse four speaks of humans, and then it switches over and speaks of Christ, the Son of Man. The other change that I made is I added the words "for" and "while" in verse five. This is because the Hebrew word "meat" can mean either "little (of size), few (of quantity), or short (of time)."[8] One must determine, by the context, which is in view. And since Christ **emptied** Himself and took on the form of a **bond-servant**, I would say that He was made more than just "a little" lower than God. Therefore, I believe that "meat" means "short (of time)" here, and is referring to the time that Christ was on earth. Thus, I believe that the Hebrew word "meat" should be translated as "for a little while" in verse five, not as "a little."

I also want to point out that this prophecy of David's (Ps. 8:4–6) is also in harmony with Daniels prophecy, which states:

> [13]"I kept looking in the night visions, and behold, with the clouds of heaven One like a Son of Man was coming, and He came up to the Ancient of Days and was presented before Him. [14]And to Him was given dominion, glory, and a kingdom, that all the peoples, nations and *men of every* language might serve Him. His dominion is an everlasting dominion which will not pass away; and His kingdom is one which will not be destroyed" (Dan. 7:13–14).

Here, in Daniels prophecy, we see that the Ancient of Days, the Father, is giving the Son of Man, Christ, dominion (ruling control), glory (crowned with glory and majesty), and a kingdom (the works of God's hands) just as He has in David's prophecy. Therefore, these two prophecies are extremely significant to note and are two examples of why it is so vital to compare Scripture with Scripture. For we should not see Paul's detailed explanation to those in Corinth veer from these two prophecies. And indeed, Paul's teaching corresponds to both. For neither prophecy shows any subjection of Christ by God, and both prophecies show that the Father will one day hand over the "kingdom, kingship, royal or sovereign rule" to Christ.

Also, Revelation 11:15–17 says concerning Christ:

> [15]"Then the seventh angel sounded; and there were loud voices in heaven, saying, 'The kingdom [basileia] of the world has become *the kingdom* of our Lord [Christ] and of His [the Father's] Christ;

and He [Christ] will reign forever and ever.' [16]And the twenty-four elders, who sit on their thrones before God, fell on their faces and worshiped God, [17]saying, 'We give You thanks, O Lord God [Christ], the Almighty, who are and who were [who is and who was], because You have taken Your great power and have begun to reign.'"

Here, in Revelation, we can see that Christ **RECEIVES** the "basileia" at the end. This is further proof that in 1 Corinthians 15:24, the God and Father hands over the "basileia" to Christ at the end. For if Christ were handing it over to the Father, as it is translated in 1 Corinthians 15:24, then it would mean that Christ "had" the kingdom, kingship, royal or sovereign rule up until the time when He handed it to the Father. However, Revelation 11:15–17 makes it clear that the kingdom of the world "has become" Christ's, that He "has begun" to reign, meaning Christ did not have the kingdom, kingship, royal or sovereign rule in the past, but the Father did. So again, in Revelation, at the end, we see the "kingdom, kingship, royal or sovereign rule" of the world being given to Christ by the Father. And we see Christ reigning, from this time forth, forever and ever.

And finally, I would like to go over Hebrews 2:5–9 because the author of Hebrews tells us some very important things. In this portion of Scripture, the word "hypotasso" is used three times, and the word "hypotage" is used once. Here, the author of Hebrews also quotes King David in Psalm 8:4–6. It reads (with my modifications), *[5]"For He did not **place** [hypetaxen] to angels the world to come, concerning which we are speaking. [6]But one [King David] has testified somewhere, saying, 'WHAT IS MAN, THAT YOU REMEMBER HIM? OR THE SON OF MAN, THAT YOU CARE FOR HIM? [7]YOU HAVE MADE HIM FOR A LITTLE WHILE LOWER THAN GOD; YOU HAVE CROWNED HIM WITH GLORY AND HONOR, AND HAVE APPOINTED HIM OVER THE WORKS OF YOUR HANDS; [8]YOU **HAVE PLACED** [hypetaxas] ALL THINGS UNDER HIS FEET.' For in **placing** [hypotaxai] all things to Him, He left nothing to Him that is disobedient [anypotakton]. But at this present time, we do not yet see all things **willed** [hypotetagmena] to Him. [9]But we do see Jesus, the One having been made for a little while lower than God, now crowned with glory and honor because of the suffering of death, so that by the grace of God on behalf of everyone He might taste death."* (Note: The NASB translators have translated the Greek word "anypotakton" as "not subject." The Greek word "anypotaktos" means "rebellious, disobedient, not made subject to."[9] "Anypotaktos" is listed as a separate word in the Strongest NIV Exhaustive concordance and is not listed under the word "hypotasso.")

Here, we can clearly see once again that Christ will be appointed by the will of the Father after all things have been placed under His feet. Nowhere in this passage does it speak of the subjection of Christ after all things have been placed under His feet. So again, Paul is not saying that Christ will be subjected by the One who placed all things to Him, but rather that He will be appointed by the will of the One who placed all things to Him. We can also see by this passage that when all things are placed to Christ by the Father, nothing will be left to Him that is rebellious, disobedient, or not made subject to Him. This also matches what Paul has stated in 1 Corinthians 15. For Paul has stated in verse twenty-four that the Father will abolish all rule and all authority and power before He hands over the sovereign rule to Christ. Furthermore, the author of Hebrews tells us that at this present time, we do not yet see all things willed to Christ. This means that the Father is still reigning and has not yet handed over the sovereign rule to Christ, which also matches what Paul has stated in 1 Corinthians 15. In verses 24–25, Paul has stated that the God and Father will hand over the sovereign rule at the end. As Hebrews 10:12–13 says, [12]"…but He, having offered one sacrifice for sins for all time, SAT DOWN AT THE RIGHT HAND OF GOD, [13]waiting from that time onward UNTIL HIS ENEMIES BE MADE A FOOTSTOOL FOR HIS FEET." And finally, the author of Hebrews tells us that although all things have not yet been willed to Christ, He has now been crowned with glory and honor because He suffered death. He has made purification of sins and has been exalted to the right hand of the Father. The glory that He shared with the Father before the world was, has been restored.

I would also like to explain, in reference to my translation of Hebrews 2:5–9, why I believe the author of Hebrews, in verse seven (also verse nine), is saying that Jesus Christ was made for a little while lower than God, not angels as the NASB has rendered. The reason why I believe the author of Hebrews is saying that Jesus Christ was made for a little while lower than God is because the author of Hebrews is *directly quoting* King David in Psalm 8:4–6. And King David clearly stated that Christ would be made for a little while lower than "Elohim," which means "God; plural of majesty." But the question is, "Why would the author of Hebrews choose the word 'angelous,' meaning 'messengers,' when referencing God?" I believe it was to emphasize the fact that Elohim was the "Messengers" of long ago. For the author did say in Hebrews 1:1, [1]"God, after He spoke long ago to the fathers in the prophets in many portions and in many ways, [2]in these last days has spoken to us in His Son...." And since the people he/she was writing to would have been familiar with King David's prophecy, they would have understood the point that was being made. They would have understood that Christ was made for a little while lower than the One (Elohim; plural of majesty) who spoke to their forefathers many years before. For just as the apostle John refers to Christ as the "Light" to stress that He is the Light of the world in the first chapter of John, so also the author of Hebrews refers to God as "Messengers" to stress that He is the One who spoke to their forefathers many years before.

(Note: I chose to translate the Greek word "angelous" as "God" instead of as "Messengers" in Hebrews 2:7, 9 because there is no article (tous/the) before the word "angelous" in these verses as there is in 1 Corinthians 11:10.)

I also want to point out one more thing concerning the prophecy of King David. It is obvious that the translators of the NASB think that David's prophecy is referring to man, not Christ. They believe that all things will one day be put under man's feet, not Christ's feet. This is evident by the lower-case letters in Psalm 8:4–6 and is confirmed by the lower-case letters (and lower-case capital letters) in Hebrews 2:6–8 and the upper-case letters in Hebrews 2:9. (They believe that Hebrews 2:6–8 is speaking of man and that Hebrews 2:9 is speaking of Christ.) However, it is also clear that the translators of the NASB believe that 1 Corinthians 15:27–28 is referring to all things being placed under Christ's feet because of the upper-case letters in verses 27–28. So let me ask a simple question. If 1 Corinthians 15:27–28 is referring to all things being placed under Christ's feet, then wouldn't the *original prophecy*, from which Paul is quoting, also be talking about all things being placed under Christ's feet? And if all things are placed under Christ's feet, then how can all things be placed under man's feet? Which is it? Are all things placed under Christ's feet? Or are all things placed under man's feet? Indeed, the prophecy in Psalm is referring to Christ because Paul is talking about Christ when he quotes King David's words. Furthermore, throughout the first two chapters of Hebrews, the author explains that Christ is far superior to angels. Would then, the author of Hebrews, in chapter two verses 5–8, veer from this topic to explain how the world will one day be placed to man instead of angels? Indeed, no! In these verses, the author of Hebrews is still explaining that Christ is superior to angels. The world to come will be placed to Christ.

Indeed, all things will one day be placed under Christ's feet! In addition, the author of Hebrews, after quoting David's prophecy (vv. 6–8), then explicitly names Jesus as the One who was spoken of in David's prophecy (v. 9). Therefore, there is no disputing that King David's prophecy is referring to Christ.

When King David uttered his prophecy many years ago, he spoke of the future to come. But now, two parts of David's prophecy have been fulfilled. Christ was made for a little while lower than God when He emptied Himself on our behalf, and Christ has been crowned with glory and majesty after being exalted to the right hand of the Father. But also, two parts have not yet been fulfilled. Not yet are all things placed under Christ's feet, and as a result, the sovereign rule has not yet been handed over to Him; for that will happen when the end comes as Paul has explained to those in Corinth.

In ending, I would like to say that the presented rendering of 1 Corinthians 15:20–28 is in complete harmony with the rest of Scripture. The mistranslation of the word "hypotage" has our wonderful Savior in a position of subjection when, in reality, He will be appointed over the works of God's hands by the will of the Father. Furthermore, the word "hypotasso" is a word of placement, not a word of subjection. Thankfully, God has preserved the true meaning of the word "hypotasso" for us through Paul's quote of Scripture. For we need to understand that David wrote the Psalms because he was moved by the Holy Spirit. David did not prophesy by his own will, but by God. The divine prophecy given to him was the Word of God, and he wrote it down in a Scroll for future generations to come. Many centuries later, Paul quoted the Scripture that had been written by the hand of David, because he was teaching those in Corinth about what would happen when the end comes. Certainly, Paul, the servant of the Lord, would not have changed or misquoted God's inerrant Word that had been written in the Scroll from many centuries earlier. But over the centuries, men have changed God's inerrant Word to suit their own agenda. They have not held God's inerrant Word in high esteem but have shown their contempt by changing its words. They have kept women in bondage when Christ has set them free. Many men want desperately to hold to their doctrine of lies in order to keep women in bondage so that they can have control. But bondage is not God's will for His beloved daughters, and as we go along, we will see the proper placement of the daughters that He so cherishes.

PSALM 8:4–6
(Prophecy given through King David)

[4]"What is man [enos] that You take thought of him, and the Son of Man [adam] that You care for Him? [5]Yet You have made Him for a little while lower than God, and You crown Him with glory and majesty! [6]You make Him to rule over the works of Your hands; You have put all things under His feet."

1 CORINTHIANS 15:20–28
(Paul expounds upon King David's prophecy)

[20]"But now Christ has been raised from the dead, the first fruits of those who are asleep. [21]For since by a man *came* death, by a man also *came* the resurrection of the dead. [22]For as in Adam all die, so also in Christ all will be made alive. [23]But each in his own order: Christ, the first fruits, after that those who are Christ's at His coming, [24]then *comes* the end, when the God and Father hands over the sovereign rule, as soon as He [Father] abolishes all rule and all authority and power. [25]For He [Father] must reign until He has put all His [Christ's] enemies under His [Christ's] feet. [26]The last enemy that will be abolished is death. [27]'For HE [Father] HAS PLACED ALL THINGS UNDER HIS [Christ's] FEET.' But when He says, 'All things are placed,' it is clear that it is apart from the One [Father] who placed all things to Him [Christ]. [28]But as soon as all things are willed to Him [Christ], then also the Son Himself will be appointed by the will of the One [Father] who placed all things to Him [Christ], so that God may be all in all."

HEBREWS 2:5–9
(Author of Hebrew's expounds upon King David's prophecy)

[5]"For He did not place to angels the world to come, concerning which we are speaking. [6]But one has testified somewhere, saying, 'WHAT IS MAN, THAT YOU REMEMBER HIM? OR THE SON OF MAN, THAT

YOU CARE FOR HIM? 7YOU HAVE MADE HIM FOR A LITTLE WHILE LOWER THAN GOD; YOU HAVE CROWNED HIM WITH GLORY AND HONOR, AND HAVE APPOINTED HIM OVER THE WORKS OF YOUR HANDS; 8YOU HAVE PLACED ALL THINGS UNDER HIS FEET.' For in placing all things to Him, He left nothing to Him that is disobedient. But at this present time, we do not yet see all things willed to Him. 9But we do see Jesus, the One having been made for a little while lower than God, now crowned with glory and honor because of the suffering of death, so that by the grace of God on behalf of everyone He might taste death."

7

HYPOTASSO

(Part II)

In the previous chapter, "Hypotasso (Part I)," I explained how a quote of Old Testament Scripture (by Paul) reveals to us that the word "hypotasso" is a word of placement, not a word of subjection. I also explained that I believe the word "hypotage" means "will, willed, appointed by the will of, willing, willingness, etc.," which, in turn, showed us that Christ will not be subjected by God after all things are placed under His feet, but rather, that He will be appointed by the will of God (over the works of His hands) after all things are placed under His feet. Furthermore, I showed that the translation of 1 Corinthians 15:24, in which Christ hands over the "basileia" to the God and Father at the end, is inconsistent with the rest of Scripture, which states that it is the God and Father who hands over the "basileia" to Christ at the end. Indeed, it is the God and Father who will hand over the "kingdom, kingship, sovereign rule" to Christ at the end after He (Father) puts all things under His (Christ's) feet.

In this chapter, I will go over the remaining uses of the words "hypotasso" and "hypotage" (except for two, which will be discussed in the following chapters) in order to show how their true meanings harmonize perfectly with God's Word. At times, the insertion of the new meaning will bring a drastic change to the passage, in which case, I will give an explanation along with my translation. At other times the insertion of the new meaning will bring only a slight change, in which case, I will provide only the translation of the NASB and my translation underneath as they are self-explanatory. Furthermore, you will see that at times I will translate the word "hypotasso" as "to place, to put, to set," while at other times, I will translate it as "to be set in this way." This latter translation is for better flow in the English language and is consistent with the most prevalent meaning of "hypo," which is "by or by means of." And as I mentioned previously, one must read the context to see just how something is being placed.

(Note: The word "tasso" means "to arrange, assign, appoint, determine, ordain, set,[1] devote, establish."[2] The word "hypo" means "by, by means of; under; at."[3] The translators have taken the word "hypo" to mean "under" when used in conjunction with the word "tasso" ["to be set under, to arrange under, to be subject, etc."]. However, we know from Paul's quote of Old Testament Scripture that the word "hypotasso" is a word of placement. Therefore, the word "hypo" when used in conjunction with the word "tasso" means "by means of" ["to be set by means of, to arrange by means of, etc."]. However, in the English language, the words "by means of" often do not need to be translated.)

Thus far, we have gone over ten of the forty-two total uses of the words "hypotasso" and "hypotage." Six in 1 Corinthians 15:27–28 and four in Hebrews 2:5, 8. From here on out, I will go over the words in chronological order, which will bring us to the gospel of Luke.

The first passage in Luke that we will go over is Luke 2:41–52. Here we have the story about Jesus going to Jerusalem with His parents for the Feast of the Passover when He was a boy. In this passage, the word "hypotasso" is used once in verse fifty-one. In fact, the word that is actually used is "hypotassomenos." And the Greek word "meno" means "to stay, remain, or continue."[4] This is why the NASB translators have translated the word "hypotassomenos" as "continued in subjection." But the question is, "Do we see Jesus being subject to His parents in this passage?" Or do we see something else? What did Jesus really continue to do? Let us take a look.

Starting with verse forty-one, it says, [41]"Now His parents went to Jerusalem every year at the Feast of the Passover. [42]And when He became twelve, they went up *there* according to the custom of the Feast; [43]and as they were returning, after spending the full number of days, the boy Jesus stayed behind in Jerusalem. But His parents were unaware of it...." Now, the word that is translated as "stayed behind" in verse forty-three is "hypomeno" in Greek. The word "hypomeno" is used eighteen times in the New Testament. The Strongest NIV Exhaustive Concordance lists the meaning of this word as "to stay behind; to stand firm, endure, persevere."[5] However, if one looks at this word and its context in the other passages that it is used, it undoubtedly, and without exception, means "to stand firm, endure, persevere." It does not mean to "stay behind." Consequently, Luke 2:43 is saying that Jesus "stood firmly" in Jerusalem. For it is quite apparent that after Mary and Joseph had spent the full number of days, they directly told Jesus that they were returning. And Jesus, in reply, obviously told them that He was to stay to do His Father's will; for He would not have deceived His parents, either by words or by silence, into thinking that He was following them when He wasn't. Instead, He would have made His intentions quite clear to them. However, His parents either did not grasp that He intended to stay or if they did, they were in disagreement and restated that it was time to go. Either way, His parents set out on their way to return to Nazareth and were unaware that Jesus did not follow them as they had requested because He was standing firm in Jerusalem.

Now it is essential for us to understand that the reason Jesus stood firmly to them is that He came to do the will of His Father, who sent Him. He did not come to do the will of Mary and Joseph. He did not come to do the will of sinners. Jesus, at the age of twelve, was **SINLESS**. He had not committed even one single sin because He had a deep understanding of the Father and that which was righteous in His eyes. The Father revealed His will to Jesus. He was One with the Father. He had wisdom and an understanding of God's Word that far surpassed that of any human. And at this tender age of twelve, Jesus had already far surpassed Mary and Joseph in wisdom and understanding, for they did not even understand the statement that He made to them (Luke 2:50). So Jesus stood firmly to them because they needed to know that He was sent for a purpose. And that purpose was not theirs. Jesus was sent for a higher purpose. He was sent to reach the lost. However, they did not understand His mission, but Jesus knew. Even at the tender age of twelve, He knew He was to die for the sins of the many; He was to die for the sins of Mary and Joseph. But Mary and Joseph did not understand, for they were human; they were sinners. And just as they did not understand Christ's mission, they also did not understand God's purpose at that time in Jerusalem. They had a different schedule in mind than God did. They wanted Jesus to return to Nazareth with them, but He did not follow right away, for He was on His Father's timeline. The Father had willed it for Jesus to stay as part of that plan to reach the lost. Everything that Jesus did was part of God's plan to reach the lost. So Jesus knew full well that His parents were leaving and wanted Him to return with them. But He made a conscious decision to "stand firm" in order to do His Father's will. Jesus never yielded His will to the authority and control of sinful humans. His will was only to do that of His Father's. Jesus never did anything on His own initiative but always what the Father taught Him; the Father was always with Christ, and Christ always did the things that were pleasing to Him (John 8:28–29). So we do not see Jesus being subject to Mary and Joseph in this passage, but quite the opposite. Jesus stood firmly to them.

As we continue in this passage, we see that after Jesus' parents went a day's journey, they discovered that He was not among their relatives and acquaintances, so they returned to Jerusalem looking for Him. Then in verse forty-six, it says, [46]"Then, after three days they found Him in the temple, sitting in the midst of the teachers, both listening to them and asking them questions." So here, we can see that Jesus was doing the will of His Father who sent Him; for it was not by accident that He was in the temple, sitting in the midst of the teachers. He was precisely where His Father wanted Him to be. Now I would also like to point out that when it says, in verse forty-six, that Jesus was sitting in the temple both listening to the teachers and asking them questions, He was not asking them questions because He needed answers. Jesus had His Father for that. But His questions were of a rhetorical nature. The fact that it says, in verse forty-seven, that all who heard Him were amazed at His understanding and His **answers** is confirmation of this. If Jesus were asking them questions because He did not know the answers, the teachers would have given Him the answers. But it says that Jesus gave them the answers even though He was the one asking the questions. For Jesus listened to what they had to say and then asked them questions to see what their response would be. He asked them questions to make a point and to teach them. He did not desire to know anything from these teachers of the Law, for they would not have had answers that would have been in accordance with God. But He asked them questions to initiate a response from them so that He could answer them back, for how else could they have been amazed at His understanding and His answers. So, in reality, Jesus was teaching those in the temple, but He initiated it in a question format. Jesus did this many times as an adult also. Jesus always asked questions to elicit a response from those He was teaching.

Next, in verse forty-eight, it says, [48]"When they saw Him, they were astonished; and His mother said to Him, 'Son, why have You treated us this way? Behold, Your father and I have been anxiously looking for You.'" Now I would like to point out that the wording of verse forty-eight makes it sound as though the reason Mary and Joseph were astonished was that Jesus had not gone with them to Nazareth. But I believe the astonishment is in relation to seeing His wisdom, along with all who heard Him. The word that is translated as "astonished" in Luke 2:48 is "ekplesso" in Greek, and almost every time it is used, it is in relation to being astonished or amazed at the teachings of Jesus. And when Mary and Joseph saw Him sitting in the temple in the midst of the teachers, I am sure that they did not disrupt the conversation. I'm sure they listened to Him and waited until an appropriate time to see why He had not gone with them. So they had time to see their Son and to observe His wisdom. And I believe this is the reason that they were astonished.

Next, in verse forty-nine, it says, [49]"And He said to them, 'Why is it that you were looking for Me? Did you not know that I had to be in My Father's *house*?'" But I believe a more accurate translation would be, [49]"Why is it that you were looking for Me? Did you not know that I had to be doing that of My Father's?" And I believe the reason Jesus asked Mary and Joseph these questions was because He had expressed to them previously that He was to stay to do the will of His Father. Therefore, they should have known where He was. If we notice, Jesus offered no apology for not following them, for He had done nothing wrong. He did what was right in His Father's sight. He was obedient to the Father and the Father alone, for He came to do His will.

Then in verse fifty-one, it says, [51]"And He went down with them and came to Nazareth, and He **continued in subjection** [hypotassomenos] to them...." But as we can see, Jesus is not seen as being subject to Mary and Joseph anywhere in this passage. Therefore, Luke 2:51 should instead be translated as, [51]"And He went down with them and came to Nazareth, and He **continued to be set in this way** [hypotassomenos] to them..." meaning that He was continuing to do that of His Father's. So when it says, [51]"...and He CONTINUED..." the continuation is not in reference to the fact that He went down with them, as is supposed due to the mistranslation of the word "hypotasso"; instead, it is referring to the fact that He was doing the will of His Father who sent Him. For Jesus stood firmly to Mary and Joseph in Jerusalem in doing His Father's will, and He continued to be set in this way to them in Nazareth and throughout His life, so that He could accomplish the will of His Father who sent Him. Also, when it says that Jesus went down with them and came to Nazareth, it doesn't mean that they left the temple right away. The Bible doesn't give a timeline. I am sure that Jesus did not leave before ensuring that His Father's will had been done. If there was more to be done at the temple, Jesus would not have left until it had been fulfilled. It may have been completed upon Mary and Joseph's arrival, or Mary and Joseph may have stayed a while longer until it was carried out. But without a doubt, He did not leave before completing His Father's will.

Therefore, I would translate Luke 2:41–52 as follows:

[41]"Now His parents went to Jerusalem every year at the Feast of the Passover. [42]And when He became twelve, they went up there according to the custom of the Feast; [43]and as they were returning, after spending the full number of days, the boy Jesus stood firmly in Jerusalem. But His parents were unaware of it, [44]and thought Him to be in the company of travelers and went a day's journey; and they began looking for Him among their relatives and acquaintances. [45]When they did not find Him, they returned to Jerusalem looking for Him. [46]Then, after three days, they found Him in the temple, sitting in the midst of the teachers, both listening to them and asking them questions. [47]And all who heard Him were astonished at His understanding and His answers. [48]Also seeing Him, they were amazed. Then His mother said to Him, 'Son, why have You treated us this way? Behold, Your father and I have continued in agony looking for You.' [49]And He said to them, 'Why is it that you were looking for Me? Did you not know that I had to be doing that of My Father's?' [50]But they did not understand the statement which He had spoke to them. [51]And He went down with them and came to Nazareth, and He **continued to be set in this way** [hypotassomenos] to them; and His mother treasured all His words in her heart. [52]And Jesus kept increasing in wisdom and stature and favor with God and people."

The next passage that we come to is Luke 10:17–20. In this passage, the word "hypotasso" is used twice.

[17]"The seventy returned with joy, saying, 'Lord, even the demons **are subject** [hypotassetai] to us in Your name.' [18]And He said to them, 'I was watching Satan fall from heaven like lightning. [19]Behold, I have given

94

you authority to tread on serpents and scorpions, and over all the power of the enemy, and nothing will injure you. ²⁰Nevertheless do not rejoice in this, that the spirits **are subject** [hypotassetai] to you, but rejoice that your names are recorded in heaven'" (Luke 10:17–20).

¹⁷"The seventy returned with joy, saying, 'Lord, even the demons **are placed** [hypotassetai] to us in Your name.' ¹⁸And He said to them, 'I was watching Satan fall from heaven like lightning. ¹⁹Behold, I have given you authority to tread on serpents and scorpions, and over all the power of the enemy, and nothing will injure you. ²⁰Nevertheless do not rejoice in this, that the spirits **are placed** [hypotassetai] to you, but rejoice that your names are recorded in heaven'" (Luke 10:17–20).

Next, we come to Romans 8:6–8. In this passage, the word "hypotasso" is used once in verse seven.

⁶"For the mind set on the flesh is death, but the mind set on the Spirit is life and peace, ⁷because the mind set on the flesh is hostile toward God; for **it does** not **subject itself** [hypotassetai] to the law of God, for it is not even able *to do so*, ⁸and those who are in the flesh cannot please God" (Rom. 8:6–8).

⁶"For the mind set on the flesh is death, but the mind set on the Spirit is life and peace, ⁷because the mind set on the flesh is hostile toward God; for **it is** not **set** [hypotassetai] to the law of God, neither indeed can it, ⁸and those in the flesh cannot please God" (Rom. 8:6–8).

(Note: The NASB translators have added the word "set" three times in verses 6–7, where it does not appear in the Greek. However, the translators have added it because they understand that Paul is talking about a person's "mindset." Therefore, I have kept the three uses of the word "set" in my translation to reinforce the understanding that the word "hypotasso" is a word of placement. Indeed, the mind set on the flesh is hostile toward God; for it [the mind] is not set to the law of God.)

Next, we come to Romans 8:20–21. In this passage, the word "hypotasso" is used once, and the word "hypotage" is used once.

²⁰"For the creation **was subjected** [hypetage] to futility, not willingly, but because of Him who **subjected** [hypotaxanta] it, in hope ²¹that the

creation itself also will be set free from its slavery to corruption into the freedom of the glory of the children of God" (Rom. 8:20–21).

[20]"For the creation **was willed** [hypetage] to futility, not by their own choice, but by the One who **placed** [hypotaxanta] it, in hope [21]that the creation itself then will be set free from its slavery to corruption into the freedom of the glory of the children of God" (Rom. 8:20–21).

Next, we come to Romans 10:1–3. In this passage, the word "hypotage" is used once in verse three.

[1]"Brethren, my heart's desire and my prayer to God for them is for *their* salvation. [2]For I testify about them that they have a zeal for God, but not in accordance with knowledge. [3]For not knowing about God's righteousness and seeking to establish their own, **they did** not **subject themselves** [hypetagesan] to the righteousness of God" (Rom. 10:1–3).

[1]"Brethren, my heart's desire and my prayer to God for them is for *their* salvation. [2]For I testify about them that they have a zeal for God, but not in accordance with knowledge. [3]For not knowing about God's righteousness and seeking to establish their own [will], **they did** not **will** [hypetagesan] the righteousness of God" (Rom. 10:1–3).

The next passage that we come to is Romans 13:1–7. In this passage, the word "hypotasso" is used twice. Now before I begin, I would like to say that this passage, as translated, makes little sense given the fact that we have seen many evil governments arise over the centuries. But the reason it makes little sense is that the translators have incorrectly defined the word "hypotasso." Hence, this ill-defined word has caused them to mistranslate portions of this passage, and the result is a passage that is in opposition to Scripture. Now before I get into what I believe this passage is saying, I would first like to go over this passage as it is translated so that we can see for ourselves just how much it contradicts Scripture.

Verse one says, [1]"Every person **is to be in subjection** [hypotassestho] to the governing authorities. For there is no authority except from God, and those which exist are established by God." So, this verse, as translated, tells us that all authorities which exist have been established by God. But if this is true, then did God establish the corrupt governments that were in power at the time of Christ? Did God establish the very governments that crucified our Lord? Should the apostles have been in subjection to them as this verse says? If so, then the apostles themselves did not heed their own words because we do not see the apostles submitting to them in Scripture. The apostles instead withstood these evil governments, and many went to their very deaths because they did not submit. For the apostles themselves said in Acts 5:29, [29]"…We must obey God rather than men." And obeying God rather than men is what we see them doing throughout Scripture. Furthermore, what about Hitler? Did God establish Hitler to be in power? Should believers have been in subjection to him as this verse says since he was from God? Absolutely not! Hitler was not from God; Hitler was from Satan, along with the governments that crucified Jesus. And to suggest that Paul here is asking us to do something that he, along with the other apostles, did not do, is ridiculous, to say the least.

Next, verse two says, [2]"Therefore whoever resists authority has opposed the ordinance of God; and they who have opposed will receive condemnation upon themselves." Now again, we can see clearly in Scripture that the apostles did resist the governing authorities. In fact, in Acts 5:27–28 and Acts 5:40–42, we can see that the Council and the High priest had given them strict orders not to continue teaching in the name of Christ, yet the apostles continued to do just that. Now, did the apostles oppose the ordinance of God by resisting the governing authorities? Or did they do what was right in the sight of God? Also, did those in Hitler's day who refused to go along with his murderous rants oppose the ordinance of God? Or did they do what was right in the sight of God? In both cases, I believe it is the latter.

Continuing, in verse three, it says, [3]"For rulers are not a cause of fear for good behavior, but for evil. Do you want to have no fear of authority? Do what is good and you will have praise from the same…." So again, we can see that this verse is at odds with Scripture. In Acts 5:40, when the apostles had resisted the governing authorities and had continued to teach in the name of Christ, they were flogged. Therefore, the authorities were a cause of fear for good behavior. And since it was the authorities who flogged them, they surely did not receive any praise from them. Furthermore, Hitler certainly was a cause of fear for good behavior. If you hid a Jewish person, he would have killed you too. And he most certainly would not have given anyone praise for doing what was good.

Next, in verse four, it says, [4]"…for it is a minister of God to you for good. But if you do what is evil, be afraid; for it does not bear the sword for nothing; for it is a minister of God, an avenger who brings wrath on the one who practices evil." Now, are we expected to believe that the Council and High Priest were ministers of God to the apostles for good? The very ones who did not want the apostles to teach in the name of Christ and who crucified our Lord? Were they avengers of God who brought wrath on the one who practiced evil? Most certainly, they were not. As I said before, many of the apostles were put to death by this very government for doing what was good. And was Hitler a minister and an avenger of God who brought wrath on the one who practiced evil? No, Hitler was an enemy of God, not a minister of God. He was on the side of Satan and brought wrath on the one who practiced what was good, not evil. The truth is that no unbeliever could ever be a minister of God to us for good. Therefore, both of these governments were set up by human hands and human will. They were not established by God.

And continuing, verse five says, [5]"Therefore it is necessary **to be in subjection** [hypotassesthai], not only because of wrath, but also for conscience' sake." So, this verse tells us that we should be in subjection to these supposed ministers of God because of wrath and also for conscience' sake? Certainly, believers would have a guilty conscience if they ever submitted to one of these evil governments. And one would have to submit to their evil ways in order to keep from feeling their wrath. Therefore, we can clearly see that this passage, as it is translated, makes no sense from a Christian perspective because its directives go entirely against God's Word. Accordingly, then, what does make sense from a Christian perspective, are the words of Paul in Romans 12:1–2. He states:

> [1]"Therefore I urge you, brethren, by the mercies of God, to present your bodies a living and holy sacrifice, acceptable to God, *which is* your spiritual service of worship. [2]And do not be conformed to this world, but be transformed by the renewing of your mind, so that you may prove what the will of God is, that which is good and acceptable and perfect."

The directives given to us by Paul in Romans 12:1–2 are what believers should always follow, even when dealing with governing authorities. Indeed, living in a way that is holy is the way that believers are to be in relation to those in authority, and this is what we will see Paul tell those in Rome.

Before I begin explaining this passage, I would just like to say that I believe the main reason this passage does not make sense is that verses one and two are, to a great extent, mistranslated. And the mistranslation of these two verses throws off the whole passage because the remaining verses are, for the most part, translated accurately, with the exception of the word "hypotasso" in verse five and an "added word" in verse six. Therefore, I will now explain what I believe this passage is saying. Again, the first sentence in verse one says, [1]"Every person **is to be in subjection** [hypotassestho] to the governing authorities." The word that is translated as "person" is "psyche" in Greek. The word "psyche" means "life, soul, heart, mind; the immaterial part and eternal part of the inner person."[6] Now, I believe the reason the translators have translated the word "psyche" as "person" is that it would seem odd for Paul to tell believers to submit their lives, their souls, their hearts, or their minds to the governing authorities, especially in light of the words he stated in Romans 12:1–2. However, translating it as "person" is not an accurate rendering because, again, "psyche" means "life, soul, heart, mind; the immaterial part and eternal part of the inner person."

The next word, hypotasso, again, is a word of placement, not a word of subjection. Therefore, Paul wants believers to have their minds (in the way that they think) and their hearts (in the way that they feel), etc., set on something. Now, does Paul want believers to have their minds set on the governing authorities? No! The word that is translated as "governing" is "hyperecho" in Greek and also means "to be better than, to transcend."[7] Therefore, I believe that Paul is telling the believers in Rome to have their minds set on transcending the authorities. In other words, Paul wants the believers to be set apart from the authorities; to be beyond them; to exist above them. For God's people are set apart unto Him. They are a chosen race, a royal priesthood, a holy nation, and a people for God's own possession (1 Pet. 2:9). And since the Roman authorities that were in power were against God, as they persecuted believers and committed many evil atrocities, Paul wanted God's chosen to be set apart from them and to rise above them. He wanted believers to be set in such a way that was honoring to God. He wanted them to be better than the authorities in the way they lived their lives. And he wanted them to distinguish themselves from the authorities to show that they were separate unto God by refusing to give in to their ungodly ways. And this, by the way, is what the apostles themselves did. It is also what Corrie ten Boom did during Hitler's reign of terror. Corrie ten Boom refused to give in to the evil acts of Hitler. As a woman set apart unto God, she, along with her family, risked their very lives to help Jews escape from the Nazis. She rose above and distinguished herself, the good from the evil. So the first part of verse one should be translated as, [1]"Every mind **is to be set** [hypotassestho] on transcending the authorities."

Next, in verse one, it says, [1]"…For there is no authority except from God, and those which exist are established by God." Now again, this verse tells us that all authorities which exist are established by God. However, if we turn to Hosea 8:4, we will find out that this statement is false. For God, Himself, says, [4]"They have set up kings, but not by Me. They have appointed princes, but I did not know *it*…." So this verse clearly shows us that authorities are established apart from God. Therefore, God has **NOT** established every human authority. For God only sets up righteous authorities. He appointed Deborah as judge, David as king, Esther as queen, and others like them. And although the people whom God appoints are themselves not perfect, for they too are sinners, they are those who trust in God, and He works through them. God works through believers, not unbelievers. And God does not establish evil governments, or evil people, to be in power, Satan does. However, God can use them for His purposes, and His purposes are always righteous. And since God did not establish the Roman government, it was no authority at all. God did not recognize it; He did not know it. And the same goes for Hitler's government or any other government that is against God. They have been set up apart from God and are, therefore, not recognized by God. And I believe that this is precisely what Paul is explaining in the second sentence of verse one because the Greek literally reads as, [1]"…For not it is authority if not by God, and those which are by God are ordained." So Paul explains that if the authority is not by God, then it is no authority at all. Therefore, Paul is telling the believers in Rome that the Roman government was not an actual authority (in God's sight) because it was not established by God. He also states that the authorities that are by God have been ordained by Him; they have been officially appointed. So, Romans 13:1 should be rendered as, [1]"Every mind **is to be set** [hypotassestho] on transcending the authorities. For it is not authority if *it is* not by God, and those which are by God are ordained."

Next, verse two says, [2]"Therefore whoever resists authority has opposed the ordinance of God, and they who have opposed will receive condemnation upon themselves." Here, the word that the translators have translated as "resists" is "antitassomenos" in Greek. "Anti," used in absolute or by itself, means "in place of" or "instead of." However, it can also mean "against" if it is used as part of a word as it is here.[8] "Tasso," again, means "to arrange, assign, appoint, determine, ordain, set, devote, establish." And "meno," again, means "to stay, remain, or continue." Therefore, Paul is actually saying that it is the ones who "continue to establish against" (or "continue to establish in place of") the authority of God's ordinance (what He has put into effect, e.g., righteous living; love thy neighbor) who have opposed. Indeed, it is the ones such as Hitler, with his evil pronouncements, who have opposed. Furthermore, Paul is also saying that it is the ones who have opposed the authority of God's ordinance who will receive condemnation upon themselves. Indeed, it is Hitler who will receive condemnation on himself. So verse two should be rendered as, [2]"Therefore, the one who continues to establish against the authority of God's ordinance has opposed, and those having opposed will receive condemnation on themselves."

Thus, Romans 13:1–2 should be translated as follows, [1]"Every mind **is to be set** [hypotassestho] on transcending the authorities. For it is not authority if *it is* not by God, and those which are by God are ordained. [2]Therefore, the one who continues to establish against the authority of God's ordinance has opposed, and those having opposed will receive condemnation on themselves."

Next, verses 3–4 are, for the most part, translated accurately. The only thing to understand here is that Paul is now speaking about true authorities, ones that have been set in place by God. It reads, [3]"For rulers are not a cause of fear for good behavior, but for evil. Do you want to have no fear of authority? Do what is good and you will have praise from the same; [4]for it is a minister of God to you for good. But if you do what is evil, be afraid; for it does not bear the sword for nothing; for it is a minister of God, an avenger who brings wrath on the one who practices evil." However, I believe an even more accurate translation would read as follows, [3]"For the rulers are not a cause of fear for good work, but for evil. And if you do not want to fear their authority, then do what is good and you will have praise from them. [4]For God's servant is to you for the good. But if one does evil, then be afraid. For it is not for nothing the sword they bear. For God's servant is an avenger for wrath to the one practicing evil."

Here, we can see that any authority established by God will not be a cause of fear for good work, but for evil. And throughout the Bible, we can see just this. The authorities that God had set up were avengers that brought wrath on the ones who practiced evil. Several examples of this were Deborah, who helped bring vengeance on Jabin and Sisera (Judg. 4:1–24); David, who had victory over the Amalekites (1 Sam. 30:1–20); and Esther, who helped bring vengeance on Haman in the book of Esther. Indeed, God did not bring punishment on those who practiced what was right; He brought punishment on those who practiced what was evil.

Then in verse five, Paul (supposedly) says, 5"Therefore, it is necessary **to be in subjection** [hypotassesthai], not only because of wrath, but also for conscience sake." However, verse five should instead be rendered as, 5"Therefore, it is necessary **to be set in this way** [hypotassesthai], not only because of wrath but also because of conscience." Now, when Paul says it is necessary "to be set in this way," he means it is necessary "to be set by means of" the way that he just explained. And that is, doing what is good, being set in a way that is righteous. And he explains that believers should be set in this way not only because of the punishment that can come from wrongdoing but also so that they do not have a guilty conscience before God.

Before I move on in this passage, I would like to explain the reason why Paul does not ask believers to submit to authorities that are set in place by God, and why he only asks believers to do what is good. The reason Paul does not ask believers to submit to authorities that are set in place by God is that even those who are set in place by God can stray from God's will. King David is a prime example of this. For we know from reading 2 Samuel 12:7 that God anointed David to be king over Israel. However, when David committed adultery with Bathsheba and found out that she was with child, he then commanded Joab to murder Bathsheba's husband in battle to cover up his sin (2 Sam. 11:2–17). As a result, Joab's submission to David caused him to take part in his sin, for Joab submitted to David's murderous plan, and an innocent man was struck down. So, the possibility that believers could be asked to do something sinful is why believers are not asked to submit to authorities but are only told to do what is good. And, by believers doing what is good, they submit to the ultimate and final authority, God!

Next, verse six says, [6]"For because of this you also pay taxes, for *rulers* are servants of God, devoting themselves to this very thing." Now, the problem with this verse is that the translators have inserted the word "rulers" into the text. If we notice, the word "rulers" is in italics; it is not in the original Greek. But what the translators should have done is inserted the word "believers" into the text, because the servants, or ministers, that Paul is talking about in verse six are believers, not rulers. Therefore, verse six should be rendered as, [6]"For because of this [being set righteously] you also pay taxes, for *believers are* ministers of God *who* are constantly devoting themselves for this [righteousness]." Now one thing that I want to point out is the word that is (twice) translated as "minister" in Romans 13:4 should be translated as "servant" while the word that is translated as "servants" in Romans 13:6 should be translated as "ministers." This is because the word that is (twice) translated as "minister" is "diakonos" in Greek and means "a servant; a person who renders service and help to others.[9] (See Matthew 20:26; Mark 9:35; John 2:5.) And the word that is translated as "servants" is "leitourgoi" in Greek and means "servant; minister; one who cares for another, often with a focus on a specific task or duty, which can be practical or spiritual."[10] (See Romans 15:16; Hebrews 1:7; 8:2.) The reason I point this out is that Paul is referring to believers as "ministers" in verse six. And it is important to realize this because Paul is making a similar argument to the one he made in Romans 12:1. Paul said that when believers present their bodies as a living and holy sacrifice, acceptable to God, it is their spiritual service (latreian). And the word "latreia" in Greek means "worship, ministry, or service (to God)."[11] So Paul is saying that righteousness/holiness is a believer's spiritual service (latreian) to God, which is why he then states that believers are ministers (leitourgoi) of God who devote themselves to righteousness. Indeed, believers are a chosen race, a royal priesthood, a holy nation, and a people for God's own possession (1 Pet. 2:9).

And finally, verse seven is translated accurately. Therefore, I would translate Romans 13:1–7 as follows:

[1]"Every mind **is to be set** [hypotassestho] on transcending the authorities. For it is not authority if *it is* not by God, and those which are by God are ordained. [2]Therefore, the one who continues to establish against the

authority of God's ordinance has opposed, and those having opposed will receive condemnation on themselves. ³For the rulers *set by God* are not a cause of fear for good work but for evil. And if you do not want to fear their authority, then do what is good and you will have praise from them. ⁴For God's servant is to you for the good. But if one does evil, then be afraid. For it is not for nothing the sword they bear. For God's servant is an avenger for wrath to the one practicing evil. ⁵Therefore, it is necessary **to be set in this way** [doing what is good] [hypotassesthai], not only because of wrath but also because of conscience. ⁶For because of this [being set righteously] you also pay taxes, for *believers are* ministers of God *who* are constantly devoting themselves for this [righteousness]. ⁷Render to all what is due them; to the tax the tax; to the tribute the tribute; to the respect the respect; to the honor the honor."

The next passage that we come to is 1 Corinthians 14:31–33. In this passage, the word "hypotasso" is used once in verse thirty-two. It says, ³¹"For you can all prophesy one by one, so that all may learn and all may be exhorted; ³²and the spirits of prophets **are subject** [hypotassetai] to prophets; ³³for God is not *a God* of confusion but of peace, as in all the churches of the saints."

Here, in verse thirty-two, it says that the spirits of prophets are subject to prophets. However, it makes no sense whatsoever that a prophet's spirit would be under the authority and control of prophets because the flesh does not control the spirit, but rather the spirit controls the flesh. Therefore, Paul is not saying that the spirits of prophets are subject to prophets; instead, he is saying that the spirits of prophets are set (in order) for prophets (by God). Now, the reason Paul makes this statement is that there was disorder among those in the church at Corinth. And as I stated in the 1 Corinthians 14:34–35 chapter, I believe that most of the disorderly conduct was coming from a faction of men who did not want women to prophesy. I believe that when a woman started to speak, these men spoke over them to cut them off. As a result, these men were not hearing from God and were only speaking so that they could silence the women. Therefore, Paul is explaining to them that God is the One who gives a person revelation and that He does so by speaking to that person's spirit. Thus, if they are truly hearing from God, if God is truly speaking to their spirit, then there will not be disorder among them because God will not cause them to speak all at once; for God is not of disorder but of peace, as among all the people that are holy.

So, I would translate 1 Corinthians 14:31–33 as, [31]"For you can all prophesy one by one, so that all may learn and all may be exhorted; [32]and the spirits of prophets **are set** [hypotassetai] *in order* for prophets; [33]for God is not of disorder but of peace, as among all the people that are holy."

The next passage that we come to is 1 Corinthians 14:34–35. In this passage, the word "hypotasso" is used once in verse thirty-four. (Note: The correct rendering of these verses was also given in my translation summary in the 1 Corinthians 14:34–35 chapter. These verses are, without a doubt, a quote of a faction of men who wrote Paul.)

[34]"The women are to keep silent in the churches; for they are not permitted to speak, but **are to subject themselves** [hypotassesthosan], just as the Law also says. [35]If they desire to learn anything, let them ask their own husbands at home; for it is improper for a woman to speak in church" (1 Cor. 14:34–35).

[34]*"The women are to keep silent among the people; for they are not permitted to speak, but **are to be set** [hypotassesthosan] as also the Law says. [35]If they desire to learn anything, let them ask their own husbands at home; for it is shameful for a woman to speak among the people"* (1 Cor. 14:34–35).

Next, we come to 1 Corinthians 16:15–18. In this passage, the word "hypotasso" is used once in verse sixteen. It says, [15]"Now I urge you, brethren (you know the household of Stephanas, that they were the first fruits of Achaia, and that they have devoted themselves for ministry to the saints), [16]that you also **be in subjection** [hypotassesthe] to such men and to everyone who helps in the work and labors. [17]I rejoice over the coming of Stephanas and Fortunatus and Achaicus, because they have supplied what was lacking on your part. [18]For they have refreshed my spirit and yours. Therefore, acknowledge such men."

In this passage, Paul is not asking for submission; he is asking for service. (It was for "service" [diakonia] that the household of Stephanas had devoted themselves to the saints, not "ministry.") Hence, what is happening here is that the household of Stephanas had devoted themselves for service to God's people. They had made themselves "servants" to their fellow believers and had supplied what was lacking on their part. And in return, Paul was asking those in Corinth to, likewise, be set for service to the household of Stephanas and to everyone who helps in the work and labors. So it is not submission that Paul is asking for, but servant-hood, which is also what Christ taught. For just as this family had made themselves servants for the benefit of others, so also Paul wants those in Corinth to be as servants to them and to all who do the Lord's work. Since Christ came to serve us, so also, we should serve one another.

Therefore, 1 Corinthians 16:15–18 should be translated as, ¹⁵"Now I urge you, brethren, *for* you know the household of Stephanas, that they were the first fruits of Achaia and that they have devoted themselves for service to the saints, ¹⁶that you also **be set in this way** [hypotassesthe] to such ones and to everyone who helps in the work and labors. ¹⁷I rejoice over the coming of Stephanas and Fortunatus and Achaicus, because they have supplied what was lacking on your part. ¹⁸For they have refreshed my spirit and yours. Therefore, acknowledge such ones."

Next, we come to 2 Corinthians 9:13–14. In this passage, the word "hy-potage" is used once in verse thirteen.

¹³"Because of the proof given by this ministry, they will glorify God for *your* **obedience** [hypotage] to your confession of the gospel of Christ and for the liberality of your contribution to them and to all, ¹⁴while they also, by prayer on your behalf, yearn for you because of the surpassing grace of God in you" (2 Cor. 9:13–14).

¹³"Because of the proof given by this service, they will glorify God over the **willingness** [hypotage] of your commitment to the gospel of Christ and for the liberality of your contribution to them and to all, ¹⁴while they also, by prayer on your behalf, yearn for you because of the surpassing grace of God in you" (2 Cor. 9:13–14).

The next passage that we come to is Galatians 2:4–5. In this passage, the word "hypotage" is used once in verse five.

⁴"But *it was* because of the false brethren secretly brought in, who had sneaked in to spy out our liberty which we have in Christ Jesus, in order to bring us into bondage. ⁵But we did not yield **in subjection** [hypotage] to them for even an hour, so that the truth of the gospel would remain with you" (Gal. 2:4–5).

⁴"But *it was* because of the false brethren secretly brought in, who had sneaked in to spy out our liberty which we have in Christ Jesus, in order to bring us into bondage. ⁵But we did not yield to their **will** [hypotage] for even an hour, so that the truth of the gospel would remain with you" (Gal. 2:4–5).

Next, we come to Ephesians 1:22–23. In this passage, the word "hypotasso" is used once in verse twenty-two.

²²"And He **put** [hypetaxen] all things **in subjection** under His feet, and gave Him as head over all things to the church, ²³which is His body, the fullness of Him who fills all in all" (Eph. 1:22–23).

²²"And He **placed** [hypetaxen] all things under His feet, and gave Him as head [source] for all things to believers, ²³which is His body, the fullness of Him who fills all in all" (Eph. 1:22–23).

Next, we come to Ephesians 5:18–21. In this passage, the word "hypotasso" is used once in verse twenty-one. It says, ¹⁸"And do not get drunk with wine, for that is dissipation, but be filled with the Spirit, ¹⁹speaking to one another in psalms and hymns and spiritual songs, singing and making melody with your heart to the Lord; ²⁰always giving thanks for all things in the name of our Lord Jesus Christ to God, even the Father; ²¹and **be subject** [hypotassomenoi] to one another in the fear of Christ."

If Paul were asking all believers to be subject to one another, how would this work? Because when a person is subject to someone, it means that they are under the authority and control of that person. So Paul would essentially be asking everyone to be under everyone else's authority. But the question is, "What if everyone was in disagreement?" Who would you listen to? And if you are under the authority of another person, how can that same person be under your authority? Furthermore, is the person who has been in Christ for thirty years to be subject to the authority of the one who has been in Christ for one week? Does the infant in Christ have authority over the mature person in Christ who has been in God's Word for many years? There is no distinction made here between a new believer and one who has been in Christ for many years. Paul is asking this of everyone equally.

Undoubtedly, Paul is not asking believers to be subject to one another. Instead, Paul is asking believers to **be continuously set** (hypotassomenoi) to one another in the way that he asked in verse nineteen, speaking to one another with psalms and hymns and spiritual songs. Now, when Paul asks those from Ephesus to speak to one another with psalms and hymns and spiritual songs, he is not actually expecting them to speak hymns to one another. Paul is using a metaphor here to vividly express how they are to speak to one another. And since psalms and hymns and spiritual songs are all songs that glorify God, Paul is asking them to speak to one another in a way that will glorify God. And this is how Paul wants all believers in Christ to be toward one another out of the deep respect that they have for Christ.

Thus, Ephesians 5:18–21 should be translated as, [18]"And do not get drunk with wine, for that is dissipation, but be filled with the Spirit, [19]speaking to one another with psalms and hymns and spiritual songs, singing with songs of praise in your heart to the Lord, [20]always giving thanks for all things in the name of our Lord Jesus Christ to the God and Father, [21]and **be continuously set in this way** [hypotassomenoi] toward one another out of reverence for Christ."

Next, we come to Ephesians 5:22–33. In this passage, the word "hypo-tasso" is used once in verse twenty-four. And now that Paul has just finished telling those in the body of Christ how they are to be set in relation to one another, so here also, Paul tells husbands and wives how they are to be set in relation to one another. Verse twenty-two says, [22]"Wives, *be subject* to your own husbands, as to the Lord." However, verse twenty-two should be rendered as, [22]"The wives to their own husbands, as to the Lord." As one can see, the words *"be subject"* are in italics; they are **NOT** in the original Greek. As a result, Paul is saying that he wants the wives (to be set) to their own husbands as (they would be set) to the Lord. In other words, Paul wants wives to act the same way toward their husbands that they would toward Christ if Christ were standing before them. Now it goes without saying that a woman would be kind, loving, respectful, and pure in manner toward Christ if Christ were standing before her. As a result, wives should be kind, loving, respectful, and pure in manner toward their husbands as well. And this is what Paul means when he says, [22]"The wives to their own husbands, as to the Lord."

Next, verse twenty-three says, [23]"For the husband is the head of the wife, as Christ also is the head of the church, He Himself *being* the Savior of the body." Now in this verse, the translators should have rendered the words "aner/gunaikos" as "man/woman," not as "husband/wife." (Note: In the Greek, the word "aner" means "man/husband," and the word "gunaikos" means "woman/wife"; there is not a separate word for each. As a result, the context determines how these words are rendered.) It is also imperative to understand here that the word "head" means "source," as was discussed in my earlier chapter "Head—Source or Leader?" Therefore, Ephesians 5:23 should be rendered as, [23]"For the man is the head [source] of the woman, as Christ also is the head [source] of the church, He Himself *being* the Savior of the body." Now, verse twenty-three should be rendered this way because Paul wants wives to understand that the man is the source of the woman (as she is flesh of HIS flesh and bone of HIS bone), just as Christ is the source of the church, He Himself being the Savior of the body; for there would be no church if Christ did not shed His blood on the cross for her. Now Paul wants wives to understand this because he is making the point that because the man is the source of the woman as Christ also is the source of the church, the wife is to be toward her husband as the church is toward Christ. This is why Paul concludes by saying, [24]"So as the church **is set** [hypotassetai] to Christ, so also the wives to their husbands in everything."

I would like to clarify that when Paul says "in everything" in verse twenty-four, he is speaking in the context of the way a woman is to "act" toward her husband. In other words, Paul wants wives to "always," "in all things," "in all situations," be kind, loving, respectful, and pure in manner toward their husbands. "Everything" does not mean that wives are to submit to their husbands. And we must make this indisputably clear because there is no doubt that some men will insist that submission is included. For if Paul meant "everything" outside the context of the way a woman is to "act" toward her husband, then one could contend that it also means that a woman is to worship her husband since the church worships Christ (Matt. 2:11; 14:33; 28:9; Luke 24:52; John 9:38). However, we know from Scripture that only God is to be worshiped (Matt. 4:10; Rev. 19:10). Therefore, we know that "everything" cannot mean "worship." And since we likewise know from Scripture that we are to obey God rather than men (Acts 5:29), we know that "everything" cannot mean "submission" either. Therefore, when Paul says "everything," he is speaking in the context of the way a woman is to "act" toward her husband. It is true that wives are called to serve their husbands, but submission is only to God.

So, Ephesians 5:22–24 should be translated as, 22"The wives to their own husbands, as to the Lord. 23For the man is the head [source] of the woman, as Christ also is the head [source] of the church, He Himself *being* the Savior of the body. 24So as the church **is set** [hypotassetai] to Christ, so also the wives to their husbands in everything."

Moving along in this passage, Paul then goes on to say in verses 25–30, 25"Husbands, love your wives, just as Christ also loved the church and gave Himself up for her, 26so that He might sanctify her, having cleansed her by the washing of water with the word, 27that He might present to Himself the church in all her glory, having no spot or wrinkle or any such thing; but that she would be holy and blameless. 28So husbands ought also to love their own wives as their own bodies. He who loves his own wife loves himself; 29for no one ever hated his own flesh, but nourishes and cherishes it, just as Christ also *does* the church, 30because we are members of His body."

When most people read this portion of Ephesians, they mistakenly think that Paul is asking husbands to love their wives. However, the command to husbands is not to "love their wives"; rather, the command to husbands is to "love their wives AS CHRIST LOVED THE CHURCH." As a result, Paul is asking husbands to treat their wives the same way that Christ treats the church out of the deep love that He has for her. Otherwise, it means that a man can demean his wife as long as he loves her; it means that a man can speak disrespectfully to his wife as long as he loves her; it means that a man can act immorally toward his wife as long as he loves her. But love and demeaning, disrespectful, and immoral behavior do not go hand in hand, as they are at opposite ends of the spectrum. Therefore, a man cannot do these things if he loves his wife as Christ loved the church; for loving one's wife as Christ loved the church embodies and encompasses the whole realm of behavior that Christ portrayed. And Christ portrayed all godly characteristics. He modeled righteous behavior so that we would know what righteous behavior is. So that we would know what love is, Christ first loved us. So that we would know what kindness is, Christ first showed us kindness. So that we would know what respect is, Christ first showed us respect. So that we would know God's righteousness, Christ was righteous and pure before us. Christ never said, "Do as I say and not as I do." Instead, He modeled righteous behavior so that we could emulate His behavior. Indeed, Christ treated His bride with the utmost love, kindness, respect, and purity and is the model for the way husbands are to be toward their wives. As a result, Paul is asking husbands not only to love their wives but also to treat them in a kind, respectful, and pure manner as Christ also does the church. When a husband does this, he is nourishing and cherishing his wife. So, in reality, Paul is asking for the exact same thing from both husbands and wives. He wants kind, loving, respectful, and pure behavior from each toward their spouse. The only thing is he explains it from a different standpoint for each. For Paul wants wives to understand that a woman CAME FROM a man's own flesh and bone just as the church CAME FROM Christ, and he wants the husbands to realize that their wives ARE their own flesh and bone, their own bodies, just as the church IS the body of Christ. As a result, Paul wants wives to ask themselves how they would treat Christ and therefore act accordingly to their husbands, and Paul wants husbands to ask themselves how Christ would treat the church and therefore act accordingly to their wives.

On the following page, I have given a visual aid to help husbands and wives better understand what Paul is asking of them and why. Notice Paul has used the one-flesh relationship scenario for each, only from a different standpoint.

To Wives:

²²"The wives to their own husbands,
as to the Lord" (Eph. 5:22).

The man is the source of the woman as
Christ also is the source of the church.

To Husbands:

²⁵"Husbands love your wives, just as Christ
also loved the church…" (Eph. 5:25).

The woman is the body of man as the
church is the body of Christ.

When dealing with their husband's women should always ask themselves, "How would I be toward Christ?" And when dealing with their wives, men should always ask themselves, "How would Christ be toward the church?"

Below I have asked a series of questions from the viewpoint of the wife and the viewpoint of the husband to give some examples.

Wife — Would I demean Christ?

Would I slander Christ?

Would I speak to Christ in an angry tone?

Would I speak to Christ in a disrespectful tone?

Would I lie to Christ or ask Him to lie for me?

Would I curse at Christ?

Would I strike Christ?

If the answer to any of the above is "no," then neither shall I to my husband.

Husband — Would Christ demean the church?

Would Christ slander the church?

Would Christ speak to the church in an angry tone?

Would Christ speak to the church in a disrespectful tone?

Would Christ lie to the church or ask her to lie for Him?

Would Christ curse at the church?

Would Christ strike the church?

If the answer to any of the above is "no," then neither shall I to my wife.

Likewise, the reverse questions should be asked.

Wife — Would I be kind to Christ?

Would I love Christ?

Would I be respectful toward Christ?

Would I be pure in manner toward Christ?

Would I serve Christ?

If the answer to any of the above is "yes," then also shall I to my husband.

Husband — Would Christ be kind to the church?

Would Christ love the church?

Would Christ be respectful toward the church?

Would Christ be pure in manner toward the church?

Would Christ serve the church?

If the answer to any of the above is "yes," then also shall I to my wife.

Again, wives are to picture Christ as their model on how to act toward their husbands. They should act toward their husbands the same way that they would act toward Christ, in a kind, loving, respectful manner with all purity. Wives are to do this because the woman came from the man just as the church came from Christ. Likewise, husbands are to picture Christ as their model in the treatment of their wives. Husbands are to treat their wives the same way that Christ treats the church, in a kind, loving, respectful manner with all purity. Husbands are to do this because the woman is a man's own flesh and bone just as the church is the body of Christ.

I also want to point out a mistranslation in verse thirty-three. In verse thirty-three, the translators have made it appear as though Paul is summing up the command to both the husband and wife. However, Paul is only summing up the command to the husband here because he has already summed up the command to the wife in verse twenty-four. Furthermore, if Paul were summing up the command to the wife, then it would have been reflective of what he had stated earlier, that the wife is to be set to her husband as she, or the church, is set to Christ. Verses 25–33, then, are strictly to the husband. Now, the reason verse thirty-three is mistranslated is that the translators have translated the Greek word "hina" as "must see to it." However, "hina" is a marker that shows purpose or result. It means "in order that, in order to, so that, then."[12] Hence, verse thirty-three should be translated as, [33]"Nevertheless, each one of you also is to love his own wife as himself, and the wife will then have a deep respect for her husband." Now, I believe the reason Paul says this is because men had for so long demanded respect from their wives. They had a sense of entitlement simply because they were male. However, Paul knows that demanding respect only causes superficial respect, for appearance's sake, to occur. It does not cause a true feeling of respect to be gained. Therefore, Paul does not want men to demand respect from their wives, but rather, Paul wants men to treat their own wives as they would themselves, so their wives would then have a true feeling of respect for them in their hearts just as the church does for Christ. In essence, Paul is telling men that they are not to demand respect; they are to earn it.

Therefore, Ephesians 5:22–33 should be translated as, [22]"The wives to their own husbands, as to the Lord. [23]For the man is the head [source] of the woman, as Christ also is the head [source] of the church, He Himself *being* the Savior of the body. [24]So as the church **is set** [hypotassetai] to Christ, so also the wives to their husbands in everything. [25]You husbands love your wives just as Christ also loved the church and gave Himself up for her, ²⁶so that He might sanctify her, having cleansed her by the washing of water with the Word, ²⁷so that He might present to Himself the church in all her glory, having no spot or wrinkle or any such thing; but that she would be holy and blameless. ²⁸So husbands ought also to love their own wives as their own bodies. He who loves his own wife loves himself; ²⁹for no one ever hated his own flesh, but nourishes and cherishes it, just as Christ also *does* the church, ³⁰because we are members of His body. ³¹'FOR THIS REASON A MAN SHALL LEAVE HIS FATHER AND MOTHER AND SHALL HOLD FAST TO HIS WIFE AND THE TWO SHALL BECOME ONE FLESH.' ³²This mystery is great; but I am speaking with reference to Christ and the church. ³³Nevertheless, each one of you also is to love his own wife as himself, and the wife will then have a deep respect for her husband."

Next, we come to Philippians 3:20–21. In this passage, the word "hypotasso" is used once in verse twenty-one.

²⁰"For our citizenship is in heaven, from which also we eagerly wait for a Savior, the Lord Jesus Christ; ²¹who will transform the body of our humble state into conformity with the body of His glory, by the exertion of the power that He has even **to subject** [hypotaxai] all things to Himself" (Phil. 3:20–21).

²⁰"For our citizenship is in heaven, from where also we eagerly wait for a Savior, the Lord Jesus Christ; ²¹who will transform the body of our low state into conformity with the body of His glory, according to the power that He has even **to place** [hypotaxai] all things to Himself" (Phil. 3:20–21).

Next, we come to Colossians 3:18. In this verse, the word "hypotasso" is used once. It says, ¹⁸"Wives, **be subject** [hypotassesthe] to your husbands, as is fitting in the Lord." However, Paul is not asking wives to be subject to their husbands here, but rather, he is asking them to be set to their husbands in a way that is proper or right in the Lord's sight. Hence, Paul is once again asking wives to be kind, loving, respectful, and pure in manner toward their husbands. As a result, Colossians 3:18 should be translated as, ¹⁸"Wives, **be set** [hypotassesthe] to your husband's **in a way** that is fitting in the Lord."

The next passage that we come to is 1 Timothy 2:8–15. In this passage, the word "hypotage" is used once in verse eleven. However, this passage will be discussed and the interpretation given in the eighth chapter.

The next passage that we come to is 1 Timothy 3:1–7. In this passage, the word "hypotage" is used once in verse four. However, this passage will be discussed and the interpretation given in the ninth chapter.

Next, we come to Titus 2:3–5. In this passage, the word "hypotasso" is used once in verse five. It says, ³"Older women likewise are to be reverent in their behavior, not malicious gossips nor enslaved to much wine, teaching what is good, ⁴so that they may encourage the young women to love their husbands, to love their children, ⁵*to be* sensible, pure, workers at home, kind, **being subject** [hypotassomenas] to their own husbands, so that the word of God will not be dishonored."

Here, once again, Paul is not asking women to be subject to their husbands. Paul is asking older women to act in a way that is holy and be teachers of what is good so that they can encourage the young women to gain godly attributes. Paul also wants the older women to portray the same godly attributes that he lists for the younger women so that the Word of God will not be dishonored. In other words, Paul does not want older women to teach one thing and do another. He wants the older women to live out what they teach.

Thus, Titus 2:3–5 should be translated as, ³"Older women, likewise, are to be with behavior appropriate to holiness, not false accusers, nor enslaved by much wine, *being* teachers of what is good, ⁴so that they may encourage the young women to love their husbands, love their children, ⁵to exercise sound judgment, to be pure, diligent at home, kind, **being set in this way** [hypotassomenas] to their own husbands so that the Word of God will not be dishonored."

Also, I want to say one more thing concerning this passage before moving on. Many men maintain that Paul, in verse five, is saying that a woman's place is in the home and that a woman should not work outside of the home. However, Paul is not saying this at all. He was simply giving women instructions for righteous living in the situation that they were in. Since women were typically relegated to the home, Paul was making the point that he wanted women to be hard-working in the home as opposed to being idle. He was not telling them that they were not allowed to work outside of the home. Now, there are two reasons how I know that Paul was simply speaking to women in the situation that they were in and was not telling them that they were not allowed to work outside of the home. The first reason is that many women in the Bible worked outside of the home. We know from Scripture that Shiphrah and Puah, along with many other women, were midwives (Exod. 1:15; Gen. 35:17; 38:28). Women served at the doorway of the tent of meeting (Exod. 38:8; 1 Sam. 2:22). Deborah was a judge and a prophetess and went into battle (Judg. 4:4–5; 6–14). Priscilla was a tentmaker (Acts 18:2–3). Lydia was a seller of purple fabrics (Acts 16:14). And the woman of Proverbs 31 bought a field and planted a vineyard from her earnings and made linen garments to sell them (Prov. 31:16, 24). Indeed, in just these few examples, we can see that women worked in the profession of health care, women served as priests, women served in judicial office and military operations, women worked trades that involved manual labor, women were merchants, and women owned and worked in agriculture. Furthermore, there are three things to note in these scenarios. First, most of the women were married, which would mean that they also had children unless they were barren. Secondly, the women had to leave their homes to accomplish part or all of their occupations, which would have taken them away from home for many hours at a time. And thirdly, God's blessing was upon these women as they worked outside of the home.

The second reason that I know that Paul was simply speaking to women in the situation that they were in is that I know that Paul would not teach against God's Word. God's Law clearly states that there is to be an equal balance of power over all the earth between male and female (Gen. 1:26). This means both in the home and out of the home. God did not give man authority to rule over the earth by himself. Indeed, God created the woman because He saw that it was not good for the man to be alone (Gen. 2:18–22). And it was only when the woman was placed beside the man that God gave them equal authority to rule (Gen. 1:27–28). God knows that only when men and women rule together, both inside and outside of the home, are the necessary checks, balances, and safeguards obtained. Indeed, God has given women wisdom and insight, which often escapes that of man (1 Sam. 25:2–38). As a result, when a woman's voice is silenced, "evil" is often the outcome (Matt. 27:19). Indeed, many heinous practices have emerged over the centuries because women did not have a voice. Therefore, in order to fulfill God's Law, women (in general) must work outside of the home. This means in positions of government and other administration. The balance of power needs to be equal. Likewise, just as women need to have more responsibilities outside of the home, so also men need to have more responsibilities within the home. For men have long been abrogating their duties in the home and have been laying them entirely on the woman. As a result, so that a woman can work outside of the house, it may be necessary for the man to be the primary one to stay at home. However, both men and women are to use the talents that God gave them accordingly, and servanthood must always play a role. Furthermore, I would like to say that family, friends, and trustworthy babysitters are not to be looked upon as being evil. As I stated previously, many married women in the Bible worked away from their homes for many hours at a time. As a result, one of several things had to happen. The children tagged along with their mother, stayed at home with the father, or family, friends, maidservants, or menservants (in essence, babysitters) watched the children while they were gone. Indeed, just as these were necessary options in the Bible, so also, they are necessary options today.

It is indeed God's plan that women rule over all the earth on an equal basis to that of men. God never intended the man to have free reign to rule over the earth by himself. Therefore, women should not be persuaded by guilt into staying at home if God is calling them otherwise. It is a grave misinterpretation of Paul's words to teach that women must remain at home. Indeed, the reason that God's blessing was upon these women and mothers in the Bible who worked outside of the home was that God had deemed it to be right from the beginning. Indeed, a woman's voice outside of the home, as in the home, is necessary to fulfill God's Law.

The next passage that we come to is Titus 2:9–10. In this passage, the word "hypotasso" is used one time. It says, [9]*"Urge* bondslaves **to be subject** [hypotassesthai] to their own masters in everything, to be well-pleasing, not argumentative, [10]not pilfering, but showing all good faith so that they will adorn the doctrine of God our Savior in every respect."

Here, Paul is not asking bondslaves to be subject to their masters. Instead, he is asking them to be set to their masters in a way that is righteous. For the Greek literally reads as, [9]"Bondslaves to their own masters **are to be set** [hypotassesthai] in all things well-pleasing to be, not argumentative, [10]not pilfering, but all faith showing good, in order that the teaching of the Savior of us, God, will be made attractive in all things." Consequently, we can see that Paul, as he previously did with women, was giving bondslaves instructions for righteous living in the situation that they were in. For one can see by reading Philemon that Paul did not condone slavery. Paul made it clear that people are not to be treated as slaves, but as beloved brothers and sisters (Philem. 1:15–16).

So, I would translate Titus 2:9–10 as, [9]"Bondslaves to their own masters, in all things, **are to be set in a way** [hypotassesthai] that is well-pleasing, not argumentative, [10]not pilfering, but showing all good faith so that the teaching of God our Savior will be made attractive in all things."

Next, we come to Titus 3:1–2. In this passage, the word "hypotasso" is used one time. It says, [1]"Remind them **to be subject** [hypotassesthai] to rulers, to authorities, to be obedient, to be ready for every good deed, [2]to malign no one, to be peaceable, gentle, showing every consideration for all men."

Here, once again, Paul is not asking believers to be subject to rulers and authorities; nor is he asking them to be obedient (to rulers and authorities). Instead, Paul is asking believers to be set to rulers and authorities in a way that they are ready to be obedient to every good work. For the Greek of verse one literally reads as, [1]"Remind them, to rulers to authorities **to be set** [hypotassesthai] to be obedient to every work good ready to be…." So the obedience is in reference to the "good work," not rulers and authorities. In other words, Paul is saying that if anyone in authority asks a believer to do something that is righteous in God's sight, the believer is to do it; they are to be obedient to every good work. This way, obedience is to God and not to man, for no one can serve two masters.

Thus, I would translate Titus 3:1–2 as, [1]"Remind them **to be set** [hypotassesthai] to rulers and authorities **in a way** that they are ready to be obedient to every good work, [2]to malign no one, to be peaceable, gentle, showing every consideration for all people."

The next passage that we come to is Hebrews 12:4–11. In this passage, the word "hypotage" is used once in verse nine.

[4]"You have not yet resisted to the point of shedding blood in your striving against sin; [5]and you have forgotten the exhortation which is addressed to you as sons, 'MY SON, DO NOT REGARD LIGHTLY

THE DISCIPLINE OF THE LORD, NOR FAINT WHEN YOU ARE REPROVED BY HIM; ⁶FOR THOSE WHOM THE LORD LOVES HE DISCIPLINES, AND HE SCOURGES EVERY SON WHOM HE RECEIVES.' ⁷It is for discipline that you endure; God deals with you as with sons; for what son is there whom *his* father does not discipline? ⁸But if you are without discipline, of which all have become partakers, then you are illegitimate children and not sons. ⁹Furthermore, we had earthly fathers to discipline us, and we respected them; shall we not much rather **be subject** [hypotagesometha] to the Father of spirits, and live? ¹⁰For they disciplined us for a short time as seemed best to them, but He *disciplines us* for our good, so that we may share His holiness. ¹¹All discipline for the moment seems not to be joyful, but sorrowful; yet to those who have been trained by it, afterwards it yields the peaceful fruit of righteousness" (Heb. 12:4–11).

⁴"You have not yet resisted to the point of shedding blood in your struggle against sin; ⁵and you have forgotten the exhortation which is addressed to you as children, 'MY CHILD, DO NOT DESPISE THE CORRECTION OF THE LORD, NOR LOSE HEART WHEN YOU ARE REPROVED BY HIM; ⁶FOR THOSE WHOM THE LORD LOVES HE CORRECTS, AND HE SCOURGES EVERY CHILD WHOM HE RECEIVES.' ⁷God deals with you as with children, so endure correction for this reason. For what child is there whom their father does not correct? ⁸But if you are without correction, of which you all have taken part in, then you are illegitimate and not children. ⁹Furthermore, we had fathers of our flesh to correct us, and we respected them. Shall we not, even more than, also live **to do the will** [hypotagesometha] of the Father of our spirits? ¹⁰For they corrected us for a short time according to what seemed best to them, but He for our benefit so that we can share in His holiness. ¹¹All correction at the moment seems not to be pleasant, but sorrowful; yet to those who have been trained by it, afterwards it yields the peaceful fruit of righteousness" (Heb. 12:4–11).

The next passage that we come to is James 4:7–8. Here, the word "hypotage" is used once.

⁷"**Submit** [hypotagete] therefore to God. Resist the devil and he will flee from you. ⁸Draw near to God and He will draw near to you" (James 4:7–8).

121

[7]**Do the will** [hypotagete], then, of God. Resist the devil and he will flee from you. [8]Draw near to God, and He will draw near to you" (James 4:7–8).

The next passage that we come to is 1 Peter 2:13–17. In this passage, the word "hypotage" is used once in verse thirteen. It says, [13]**"Submit yourselves** [hypotagete] for the Lord's sake to every human institution, whether to a king as the one in authority, [14]or to governors as sent by him for the punishment of evildoers and the praise of those who do right. [15]For such is the will of God that by doing right you may silence the ignorance of foolish men. [16]Act as free men, and do not use your freedom as a covering for evil, but *use it* as bondslaves of God. [17]Honor all people, love the brotherhood, fear God, honor the king."

I would like to start explaining this passage by bringing attention to the obvious contradiction within it. In verse thirteen, Peter (supposedly) asks believers to submit to EVERY human institution. Then, in verse fifteen, he states that by doing right, they may silence the ignorance of foolish men. However, a believer can't submit to every human institution and do what is right at the same time because many human institutions are evil. Indeed, any submission to an evil institution will not cause a believer to do what is right but rather to do what is wrong. I also want to say that one's submission will never silence the ignorance of foolish men. For foolish men only grow more proud and evil in their ways when people yield their will to them. Hitler is a prime example of this. Indeed, their ignorance will only be silenced when one stands their ground to them against all unrighteousness by following the ways of God so as to be an example.

So clearly, Peter is not asking believers to submit to every human institution. I believe, then, that Peter is asking believers to "be willing" toward every human institution because of the Lord. In other words, Peter wants all believers to give readily of themselves in good works and to do what is right toward all who are in authority so that they will know, by our example, what is right in the sight of God and act accordingly in their authority. One can even see in the verse that immediately precedes verse thirteen that Peter is asking believers to keep their behavior excellent among the Gentiles (pagans, foreign nations) so that they may glorify God in the day of visitation because of their good works. Therefore, Peter carries over this teaching of how believers are to behave amongst unbelievers and applies it to all human institutions as well. Indeed, believers are a chosen race, a royal priesthood, a holy nation, a people for God's own possession. Therefore, they prove to both the layperson and those in authority what the will of God is, that which is good and acceptable and perfect.

Therefore, I would translate 1 Peter 2:13–17 as, [13]"**Be willing** [hypotagete] *to do good* toward every human institution because of the Lord, whether to a king as the one in authority, [14]or to governors as sent by him, so that punishment will come on those who do evil and praise will come on those who do good. [15]For such is the will of God that by doing good, you may silence the ignorance of foolish people. [16]Act as free people, and do not use your freedom as a covering for evil, but use it as bondslaves of God. [17]Honor all people, love fellow believers, fear God, show proper respect to the king."

The next passage that we come to is 1 Peter 2:18–20. In this passage, the word "hypotasso" is used once in verse eighteen. It reads as, [18]"Servants, **be submissive** [hypotassomenoi] to your masters with all respect, not only to those who are good and gentle, but also to those who are unreasonable. [19]For this *finds* favor, if for the sake of conscience toward God a person bears up under sorrows when suffering unjustly. [20]For what credit is there if, when you sin and are harshly treated, you endure it with patience? But if when you do what is right and suffer *for it* you patiently endure it, this *finds* favor with God."

I want to begin this passage by saying that the NASB, along with many other translations, mistranslate a word in this passage to make it appear doctrinally sound. They translate the Greek word "skolios" as "unreasonable (NASB, WNT), ill-tempered (DBT), cross (YLT), froward, (ASV, DRB, ERV, KJB), harsh (NIV, NJKV), unfair (GWT), or cruel (NLT)."[13] However, the Greek word "skolios" means "crooked; corrupt."[14] But again, the reason why the translators mistranslate the word "skoliois" is that they are trying to make this passage appear doctrinally sound. If Peter were asking servants to submit to crooked and corrupt masters, then he would be asking them to submit to that which is crooked and corrupt. For if the masters themselves are crooked and corrupt, would they not ask their servants for that which is unrighteous? However, Peter is not asking servants to submit to corrupt masters. Instead, Peter is asking servants to be set to their masters with all respect, not only to those that are good and gentle but also to the corrupt. For, indeed, respectful behavior is godly behavior.

So, 1 Peter 2:18–20 should be translated as, ¹⁸"Servants, **be set** [hypotassomenoi] to your masters with all respect, not only to those who are good and gentle but also to those who are corrupt. ¹⁹For this *finds* favor if, for the sake of conscience toward God, a person bears up under sorrows when suffering unjustly. ²⁰For what honor is there if, when you sin, you endure harsh treatment *for it*? But if when you do what is right and endure suffering *for it*, this *finds* favor with God."

The next passage that we come to is 1 Peter 3:1–6. In this passage, the word "hypotasso" is used two times. It states, ¹"In the same way, you wives, **be submissive** [hypotassomenai] to your own husbands so that even if any *of them* are disobedient to the word, they may be won without a word by the behavior of their wives, ²as they observe your chaste and respectful behavior. ³Your adornment must not be *merely* external—braiding the hair, and wearing gold jewelry, or putting on dresses; ⁴but *let it be* the hidden person of the heart, with the imperishable quality of a gentle and quiet spirit, which is precious in the sight of God. ⁵For in this way in former times the holy women also, who hoped in God, used to adorn themselves **being submissive** [hypotassomenai] to their own husbands; ⁶just as Sarah obeyed Abraham, calling him lord, and you have become her children if you do what is right without being frightened by any fear."

In beginning, I would like to say that this is a very dangerous passage indeed, because this passage, as translated, tells women to be submissive to their husbands even if they are disobedient to God's Word. But I must tell you that Jesus Christ did not die for our sins only to then tell women to submit to that which would be sinful. Christ died for our sins so that we might die to sin and live to righteousness. Furthermore, how would disobedient husbands be won over by the behavior of their wives if their wives did exactly as they asked? As I stated previously, one's submission will never silence the ignorance of foolish men. Indeed, their ignorance will only be silenced when one stands their ground to them against all unrighteousness by following the ways of God so as to be an example. And indeed, this is precisely what Peter is asking of wives. Peter is asking wives to stand their ground to their husbands against all unrighteousness by following the ways of God so as to be an example. Hence, as we go through this passage, we will indeed see that Peter is not asking wives to submit to their husbands, but rather, that he is asking wives to follow the example that Christ set. Let us take a look.

In verse one, when Peter addresses wives, he starts by saying, [1]**"In the same way**, you wives...."** And by this, Peter is referring to what he had just stated in the previous paragraphs (1 Pet. 2:20–25). For Peter had previously written:

> *[20]"...But if when you do what is right and endure suffering *for it*, this *finds* favor with God."*

> [21]"For you have been called for this purpose, since Christ also suffered for you, leaving you an example for you to follow in His steps..."

> [22]"...WHO COMMITTED NO SIN, NOR WAS ANY DECEIT FOUND IN HIS MOUTH..."

> [23]"...and while being reviled, He did not revile in return; while suffering, He uttered no threats, but kept entrusting *Himself* to Him who judges righteously..."

> [24]"...and He Himself bore our sins in His body on the cross, so that we might die to sin and live to righteousness; for by His wounds you were healed."

> [25]"For you were continually straying like sheep, but now you have returned to the Shepherd and Guardian of your souls."

Therefore, by studying Peter's words, we can see that Peter wants wives to follow the example that Christ set, namely in two ways. They are:

1) To commit no sin (pure behavior).

2) To not revile in return (respectful behavior).

As a result, Peter is asking wives to be set to their husbands in the same way that Christ was set, committing no sin and not reviling in return, so that even if any of their husbands are disobedient to God's Word, they will be won over by the pure and respectful behavior of their wives.

Thus, 1 Peter 3:1–2 should read as follows:

[1]"In the same way *that Christ was set,* you wives, *also* **be set** [hypotassomenai] to your own husbands, so that even if any of them are disobedient to the Word, they may be won over without a word by the behavior of their wives, [2]by observing the reverent and pure way you live your lives."

Then in verses 3–4, Peter goes on to say to wives that their beautification should not be about their outward appearance, but rather, it should be about their inward appearance with the imperishable quality of a gentle and peaceful spirit, which is of great worth in the sight of God. He then goes on to say in verse five that the holy women of old also made themselves beautiful in this way by having this inner quality of gentleness and peacefulness. They did not have a spirit of anger or resentment, nor were they inclined to quarrelsome behavior or harsh words, but instead were considerate and patient in the way that they lived with their husbands. So, in verse five, Peter is not talking about submission but rather how the holy women of old were set toward their husbands in gentleness and peacefulness.

Thus, 1 Peter 3:3–5 should read as follows:

[3]"Let it not be the outward appearance—braiding the hair and wearing gold jewelry or putting on worldly clothing, [4]but let it be the hidden person of the heart, with the imperishable quality of a gentle and peaceful spirit, which is of great worth in the sight of God. [5]For in this way in former times the holy women also, who hoped in God, used to make themselves beautiful by **being set** [hypotassomenai] to their own husbands...."

Then verse six says, [6]"...just as Sarah obeyed Abraham...." Now up to this point, Peter has not been talking about submission, so clearly, the word "obeyed" is a misfit. (In addition to this, it is clear in Acts 5:29 that we "obey" God rather than men.) For the word "obeyed" in verse six is undoubtedly connected to the word "submissive" in verse five. As a result, I believe that we have another mistranslation of a word. Hence, I believe that the Greek word "hypakouo," which is translated as "obeyed" in verse six, actually means "to answer." And the reason that I believe this to be true is because this same Greek word "hypakouo" that is used here in 1 Peter 3:6 is also used in Acts 12:13. And in Acts 12:13, this word is not translated as "to obey," but instead, it is translated as "to answer." For it says, [13]"When he knocked at the door of the gate, a servant-girl named Rhoda came **to answer** [hypakousai]." The NIV translates verse thirteen as, [13]"Peter knocked at the outer entrance, and a servant girl named Rhoda came **to answer** [hypakousai] the door." So again, I believe that the true meaning of "hypakouo" is "to answer." And to show that this word better fits the meaning of "to answer" rather than "to obey," I would like to go over all twenty-one times that it is used in the New Testament. In verse six, I do not believe that Peter is referencing Sarah "obeying" Abraham, but rather that he is referencing the way that Sarah "answered" Abraham; that is when Sarah "answered" Abraham, she did so with a spirit of gentleness and peacefulness. This way, the word "answered" in verse six correctly corresponds to the thoughts that Peter has conveyed in verses 3–5.

Below I have listed all twenty-one verses in the New Testament where the word "hypakouo" is used. The first is the translation of the NASB, and the second is a translation with the word "hypakouo" being translated as "to answer." It is also essential to understand when reading these passages that the word "answer" can be a "response by action" as well as a "verbal response." Therefore, a synonym of "respond to" would also be appropriate when it is a "response by action."

1) [27]"The men were amazed, and said, 'What kind of a man is this, that even the winds and the sea **obey** [hypakouousin] Him?'" (Matt. 8:27).

1) [27]"The men were amazed, and said, 'What kind of a man is this, that even the winds and the sea **answer** [hypakouousin] Him?'" (Matt. 8:27).

(Note: In Matthew 8:26, it says that Jesus verbally rebuked the winds and the sea. It was after this verbal rebuke that the winds and the sea answered, or responded to, His commands.)

2) [27]"They were all amazed, so that they debated among themselves, saying, 'What is this? A new teaching with authority! He commands even the unclean spirits, and they **obey** [hypakouousin] Him'" (Mark 1:27).

2) [27]"They were all amazed, so that they debated among themselves, saying, 'What is this? A new teaching with authority! He commands even the unclean spirits, and they **answer** [hypakouousin] Him'" (Mark 1:27).

127

(Note: In Mark 1:25, it says that Jesus verbally rebuked the unclean spirit. It was after this verbal rebuke that the unclean spirit answered, or responded to, His commands.)

3) [41]"They became very much afraid and said to one another, 'Who then is this that even the wind and the sea **obey** [hypakouei] Him?'" (Mark 4:41).

3) [41]"They became very much afraid and said to one another, 'Who then is this that even the wind and the sea **answer** [hypakouei] Him?'" (Mark 4:41).

(Note: Here again, in Mark 4:39, it says that Jesus rebuked the wind and said to the sea, "Hush, be still." Both the wind and the sea answered Him by becoming calm.)

4) [25]"And He said to them, 'Where is your faith?' They were fearful and amazed, saying to one another, 'Who then is this that He commands even the winds and the water, and they **obey** [hypakouousin] Him?'" (Luke 8:25).

4) [25]"And He said to them, 'Where is your faith?' They were fearful and amazed, saying to one another, 'Who then is this that He commands even the winds and the water, and they **answer** [hypakouousin] Him?'" (Luke 8:25).

(Note: Here again, Jesus spoke to the wind and the waves, and they answered Him by becoming calm.)

5) [6]"And the Lord said, 'If you had faith like a mustard seed, you would say to this mulberry tree, 'Be uprooted and be planted in the sea'; and it would **obey** [hypekousen] you'" (Luke 17:6).

5) [6]"And the Lord said, 'If you had faith like a mustard seed, you would say to this mulberry tree, 'Be uprooted and be planted in the sea'; and it would **answer** [hypekousen] you'" (Luke 17:6).

6) [7]"The word of God kept on spreading; and the number of the disciples continued to increase greatly in Jerusalem, and a great many of the priests **were becoming obedient** [hypekouon] to the faith" (Acts 6:7).

6) [7]"The Word of God kept on spreading; and the number of the disciples continued to increase greatly in Jerusalem, and a great many of the priests **were answering** [hypekouon] the faith" (Acts 6:7).

7) [13]"When he knocked at the door of the gate, a servant-girl named Rhoda came **to answer** [hypakousai]" (Acts 12:13).

7) [13]"When he knocked at the entryway door, a servant-girl named Rhoda came **to answer** [hypakousai]" (Acts 12:13).

8) [12]"Therefore, do not let sin reign in your mortal body so that you **obey** [hypakouein] its lusts..." (Rom. 6:12).

8) [12]"Therefore, do not let sin reign in your mortal body so that you **answer** [hypakouein] its lusts..." (Rom. 6:12).

9) [16]"Do you not know that when you present yourselves to someone *as* slaves for obedience, you are slaves of the one whom you **obey** [hypakouete], either of sin resulting in death, or of obedience resulting in righteousness?" (Rom. 6:16).

9) [16]"Do you not know that when you present yourselves to someone *as* slaves for obedience, you are slaves of the one to whom you **answer** [hypakouete], either of sin resulting in death, or of obedience resulting in righteousness?" (Rom. 6:16).

10) [17]"But thanks be to God that though you were slaves of sin, you **became obedient** [hypekousate] from the heart to that form of teaching to which you were committed, [18]and having been freed from sin, you became slaves of righteousness" (Rom. 6:17–18).

10) [17]"But thanks be to God that though you were slaves of sin, you **answered** [hypekousate] from the heart to that form of teaching to which you were committed, [18]and having been freed from sin, you became slaves of righteousness" (Rom. 6:17–18).

11) [16]"However, they did not all **heed** [hypekousan] the good news; for Isaiah [53:1] says, 'LORD, WHO HAS BELIEVED OUR REPORT?'" (Rom. 10:16).

11) [16]"However, they did not all **answer** [hypekousan] the good news; for Isaiah [53:1] says, 'LORD, WHO HAS BELIEVED OUR MESSAGE?'" (Rom. 10:16).

12) [1]"Children, **obey** [hypakouete] your parents in the Lord, for this is right. [2]HONOR YOUR FATHER AND MOTHER (which is the first commandment with a promise), [3]SO THAT IT MAY BE WELL WITH YOU, AND THAT YOU MAY LIVE LONG ON THE EARTH" (Eph. 6:1–3).

12) [1]"Children, **answer** [hypakouete] your parents in the Lord, for this is right. [2]HONOR YOUR FATHER AND MOTHER (which is the first commandment with a promise), [3]SO THAT IT MAY BE WELL WITH YOU, AND THAT YOU MAY LIVE LONG ON THE EARTH" (Eph. 6:1–3).

Here, Paul is asking children of all ages, including adult children, to answer their parents in the Lord, meaning that they are to answer their parents in a way that is Christ-like. In other words, Paul is asking children to answer their parents in a respectful and honoring way. This is why Paul then quotes one of the Ten Commandments (Exod. 20:12). And notice that the commandment given by God in the Old Testament is not for children to obey their parents, but rather to honor. So Paul is not making up a new commandment for children but is reiterating the commandment that was given by God in the Old Testament, because to answer your parents in a Christ-like manner is to honor them.

I also want to stress that there is a good reason why God does not give a commandment to children to obey their parents. And it is simply that parents' sin. If God gave a commandment to children to obey their parents, then inevitably, their children would sin. What parents should do is bring them up in the training and instruction of the Lord and then encourage them to do what is right at all times. If parents do this, then I am sure that even they will be reminded by their children now and then that some of their own actions are not honoring in God's sight. And for people who make the argument that Paul is telling (underage) children to obey their parents in the Lord, meaning that children are to obey only the righteous commands of their parents, then it puts the burden on children to know the difference between right and wrong. It is asking the child, who themselves are in the stage of learning right from wrong, to know the difference between right from wrong. So, I believe that Paul is asking children of all ages to answer their parents in a way that is honoring.

13) ⁵"Slaves, **be obedient** [hypakouete] to those who are your masters according to the flesh, with fear and trembling, in the sincerity of your heart, as to Christ; ⁶not by way of eyeservice, as men-pleasers, but as slaves of Christ, doing the will of God from the heart" (Eph. 6:5–6).

13) ⁵"Slaves, **answer** [hypakouete] those who are your masters according to the flesh, with respect and fear, in the sincerity of your heart, as to Christ; ⁶not by way of eyeservice, as men-pleasers, but as slaves of Christ, doing the will of God from the heart" (Eph. 6:5–6).

Here again, Paul is not asking slaves to obey their masters because Scripture teaches us that we are to obey God rather than men. And obeying God rather than men is why Paul tells slaves, in verse six, that they are to do the will of God from the heart; for no one can serve two masters. As a result, Paul is asking slaves to answer their earthly masters with respect and fear. He is giving them instructions for righteous living in the situation that they were in. And to confirm that it is a respectful tone (and servanthood, v. 7), and not obedience that Paul is asking for, Paul also, in verse nine, asks masters to do the same things to their slaves. If it were obedience that Paul was asking for, then Paul would be asking masters to obey their slaves in return. But since it is a respectful tone and servant-hood that Paul is asking for, Paul is also asking masters to be respectful of their slaves and to serve them as well, because when we are in Christ, there is no longer a master-slave relationship but rather a brother-brother relationship. This is why, in Philemon 1:15–16, Paul asks Philemon to take Onesimus back forever, no longer as a slave, but as a beloved brother. We also must understand that it is our hard-heartedness and disobedience to Christ that has caused us to have these kinds of relationships in the first place, of masters over slaves and of men over women. But Paul is trying to steer them in a new direction, appealing to them in love to serve one another and to treat one another with respect because this is the way it is in the family of God. For respecting and serving one another is doing the will of God from the heart.

It is also essential to understand that Paul refers to slave owners as "masters" only because that is what they were called on earth. He does not refer to them as "masters" because they were in any way legitimate in God's sight. In fact, in verse nine, Paul is trying to get masters to understand that their slave's true Master is God, who is in heaven, and that they are their slave's master only by way of their own disobedience to God.

14) [12]"So then, my beloved, just as you have always **obeyed** [hypekousate], not as in my presence only, but now much more in my absence, work out your salvation with fear and trembling; [13]for it is God who is at work in you, both to will and to work for *His* good pleasure" (Phil. 2:12–13).

14) [12]"So then, my beloved, just as you have always **answered** [hypekousate], not as in my presence only, but now much more in my absence, with respect and fear, accomplish much with your salvation; [13]for it is God who is at work in you, both to will and to work for *His* good pleasure" (Phil. 2:12–13).

15) [20]"Children, **be obedient** [hypakouete] to your parents in all things, for this is well-pleasing to the Lord" (Col. 3:20).

15) [20]"Children, **answer** [hypakouete] your parents in all things, for this is well-pleasing to the Lord" (Col. 3:20).

Here, Paul does not want children to ignore their parents or give them the silent treatment. He wants them always to answer their parents.

16) [22]"Slaves, in all things **obey** [hypakouete] those who are your masters on earth, not with external service, as those who *merely* please men, but with sincerity of heart, fearing the Lord" (Col. 3:22).

16) [22]"Slaves, in all things **answer** [hypakouete] those who are your masters on earth, not with eyeservice, as those who *merely* please men, but with sincerity of heart, fearing the Lord" (Col. 3:22).

17) [6]"For after all it is *only* just for God to repay with affliction those who afflict you, [7]and *to give* relief to you who are afflicted and to us as well when the Lord Jesus will be revealed from heaven with His mighty angels in flaming fire, [8]dealing out retribution to those who do not know God and to those who do not **obey** [hypakouousin] the gospel of our Lord Jesus" (2 Thess. 1:6–8).

17) [6]"For after all it is *only* just for God to repay with affliction those who afflict you, [7]and *to give* relief to you who are afflicted and to us as well when the Lord Jesus will be revealed from heaven with His mighty angels in flaming fire, [8]dealing out retribution to those who do not know God and to those who do not **answer** [hypakouousin] the gospel of our Lord Jesus" (2 Thess. 1:6–8).

18) [14]"If anyone does not **obey** [hypakouei] our instruction in this letter, take special note of that person and do not associate with him, so that he will be put to shame" (2 Thess. 3:14).

18) [14]"If anyone does not **answer** [hypakouei] our instruction in this letter, take special note of that person and do not associate with him, so that he will be put to shame" (2 Thess. 3:14).

19) [9]"And having been made perfect, He became to all those who **obey** [hypakouousin] Him the source of eternal salvation, [10]being designated by God as a high priest according to the order of Melchizedek" (Heb. 5:9–10).

19) [9]"And having been made perfect, He became to all those who **answer** [hypakouousin] Him the source of eternal salvation, [10]being designated by God as a high priest according to the order of Melchizedek" (Heb. 5:9–10).

20) [8]"By faith Abraham, when he was called, **obeyed** [hypekousen] by going out to a place which he was to receive for an inheritance; and he went out, not knowing where he was going" (Heb. 11:8).

20) [8]"By faith Abraham, when he was called, **answered** [hypekousen] by going out to a place which he was to receive for an inheritance; and he went out, not knowing where he was going" (Heb. 11:8).

21) [4]"...but let *it* be the hidden person of the heart, with the imperishable quality of a gentle and quiet spirit, which is precious in the sight of God. [5]For in this way in former times the holy women also, who hoped in God, used to adorn themselves, being submissive to their own husbands; [6]just as Sarah **obeyed** [hypekousen] Abraham..." (1 Peter 3:4–6).

21) [4]"...but let *it* be the hidden person of the heart, with the imperishable quality of a gentle and peaceful spirit, which is of great worth in the sight of God. [5]For in this way in former times the holy women also, who hoped in God, used to make themselves beautiful by being set to their own husbands; [6]just as Sarah **answered** [hypekousen] Abraham..." (1 Peter 3:4–6).

So again, I believe that the word "hypakouo" means "to answer," not "to obey." And again, I believe the point Peter is making in verse six is that Sarah answered Abraham with a spirit of gentleness and peacefulness.

Next, verse six says that Sarah called Abraham "lord," which is "kyrios" in Greek. Now, by the use of this word here, men of today take this to mean that Abraham was Sarah's master. However, the actual word that Sarah used in Hebrew was "adon." (See Genesis 18:12.) And "adon" was the word that Rebekah used in Genesis 24:18 to address one of Abraham's servants whom she had just met and did not know the identity of. As a result, it is apparent that this word was used as a respectful and courteous address to someone of equal standing, as well as a title of address to a person of higher status, which was also true of the Greek word "kyrios." Therefore, the point that Peter was making was not that Sarah called Abraham "kyrios" because she was subject to him, but that she called him "kyrios" because of her gentle and peaceful spirit. Her gentle and peaceful spirit prompted her to address her husband in a loving and respectful way, rather than a spiteful way which would come from an argumentative and angry spirit. As a result, the word "kyrios" needs to be translated into the English language in a way that reflects the point Peter is making. The word "lord" in the English language only refers to someone of higher status, and if translated as such, would cause the wrong conclusion to be gained. Indeed, women are not subject to their husbands but are equal in standing. As a result, I would translate the word "kyrios" as "dear husband" because this translation would reflect the intention of Peter's words. Furthermore, the word "adon" is translated as "husbands" in Amos 4:1. And the Greek word "kyria," the feminine equivalent of "kyrios," means "female lord,"[15] yet it is translated as either "lady" or "dear lady" in the New Testament. So again, I would render the word "kyrios" as "dear husband" because I believe this rendering is the closest to the meaning that Peter intended.

And finally, Peter says in verse six, [6]"...and you have become her children if you do what is right without being frightened by any fear." The NIV translates this part of verse six as, ""...You are her daughters if you do what is right and do not give way to fear." Now, it is interesting to note that Peter tells women to do what is right without giving way to fear at the end of this passage. Yet, he is seen as telling women to submit to their husbands even if they are disobedient to God's Word at the beginning of this passage. No wonder women are so confused. It is clear that there is a disparity between the beginning and ends of this passage due to the mistranslation of the word "hypotasso." But indeed, Peter has told women to do what is right at the beginning of this passage and at the end. When Peter encourages women to not give way to fear, it is obviously in reference to any threats their husbands would make because of their righteous stance. For submission was the norm of that day, and men were used to having their own way. Therefore, Peter does not want women to give way to fear and submit to their disobedient husbands and then sin. Instead, he wants them to stand firm for righteousness even if they have to endure suffering for it, for Peter made it clear that we have been called for the purpose of doing what is right and enduring suffering for it because this finds favor with God (1 Pet. 2:20–21).

Furthermore, I would also like to point out that if Peter were actually saying that the "holy" women of old used to adorn themselves by being submissive to their own husbands, and then used the example of Sarah obeying Abraham, then we would only need to turn to Genesis to see that this analogy does not even make sense. When Sarah did submit to Abraham (Gen. 12:11–20; 20:1–7), she went along with his lies (Gen. 20:5) and, as a result, was not acting in a way that was "holy." For Genesis 20:9 makes it abundantly clear that what Abraham had done was a "great sin." However, in Genesis 21:9–12, against Abraham's wishes, Sarah finally took a stand against the sinful practice of polygamy. And because Sarah finally stood up for what was right in the sight of God, God told Abraham to listen to her, whatever she told him (Gen. 21:12). So it is in the example where Sarah does not submit that she is seen as being "holy," not the examples where she is submitting.

I also want to point out that the reason we see such a stark difference between the early part of Sarah's life and the latter part is that, early on in her life, Sarah submitted to Abraham because submission was the expected role of a wife in that day. However, after God molded Sarah into a woman of godly character, she no longer submitted to Abraham's worldly behavior but instead did what was right in the sight of God. Therefore, just as God molded Sarah, Peter, too, is encouraging wives to do what is right in the sight of God. He does not want them to give in to their husband's worldly behavior, as was the cultural norm of that day, but instead, he wants them to follow the example that Christ set for them. For the holy women in former times did not yield to unrighteousness. They abided by their own moral judgment and principles even when it was at odds with their husbands. They stood firm in their conscience of doing what was right in God's sight, and they did not waver.

Therefore, I would translate this passage, starting with 1 Peter 2:20, as:

2:20"...But if when you do what is right and endure suffering *for it*, this *finds* favor with God. 21For you have been called for this purpose, since Christ also suffered for you, leaving an example for you to follow in His steps, 22WHO COMMITTED NO SIN, NOR WAS ANY DECEIT FOUND IN HIS MOUTH; 23and while being reviled, He did not revile in return; while suffering, He uttered no threats, but kept entrusting Himself to Him who judges righteously; 24and He Himself bore our sins in His body on the cross, so that we might die to sin and live to righteousness; for by His wounds you were healed. 25For you were continually straying like sheep, but now you have returned to the Shepherd and the One who cares for your souls. 3:1So in the same way *that Christ was set*, you wives, *also* **be set** [hypotassomenai] to your own husbands, so that even if any of them are disobedient to the Word, they may be won over without a word by the behavior of their wives, 2by observing the reverent and pure way you live your lives. 3Let it not be the outward appearance—braiding the hair and wearing gold jewelry or putting on worldly clothing, 4but let it be the hidden person of the heart, with the imperishable quality of a gentle and peaceful spirit, which is of great worth in the sight of God. 5For in this way in former times the holy women also, who hoped in God, used to make themselves beautiful by **being set** [hypotassomenai] to their own husbands; 6just as Sarah answered Abraham, calling him her dear husband, and you have become her children if you do what is right without giving way to fear."

Next, we come to 1 Peter 3:21–22. In this passage, the word "hypotage" is used once in verse twenty-two.

21"Corresponding to that, baptism now saves you—not the removal of dirt from the flesh, but an appeal to God for a good conscience—through the resurrection of Jesus Christ, [22]who is at the right hand of God, having gone into heaven, after angels and authorities and powers **had been subjected** [hypotagenton] to Him" (1 Pet. 3:21–22).

[21]"And this *water even* symbolizes now that you are saved. *For* baptism does not *represent* the putting away of the filth of the flesh, but *rather* a request to God for a morally good conscience through the resurrection of Jesus Christ, [22]who is at the right hand of God, having gone into heaven, **having willed** [hypotagenton] to Him angels and authorities and powers" (1 Pet. 3:21–22).

And finally, the last passage that we come to is 1 Peter 5:1–5. It says, [1]"Therefore, I exhort the elders among you, as *your* fellow elder and witness of the sufferings of Christ, and a partaker also of the glory that is to be revealed, [2]shepherd the flock of God among you, exercising oversight not under compulsion, but voluntarily, according to *the will of* God; and not for sordid gain, but with eagerness; [3]nor yet as lording it over those allotted to your charge, but proving to be examples to the flock. [4]And when the Chief Shepherd appears, you will receive the unfading crown of glory. [5]You younger men, likewise, **be subject** [hypotagete] to *your* elders; and all of you, clothe yourselves with humility toward one another, for GOD IS OPPOSED TO THE PROUD, BUT GIVES GRACE TO THE HUMBLE."

To begin this passage, I would first like to say that Peter is speaking to all of the "older" believers in verses 1–4, not a ruling class of elders; and he is speaking to all of the "younger" believers in verse five. And secondly, the words "exercising oversight" in verse two are not in the original Greek. Therefore, what Peter is asking for in this passage is simple. He wants the older believers to "voluntarily" or "willingly" take care of the younger believers. And he wants the younger believers to **likewise** "be willing" to do for the older ones.

Thus, I would translate 1 Peter 5:1–5 as:

[1]"Therefore, I exhort the older ones among you, as someone who is also older and a witness of the sufferings of Christ and a partaker also of the glory that is to be revealed, [2]take care of the flock of God among you, not under compulsion, but voluntarily, according to God; and not for sordid gain, but eagerly; [3]nor yet as lording it over those who share the inheritance

137

but being examples to the flock. [4]And when the Chief Shepherd appears, you will receive the unfading crown of glory. [5]Likewise, you younger ones **be willing** [hypotagete] toward the older ones; and all of you clothe yourselves with humility toward one another, for GOD IS OPPOSED TO THE PROUD, BUT GIVES GRACE TO THE HUMBLE."

In ending this chapter, I would like to say that Jesus never taught that certain people were to submit to others. Instead, He taught that we are to obey God rather than men, and in love, we are to serve one another. But because of the subtle tweak given the word "hypotasso," a word of placement has become a word of subjection, and a new doctrine has been created. For the doctrine of submission has brought a conflicting teaching to wives who wonder whether they are to submit to God or whether they are to submit to their husbands in everything. The doctrine of submission teaches women that they are not allowed to follow what God has convicted them to, but that they are to yield their will to what they believe is wrong. It also takes away any servanthood from the husband to the wife as she is taught to submit to her husband in everything. But the doctrine of submission is exactly why Paul and Peter take so much time to right the lies imposed on women at the time of Christ, which still go on today. Paul and Peter are trying to move wives away from submission, the norm of that day, and into righteous living before God. This is why all four passages regarding women, which use the word "hypotasso," are not about submission but are about righteous living. But the reality is that men insist on their leadership roles simply out of pride. For Christ Himself made it very clear that believers are not to be called leaders because One is our leader, Christ. Yet what do men do? They call themselves leaders. Over and over again, they call themselves leaders. They call themselves leaders in the church, and they call themselves leaders in the home. But Christ is not ONE of our leaders; He is our ONLY leader. Therefore, it is time for men to accept that Christ is every believer's sole leader. Men are not their wives leaders, and wives are not subject to their husbands. Indeed, husbands and wives are to serve one another, but submission is only to God.

Hypotasso/Hypotage (42)

Hypotasso (28) — Word of placement - To place, to put, to set; to be set in this way.

Hypotage (14) — Will, willed, appointed by the will of, willing, willingness, etc.

Luke 2:41–52 (1)

[41]"Now His parents went to Jerusalem every year at the Feast of the Passover. [42]And when He became twelve, they went up there according to the custom of the Feast; [43]and as they were returning, after spending the full number of days, the boy Jesus stood firmly in Jerusalem. But His parents were unaware of it, [44]and thought Him to be in the company of travelers and went a day's journey; and they began looking for Him among their relatives and acquaintances. [45]When they did not find Him, they returned to Jerusalem looking for Him. [46]Then, after three days, they found Him in the temple, sitting in the midst of the teachers, both listening to them and asking them questions. [47]And all who heard Him were astonished at His understanding and His answers. [48]Also seeing Him, they were amazed. Then His mother said to Him, 'Son, why have You treated us this way? Behold, Your father and I have continued in agony looking for You.' [49]And He said to them, 'Why is it that you were looking for Me? Did you not know that I had to be doing that of My Father's?' [50]But they did not understand the statement which He had spoke to them. [51]And He went down with them and came to Nazareth, and He **continued to be set in this way** [hypotassomenos] to them; and His mother treasured all His words in her heart. [52]And Jesus kept increasing in wisdom and stature and favor with God and people."

Luke 10:17–20 (2)

[17]"The seventy returned with joy, saying, 'Lord, even the demons **are placed** [hypotassetai] to us in Your name.' [18]And He said to them, 'I was watching Satan fall from heaven like lightning. [19]Behold, I have given you authority to tread on serpents and scorpions, and over all the power of the enemy, and nothing will injure you. [20]Nevertheless do not rejoice in this, that the spirits **are placed** [hypotassetai] to you, but rejoice that your names are recorded in heaven.'"

Romans 8:6–8 (1)

[6]"For the mind set on the flesh is death, but the mind set on the Spirit is life and peace, [7]because the mind set on the flesh is hostile toward God; for **it is** not **set** [hypotassetai] to the law of God, neither indeed can it, [8]and those in the flesh cannot please God."

Romans 8:20–21 (2)

[20]"For the creation **was willed** [hypetage] to futility, not by their own choice, but by the One who **placed** [hypotaxanta] it, in hope [21]that the creation itself then will be set free from its slavery to corruption into the freedom of the glory of the children of God."

Romans 10:1–3 (1)

[1]"Brethren, my heart's desire and my prayer to God for them is for *their* salvation. [2]For I testify about them that they have a zeal for God, but not in accordance with knowledge. [3]For not knowing about God's righteousness and seeking to establish their own, **they did** not **will** [hypetagesan] the righteousness of God."

Romans 13:1–7 (2)

[1]"Every mind **is to be set** [hypotassestho] on transcending the authorities. For it is not authority if *it is* not by God, and those which are by God are ordained. [2]Therefore, the one who continues to establish against the authority of God's ordinance has opposed, and those having opposed will receive condemnation on themselves. [3]For the rulers *set by God* are not a cause of fear for good work, but for evil. And if you do not want to fear

their authority, then do what is good and you will have praise from them. [4]For God's servant is to you for the good. But if one does evil, then be afraid. For it is not for nothing the sword they bear. For God's servant is an avenger for wrath to the one practicing evil. [5]Therefore, it is necessary **to be set in this way** [doing what is good] [hypotassesthai], not only because of wrath but also because of conscience. [6]For because of this [being set righteously] you also pay taxes, for *believers are* ministers of God *who* are constantly devoting themselves for this [righteousness]. [7]Render to all what is due them; to the tax the tax; to the tribute the tribute; to the respect the respect; to the honor the honor."

1 Corinthians 14:31–33 (1)

[31]"For you can all prophesy one by one, so that all may learn and all may be exhorted; [32]and the spirits of prophets **are set** [hypotassetai] *in order* for prophets; [33]for God is not of disorder but of peace, as among all the people that are holy."

1 Corinthians 14:34–35 (1)

[34]" '*The women are to keep silent among the people; for they are not permitted to speak, but* **are to be set** *[hypotassesthosan] as also the Law says.* [35]*If they desire to learn anything, let them ask their own husbands at home; for it is shameful for a woman to speak among the people.* '"

1 Corinthians 15:27–28 (6)

[27]"'For HE **HAS PLACED** [hypetaxen] ALL THINGS UNDER HIS FEET.' But when He says, 'All things **are placed** [hypotetaktai],' it is clear that it is apart from the One who **placed** [hypotaxantos] all things to Him. [28]But as soon as all things **are willed** [hypotage] to Him, then also the Son Himself **will be appointed by the will** [hypotagesetai] of the One who **placed** [hypotaxanti] all things to Him, so that God may be all in all."

1 Corinthians 16:15–18 (1)

[15]"Now I urge you, brethren, *for* you know the household of Stephanas, that they were the first fruits of Achaia and that they have devoted themselves for service to the saints, [16]that you also **be set in this way** [hypotassesthe] to such ones and to everyone who helps in the work and labors. [17]I rejoice

over the coming of Stephanas and Fortunatus and Achaicus, because they have supplied what was lacking on your part. [18]For they have refreshed my spirit and yours. Therefore, acknowledge such ones."

2 Corinthians 9:13–14 (1)

[13]"Because of the proof given by this service, they will glorify God over the **willingness** [hypotage] of your commitment to the gospel of Christ and for the liberality of your contribution to them and to all [14]while they also, by prayer on your behalf, yearn for you because of the surpassing grace of God in you."

Galatians 2:4–5 (1)

[4]"But *it was* because of the false brethren secretly brought in, who had sneaked in to spy out our liberty which we have in Christ Jesus, in order to bring us into bondage. [5]But we did not yield to their **will** [hypotage] for even an hour, so that the truth of the gospel would remain with you."

Ephesians 1:22–23 (1)

[22]"And He **placed** [hypetaxen] all things under His feet, and gave Him as head [source] for all things to believers, [23]which is His body, the fullness of Him who fills all in all."

Ephesians 5:18–21 (1)

[18]"And do not get drunk with wine, for that is dissipation, but be filled with the Spirit, [19]speaking to one another with psalms and hymns and spiritual songs, singing with songs of praise in your heart to the Lord, [20]always giving thanks for all things in the name of our Lord Jesus Christ to the God and Father, [21]and **be continuously set in this way** [hypotassomenoi] toward one another out of reverence for Christ."

Ephesians 5:22–33 (1)

[22]"The wives to their own husbands, as to the Lord. [23]For the man is the head [source] of the woman, as Christ also is the head [source] of the church, He Himself *being* the Savior of the body. [24]So as the church **is set** [hypotassetai] to Christ, so also the wives to their husbands in everything.

²⁵You husbands love your wives just as Christ also loved the church and gave Himself up for her, ²⁶so that He might sanctify her, having cleansed her by the washing of water with the Word, ²⁷so that He might present to Himself the church in all her glory, having no spot or wrinkle or any such thing; but that she would be holy and blameless. ²⁸So husbands ought also to love their own wives as their own bodies. He who loves his own wife loves himself; ²⁹for no one ever hated his own flesh, but nourishes and cherishes it, just as Christ also *does* the church, ³⁰because we are members of His body. ³¹'FOR THIS REASON A MAN SHALL LEAVE HIS FATHER AND MOTHER AND SHALL HOLD FAST TO HIS WIFE AND THE TWO SHALL BECOME ONE FLESH.' ³²This mystery is great; but I am speaking with reference to Christ and the church. ³³Nevertheless, each one of you also is to love his own wife as himself, and the wife will then have a deep respect for her husband."

Philippians 3:20–21 (1)

²⁰"For our citizenship is in heaven, from where also we eagerly wait for a Savior, the Lord Jesus Christ; ²¹who will transform the body of our low state into conformity with the body of His glory, according to the power that He has even **to place** [hypotaxai] all things to Himself."

Colossians 3:18 (1)

¹⁸"Wives, **be set** [hypotassesthe] to your husband's **in a way** that is fitting in the Lord."

1 Timothy 2:8–15 (1)

This passage will be discussed, and the interpretation given, in the eighth chapter – (hypotage).

1 Timothy 3:1–7 (1)

This passage will be discussed, and the interpretation given, in the ninth chapter – (hypotage).

Titus 2:3–5 (1)

[3]"Older women, likewise, are to be with behavior appropriate to holiness, not false accusers, nor enslaved by much wine, *being* teachers of what is good, [4]so that they may encourage the young women to love their husbands, love their children, [5]to exercise sound judgment, to be pure, diligent at home, kind, **being set in this way** [hypotassomenas] to their own husbands so that the Word of God will not be dishonored."

Titus 2:9–10 (1)

[9]"Bond slaves to their own masters, in all things, **are to be set in a way** [hypotassesthai] that is well-pleasing, not argumentative, [10]not pilfering, but showing all good faith so that the teaching of God our Savior will be made attractive in all things."

Titus 3:1–2 (1)

[1]"Remind them **to be set** [hypotassesthai] to rulers and authorities **in a way** that they are ready to be obedient to every good work, [2]to malign no one, to be peaceable, gentle, showing every consideration for all people."

Hebrews 2:5–9 (4)

[5]"For He did not **place** [hypetaxen] to angels the world to come, concerning which we are speaking. [6]But one has testified somewhere, saying, 'WHAT IS MAN, THAT YOU REMEMBER HIM? OR THE SON OF MAN, THAT YOU CARE FOR HIM? [7]YOU HAVE MADE HIM FOR A LITTLE WHILE LOWER THAN GOD; YOU HAVE CROWNED HIM WITH GLORY AND HONOR, AND HAVE APPOINTED HIM OVER THE WORKS OF YOUR HANDS; [8]YOU **HAVE PLACED** [hypetaxas] ALL THINGS UNDER HIS FEET.' For in **placing** [hypotaxai] all things to Him, He left nothing to Him that is disobedient. But at this present time, we do not yet see all things **willed** [hypotetagmena] to Him. [9]But we do see Jesus, the One having been made for a little while lower than God, now crowned with glory and honor because of the suffering of death, so that by the grace of God on behalf of everyone He might taste death."

<u>Hebrews 12:4–11</u> (1)

[4]"You have not yet resisted to the point of shedding blood in your struggle against sin; [5]and you have forgotten the exhortation which is addressed to you as children, 'MY CHILD, DO NOT DESPISE THE CORRECTION OF THE LORD, NOR LOSE HEART WHEN YOU ARE REPROVED BY HIM; [6]FOR THOSE WHOM THE LORD LOVES HE CORRECTS, AND HE SCOURGES EVERY CHILD WHOM HE RECEIVES.' [7]God deals with you as with children, so endure correction for this reason. For what child is there whom their father does not correct? [8]But if you are without correction, of which you all have taken part in, then you are illegitimate and not children. [9]Furthermore, we had fathers of our flesh to correct us, and we respected them. Shall we not, even more than, also live **to do the will** [hypotagesometha] of the Father of our spirits? [10]For they corrected us for a short time according to what seemed best to them, but He for our benefit so that we can share in His holiness. [11]All correction at the moment seems not to be pleasant, but sorrowful; yet to those who have been trained by it, afterwards it yields the peaceful fruit of righteousness."

<u>James 4:7–8</u> (1)

[7]"**Do the will** [hypotagete], then, of God. Resist the devil and he will flee from you. [8]Draw near to God and He will draw near to you."

<u>1 Peter 2:13–17</u> (1)

[13]"**Be willing** [hypotagete] *to do good* toward every human institution because of the Lord, whether to a king as the one in authority, [14]or to governors as sent by him, so that punishment will come on those who do evil and praise will come on those who do good. [15]For such is the will of God that by doing good, you may silence the ignorance of foolish people. [16]Act as free people, and do not use your freedom as a covering for evil, but use it as bondslaves of God. [17]Honor all people, love fellow believers, fear God, show proper respect to the king."

<u>1 Peter 2:18–20</u> (1)

[18]"Servants, **be set** [hypotassomenoi] to your masters with all respect, not only to those who are good and gentle but also to those who are corrupt. [19]For this *finds* favor if, for the sake of conscience toward God, a person

bears up under sorrows when suffering unjustly. ²⁰For what honor is there if, when you sin, you endure harsh treatment *for it*? But if when you do what is right and endure suffering *for it*, this *finds* favor with God."

<u>1 Peter 2:20–25; 3:1–6 (2)</u>

^{2:20}"…But if when you do what is right and endure suffering *for it*, this *finds* favor with God. ²¹For you have been called for this purpose, since Christ also suffered for you, leaving an example for you to follow in His steps, ²²WHO COMMITTED NO SIN, NOR WAS ANY DECEIT FOUND IN HIS MOUTH; ²³and while being reviled, He did not revile in return; while suffering, He uttered no threats, but kept entrusting Himself to Him who judges righteously; ²⁴and He Himself bore our sins in His body on the cross, so that we might die to sin and live to righteousness; for by His wounds you were healed. ²⁵For you were continually straying like sheep, but now you have returned to the Shepherd and the One who cares for your souls. ^{3:1}So in the same way *that Christ was set*, you wives, *also* **be set** [hypotassomenai] to your own husbands, so that even if any of them are disobedient to the Word, they may be won over without a word by the behavior of their wives, ²by observing the reverent and pure way you live your lives. ³Let it not be the outward appearance—braiding the hair and wearing gold jewelry or putting on worldly clothing, ⁴but let it be the hidden person of the heart, with the imperishable quality of a gentle and peaceful spirit, which is of great worth in the sight of God. ⁵For in this way in former times the holy women also, who hoped in God, used to make themselves beautiful by **being set** [hypotassomenai] to their own husbands; ⁶just as Sarah answered Abraham, calling him her dear husband, and you have become her children if you do what is right without giving way to fear."

<u>1 Peter 3:21–22 (1)</u>

²¹"And this *water even* symbolizes now that you are saved. *For* baptism does not *represent* the putting away of the filth of the flesh, but *rather* a request to God for a morally good conscience through the resurrection of Jesus Christ, ²²who is at the right hand of God, having gone into heaven, **having willed** [hypotagenton] to Him angels and authorities and powers."

<u>1 Peter 5:1–5</u> (1)

[1]"Therefore, I exhort the older ones among you, as someone who is also older and a witness of the sufferings of Christ and a partaker also of the glory that is to be revealed, [2]take care of the flock of God among you, not under compulsion, but voluntarily, according to God; and not for sordid gain, but eagerly; [3]nor yet as lording it over those who share the inheritance but being examples to the flock. [4]And when the Chief Shepherd appears, you will receive the unfading crown of glory. [5]Likewise, you younger ones **be willing** [hypotagete] toward the older ones; and all of you clothe yourselves with humility toward one another, for GOD IS OPPOSED TO THE PROUD, BUT GIVES GRACE TO THE HUMBLE."

HYPAKOUO (21)

(To answer)

1) ²⁷"The men were amazed, and said, 'What kind of a man is this, that even the winds and the sea **answer** [hypakouousin] Him?'" (Matt. 8:27).

2) ²⁷"They were all amazed, so that they debated among themselves, saying, 'What is this? A new teaching with authority! He commands even the unclean spirits, and they **answer** [hypakouousin] Him'" (Mark 1:27).

3) ⁴¹"They became very much afraid and said to one another, 'Who then is this that even the wind and the sea **answer** [hypakouei] Him?'" (Mark 4:41).

4) ²⁵"And He said to them, 'Where is your faith?' They were fearful and amazed, saying to one another, 'Who then is this that He commands even the winds and the water, and they **answer** [hypakouousin] Him?'" (Luke 8:25).

5) ⁶"And the Lord said, 'If you had faith like a mustard seed, you would say to this mulberry tree, 'Be uprooted and be planted in the sea'; and it would **answer** [hypekousen] you'" (Luke 17:6).

6) ⁷"The Word of God kept on spreading; and the number of the disciples continued to increase greatly in Jerusalem, and a great many of the priests **were answering** [hypekouon] the faith" (Acts 6:7).

7) ¹³"When he knocked at the entryway door, a servant-girl named Rhoda came **to answer** [hypakousai]" (Acts 12:13).

8) ¹²"Therefore, do not let sin reign in your mortal body so that you **answer** [hypakouein] its lusts…" (Rom. 6:12).

9) [16]"Do you not know that when you present yourselves to someone *as* slaves for obedience, you are slaves of the one to whom you **answer** [hypakouete], either of sin resulting in death, or of obedience resulting in righteousness?" (Rom. 6:16).

10) [17]"But thanks be to God that though you were slaves of sin, you **answered** [hypekousate] from the heart to that form of teaching to which you were committed, [18]and having been freed from sin, you became slaves of righteousness" (Rom. 6:17–18).

11) [16]"However, they did not all **answer** [hypekousan] the good news; for Isaiah says, 'LORD, WHO HAS BELIEVED OUR MESSAGE?'" (Rom. 10:16).

12) [1]"Children, **answer** [hypakouete] your parents in the Lord, for this is right. [2]HONOR YOUR FATHER AND MOTHER (which is the first commandment with a promise), [3]SO THAT IT MAY BE WELL WITH YOU, AND THAT YOU MAY LIVE LONG ON THE EARTH" (Eph. 6:1–3).

13) [5]"Slaves, **answer** [hypakouete] those who are your masters according to the flesh, with respect and fear, in the sincerity of your heart, as to Christ; [6]not by way of eyeservice, as men-pleasers, but as slaves of Christ, doing the will of God from the heart" (Eph. 6:5–6).

14) [12]"So then, my beloved, just as you have always **answered** [hypekousate], not as in my presence only, but now much more in my absence, with respect and fear, accomplish much with your salvation; [13]for it is God who is at work in you, both to will and to work for *His* good pleasure" (Phil. 2:12–13).

15) [20]"Children, **answer** [hypakouete] your parents in all things, for this is well-pleasing to the Lord" (Col. 3:20).

16) [22]"Slaves, in all things **answer** [hypakouete] those who are your masters on earth, not with eyeservice, as those who *merely* please men, but with sincerity of heart, fearing the Lord" (Col. 3:22).

17) [6]"For after all it is *only* just for God to repay with affliction those who afflict you, [7]and *to give* relief to you who are afflicted and to us as well

when the Lord Jesus will be revealed from heaven with His mighty angels in flaming fire, [8]dealing out retribution to those who do not know God and to those who do not **answer** [hypakouousin] the gospel of our Lord Jesus" (2 Thess. 1:6–8).

18) [14]"If anyone does not **answer** [hypakouei] our instruction in this letter, take special note of that person and do not associate with him, so that he will be put to shame" (2 Thess. 3:14).

19) [9]"And having been made perfect, He became to all those who **answer** [hypakouousin] Him the source of eternal salvation, [10]being designated by God as a high priest according to the order of Melchizedek" (Heb. 5:9–10).

20) [8]"By faith Abraham, when he was called, **answered** [hypekousen] by going out to a place which he was to receive for an inheritance; and he went out, not knowing where he was going" (Heb. 11:8).

21) [4]"...but let *it* be the hidden person of the heart, with the imperishable quality of a gentle and peaceful spirit, which is of great worth in the sight of God. [5]For in this way in former times the holy women also, who hoped in God, used to make themselves beautiful by being set to their own husbands; [6]just as Sarah **answered** [hypekousen] Abraham..." (1 Pet. 3:4–6).

8

1 TIMOTHY 2:11-15

Now we come to a passage that has greatly divided the body of Christ. A passage which I believe is woefully mistranslated. For this passage, as translated, states that women cannot teach nor have authority over men. This supposedly is due to the fact that Adam was physically formed first, but also because the woman was deceived and fell into transgression. Therefore, we can conclude that it is far better to sin with all premeditation and deliberateness than to be deceived since the man is not held accountable. Furthermore, we see that women will be saved through childbearing, which has not a single ounce of truth in it. Indeed, this passage as a whole makes no sense and is contradictory to teachings elsewhere in God's Word. It amazes me that the most ludicrous arguments are set forth in a futile attempt to make this distortion of God's Word even remotely make sense. Men have gone to the translation table with a preconceived bias of the superiority of man, which has resulted in a travesty of God's Word and more than half of the body of Christ being silenced.

As we know, when trying to understand difficult passages in the Bible, it is vital for us to compare Scripture with Scripture in order to come to the right conclusion. We cannot just shove certain Scriptures to the side and ignore that they exist when trying to figure out these passages but must understand that all of Scripture flows in perfect harmony. Furthermore, it is also vitally important for us to look at the clues that are given in the passage itself so that we can get a full understanding of the scenario that appears before us. Therefore, so that we can get a full understanding of the scenario that has happened in Ephesus, we will look not only at the clues given to us in the second chapter of Timothy, but we will look at the clues given to us in the first chapter of Timothy as well. The reason why it is so crucial for us to understand Paul's letter from the beginning is that we will see what Paul says here play out later in this passage. Indeed, the beginning of Paul's letter is paramount to understanding what he says in 1 Timothy 2:11–15. Therefore, we will now examine Paul's words closely, starting with verse three. He writes:

> [3]"As I urged you upon my departure for Macedonia, remain on at Ephesus so that you may instruct certain men not to teach strange doctrines, [4]nor to pay attention to myths and endless genealogies, which give rise to mere speculation rather than *furthering* the administration of God which is by faith. [5]But the goal of our instruction is love from a pure heart and a good conscience and a sincere faith. [6]For some men straying from these things, have turned aside to fruitless discussion, [7]wanting to be teachers of the Law, even though they do not understand either what they are saying or the matters about which they make confident assertions" (1 Tim. 1:3–7).

In looking at this passage, it is important to know that in both verses three and six, the Greek does not use words that identify the persons in view, nor does it identify their gender as the NASB translators have rendered. However, I agree with the NASB translators that men are in view in these verses, and I will explain why momentarily. In addition, I believe that Paul is referencing two different groups of men in these verses. This is because Paul uses the word "tines" in verse six. "Tines" means "some" in Greek and, therefore, does not refer back to the group mentioned in verses 3–4.[1] As a result, I believe that Paul is referencing believing Jewish men in verses 3–4, and that Paul is referencing unbelieving Jewish men in verses 6–7. For I believe that certain male Jewish believers were teaching strange doctrines because they were paying attention to the myths and endless genealogies that were being promoted by some unsaved Jewish men who wanted to be teachers of the Law, even though the unsaved Jewish men did not understand either what they were saying or the matters about which they made confident assertions.

I would like to clarify my reasons as to why I believe Paul is referencing believing Jewish men in verses 3–4 and unbelieving Jewish men in verses 6–7. For this, I would like to start with the second group. The reason that I believe Paul is referencing "unbelieving" Jewish men in verses 6–7 is because Paul, in verse six, states that the men were straying from love, a pure heart, a good conscience, and a sincere faith. And the word that is translated as "straying" is "astocheo" in Greek and literally means "to miss the mark."[2] So it is not that these men had strayed from these things, but instead that they "missed the mark" on them altogether. In other words, they did not have love, a pure heart, a good conscience, nor did they have a sincere or genuine faith. As a result, I believe that they were unbelievers. Furthermore, the reason that I believe Paul is referencing "Jewish men" is that he says that they wanted to be "teachers of the Law." And, of course, only Jewish men could be teachers of the Law; women and Gentile men could not. Now, the reason that I believe Paul is referencing "believing" Jewish men in verses 3–4 is because he mentions "the administration of God which is by faith." And of course, believers are the ones that further the administration of God. Believers are the ones that tell others about the saving grace of Jesus Christ. Furthermore, the reason that I believe this group also consisted of "Jewish men" is because they were paying attention to (literally devoting themselves to) the myths and genealogies that were being promoted by the unsaved Jewish men. And it is highly unlikely that unsaved Jewish men would have allowed women or Gentile men to participate in their group discussions. So again, I believe the scenario is that certain male Jewish believers were teaching things that were different from God's Word because they were paying attention to the myths and endless genealogies that were being promoted by some unsaved Jewish men. I believe that certain male Jewish believers were finding it difficult to completely break away from the traditional teachings to which they had grown accustomed.

In addition, it is also imperative to understand the urgency that Paul has to stop the believing men from teaching God's Word differently. The word that is translated as "instruct" in verse three is "parangello" in Greek. The word "parangello" comes from two Greek words— "para" and "angelos." "Para" means "from, with, before, among, in the sight of, beside, alongside, by, at," and "angelos" means "messenger."[3] So Paul literally wants Timothy to remain on at Ephesus so that he can be an "in the sight of messenger." In other words, Paul wants Timothy to tell these men "face to face" not to teach God's Word differently. Now the reason that Paul is so adamant about this is because he states that when believers teach God's Word differently, it causes "ekzeteseis." Now the Greek word "ekzeteseis" is adequately translated as "mere speculation" in verse four of the NASB. However, the Interlinear KJV-NIV Parallel New Testament in Greek and English has a much better translation. It translates the word "ekzeteseis" as "questionings." Nevertheless, neither of these translations captures the full meaning of this word. In fact, there is not a singular word in the English language that captures the full meaning of this word. The word "ekzetesis" comes from two Greek words—"ek" and "zeteo." "Ek" means "of, out of, from, away from; disassociation or separation." And "zeteo" means "to look for, seek out; to try to obtain, desire to possess, strive for."[4] So what Paul is saying here is that when believers teach God's Word differently, it causes those who are seeking (obviously for the truth) to be separated (away from the truth). For believers are the light of the world. And if believers do not teach God's Word correctly, then how will unbelievers attain the truth? So there were indeed some unsaved persons in Ephesus who were looking for the truth, seeking out the truth, trying to obtain the truth, desiring to possess the truth, striving for the truth. However, because of the false teachings of certain believers, these unsaved persons were being separated away from the truth; they were not able to come to the knowledge of the truth. So Paul wants the believing men to teach God's Word correctly so that the unsaved persons can come to know God through Jesus Christ. For Paul makes clear, in verse four, that teaching God's Word differently does not further the administration (or plan) of God. And indeed, the administration or plan of God is that people come to God by faith in Jesus Christ.

Therefore, I would translate 1 Timothy 1:3–7 as:

> [3]"As I urged you upon my departure for Macedonia, remain on at Ephesus so that you may instruct certain ones [believing Jewish men] not to teach [God's Word] differently, [4]nor to pay attention to myths and endless genealogies, because it causes those [the unsaved] who are searching for the truth to be separated away from the truth rather than *furthering* the administration of God which is [that people come to God] by faith [in Jesus Christ]. [5]But the goal of our instruction is love from a pure heart and a good conscience and a sincere faith. [6]For some [unbelieving Jewish men], missing the mark of these things, have turned to fruitless discussion, [7]wanting to be teachers of the Law, even though they do not understand either what they are saying or the matters about which they make confident assertions."

We need to understand that the very reason Paul wanted Timothy to remain on at Ephesus was that he was concerned about the salvation of the unsaved. Paul was so concerned that he not only urged Timothy to stay when he departed for Macedonia, but he also wrote to him to reiterate his concern. And if we continue reading Paul's letter, we can see that Paul's continued focus is on the salvation of the unsaved (1 Tim. 1:15–16). In fact, the very first instructions that Paul gives to the believers in Ephesus is to make earnest requests for the unsaved through prayer, because God desires all people to be saved and to come to the knowledge of the truth (1 Tim. 2:1–4). It is also important to note that Paul places emphasis on the fact that there is one God, and one mediator also between God and people, the man Christ Jesus, who gave Himself as a ransom for all (1 Tim. 2:5–6). Indeed, Paul is reminding the believers in Ephesus what the plan of God is.

As we move along in Paul's instructions, we can also see that Paul addresses the men and women individually. He does this because he is concerned that the behaviors and practices of individual believers are looking unfavorable to those who are not saved, especially among the Gentiles. For as we can see, the very last words that Paul states before he addresses the believing men and women in Ephesus is that he was appointed to teach the Gentiles in faith and truth about Jesus Christ (1 Tim. 2:7). So because he was appointed to teach the Gentiles, Paul, in verse eight, makes a specific request to all of the believing men in Ephesus to pray, lifting up holy hands without wrath and dissension. For it is clear by Paul's words that the men were not only arguing, but arguing quite angrily. It is also clear that their anger was causing them to lift their hands up to one another in unholy ways, with angry gestures and motions. As a result, Paul wants them to replace their angry arguments with prayer so that they focus their attention on God. And he does not want them to lift their hands up to one another in unholy ways, but rather, he wants them to lift up "holy" hands. Indeed, Paul wants the men who have placed their faith in Christ to model Christ-like behavior for the unsaved. He wants the believing men to set an example by having a spirit of gentleness and peacefulness.

Next, in verses 9–10, Paul now states that he would like the believing women to "likewise" have an "honorable appearance," that is, an appearance with "holiness and discretion," just as he asked the men. Unfortunately, though, the similarity of what Paul asks for among the men and women is lost in the usual translation. For the NASB translation, as well as all others that I have seen, make Paul's request to the women to be all about modest clothing, not about their appearance in the way that they act. But Paul is actually asking the women to put their focus on the way that they act and not upon the way that they dress so that they too can be examples to the unsaved.

Now, I would like to render a translation of verses 8–10 in the way that I believe is more accurate to the Greek and then will explain just why I rendered it this way.

I would translate 1 Timothy 2:8–10 as follows:

> [8]"Therefore, I want the men in every place to pray, lifting up holy hands without anger and disputing. [9]Likewise, I want the women to adorn themselves with an honorable appearance, *one* with holiness and discretion, not with braided hair and gold or pearls or costly garments, [10]but rather with what suits women who profess to worship God, by means of good works."

The reason why I translated verses nine and ten in this way, to begin, is because the word that the NASB translators translate as "clothing" in verse nine is "katastole" in Greek, and it is defined as "appearance, behavior" in the Strongest NIV Exhaustive concordance.[5] Nowhere is it defined as "clothing." Furthermore, the word following "katastole," which is translated as "proper" in verse nine, is the word "kosmios," and it is defined as "respectable, honorable" in the same concordance.[6] Thus, I translated these two words as "honorable appearance" because they are the correct definitions of the words according to the concordance. Next, Paul adds with "aidos" and "sophrosyne." Now "aidos," which is translated as "modestly" in verse nine, is defined by Spiros Zodhiates Complete Word Study Dictionary as "an innate moral repugnance to the doing of the dishonorable act."[7] It appears only this one time in the New Testament. So Paul wants the women to stay away from any action that would be dishonorable, which is why I translated "aidos" as "holiness." And finally, "sophrosyne" has to do with doing what is proper and having sound judgment and is translated as "discreetly" in the NASB. And to be discreet, or to have discretion, is to be careful about what one does or says.

Now, because the translators think that Paul is speaking of a woman's appearance in terms of clothing, and the words "katastole" and "kosmios" are translated as "proper clothing" instead of as "honorable appearance," the word "likewise" shows no logical connection between the men and women, because Paul has stated nothing about clothing when addressing the men. But Paul is actually asking for the same thing from both the men and women, that is, he wants their outward appearance to be one of holiness and discretion. The only difference between the requests is that Paul asks the men to pray and the women to do good works. Now, the reason there is a difference is because of the differing problems. The men had taken their focus off of God and had directed it toward the comments of other men, which was causing unholy and indiscreet behavior. So in order to correct the men from their dishonorable appearance, Paul asks the men to pray in every place where they went in order to get their attention back on God. For Paul knows that if these men are in constant prayer to God, it will bring a change in the way these men act. Now the women, on the other hand, had their focus on God because Paul makes clear that these women were professing to worship God, or as the NASB translators have rendered, these women were making a claim to godliness. Unfortunately, though, these women were equating godliness to the way that they dressed. They thought that by having a perfect outward appearance in terms of clothing, hair, and accessories, they were being godly examples to those who did not know Christ. But Paul explains that one's attire does not bring the unsaved to Christ, and may even have a negative effect on the unsaved if one's appearance is too ornate. Therefore, Paul is telling the women that doing good works is the way believers (those who profess to worship God) let others know of the love of Christ. So because of these mistranslations, one cannot fully understand the similarity between Paul's requests. But indeed, Paul wants both the believing men and women to appear in a way that is honorable, in terms of actions, to those who do not know Christ.

Before we come to the passage at hand, I would like to give a brief over-view of the main points in Paul's letter that we have just covered because they are extremely important to remember as we dissect verses 11–15. For Paul's whole concern, in chapters 1–2, is for the salvation of the unsaved. As we will see, verses 11–15 are connected to everything that he has just said.

Brief Overview:

1) Paul wants Timothy to remain on at Ephesus so that he can instruct certain male Jewish believers not to teach God's Word differently, nor to pay attention to the myths and endless genealogies that were being promoted by some unsaved Jewish men because it causes

those who are searching for the truth to be separated away from the truth rather than furthering the administration of God, which is that people come to God by faith in Jesus Christ.

2) Paul asks all of the believing men and women to pray for the salvation of all people, so that they can be saved and come to the knowledge of the truth.

3) Paul asks all of the believing men and women to be examples to the unsaved by acting in a way that is honoring to God, with holiness and discretion.

Now we come to 1 Timothy 2:11–15. And here we are led to believe that Paul suddenly takes his focus off of the unsaved in order to tell Christian women that they are to learn in silence with all subjection, are not allowed to teach or have authority over men, and will be saved through childbearing. But I will tell you plainly that I do not believe this is what is happening at all in this portion of Scripture. Paul has just finished asking the believers in Ephesus to act in a way that is honorable, so that they can be examples to those who do not know Christ (vv. 8–10). Paul has asked them to do this because he was appointed by God to teach the Gentiles in faith and truth about Jesus Christ (vv. 5–7). In addition to this, he also initially asked the believers to pray for the salvation of the unsaved because God desires all people to be saved and to come to the knowledge of the truth (vv. 1–4). So I believe that in this portion of Scripture, Paul is now giving instructions concerning an unsaved Gentile woman. Furthermore, I believe that this unsaved woman is the main reason why Paul has taken so much time, up to this point, to stress to believers how they are to be toward the unsaved. For I believe that Paul is concerned about this unsaved woman in particular because he knows that she is actively searching for the truth in regard to Jesus Christ. Therefore, because Paul was appointed by God to teach the Gentiles, he gives specific instructions regarding her to help ensure that she fully understands the gospel message.

I will now go through verses 11–15 to show the scenario that I believe has happened in Ephesus. As we go along, I will break down each verse separately. I will start with verse eleven, where I will first give the translation of the NASB, and then I will give what I believe to be the correct translation and an explanation of why I translated it as such. Verse eleven reads as, [11]"A woman must quietly receive instruction, with entire submissiveness." However, I believe that verse eleven should be translated as:

[11]"Let the woman learn in a peaceful atmosphere with all willingness."

As one can see, I translated the Greek word "gyne" (woman) as "the woman" instead of "a woman." I have done so because, as I previously stated, I believe that Paul is referring to a specific woman. Now the reason why I believe Paul is referring to a particular woman is that Paul, in verse fifteen, switches from the singular "she will be saved" (sothesetai) to the plural "they continue" (meinosin). Therefore, it is clear that Paul is referring to a singular woman and a plurality of people in verse fifteen because proper Greek grammar disallows referencing both "she" and "they" in the same sentence to refer to the same thing, just as it would be disallowed in English grammar. Now, most people ignore this fact and insist that Paul is speaking of all women throughout this passage due to the fact that the word "gyne" is anarthrous, meaning it lacks the article. However, in Greek, a noun doesn't need to have the article in order for it to be definite. In other words, a noun may refer to a specific person or thing, even though it lacks the article. (See Matthew 9:20; Mark 5:25; 7:25; 14:3; Luke 7:37; 11:27; 13:11; John 8:3; 8:10; Acts 17:34. In these examples, the Greek word "gyne" lacks the article, yet they are referring to a specific woman.) In fact, context is the biggest factor when determining whether a noun that lacks the article is definite or indefinite. Therefore, because a noun may be definite without the article, and proper Greek grammar disallows using a singular and plural in the same sentence to refer to the same thing, I believe that Paul is referring to a singular woman in verse eleven. As a result, I translated the word "gyne" as "the woman" instead of as "a woman" to help the reader understand that Paul is talking about a specific woman, not all women.

Next, the word "hesychia" (translated as "quietly" in the NASB) is a word that is used in relation to undisciplined behavior. (See Acts 22:2; 2 Thess. 3:12.) It does not refer to complete silence but rather to a settling down or lack of disturbance.[8] Therefore, I chose to translate "hesychia" as "peaceful atmosphere" instead of as "peacefulness" because I wanted to show that it is not the woman who is being unruly, but that it is her surroundings that are unruly. If I translated it as "peacefulness," then there is no doubt that some would attribute the disturbance to the woman. However, the only ones in this passage that are seen to be causing a disturbance are the men with their anger and disputing. The text in no way shows that this woman was being belligerent or causing a disturbance herself. Furthermore, it would be nonsensical to claim that she was both willing to learn about God and causing a disturbance at the same time. Therefore, with the translation of "peaceful atmosphere," the meaning is clear.

And finally, in verse eleven, I translated the Greek word "hypotage" as "willingness" instead of "submissiveness" because, as I stated in "Hypotasso (Part I)," I believe that the correct meaning of the word "hypotage" is "will, willed, willingness, etc.", not "obedience, submission, subjection." This is why I painstakingly went over the word "hypotage" in every single passage that it is used. See "Hypotasso (Part I and II)" for review.

So, we can see by verse eleven that this woman is a willing participant. She wants to learn about Christ. She is searching and seeking for the truth. It is also clear that Paul wants this unsaved woman to learn in a peaceful atmosphere because the chaotic atmosphere that the men were causing was making it difficult for her to learn. So again, in verse eleven, Paul is asking Timothy to ensure that this unsaved woman has an atmosphere that is conducive to learning where she can readily and willingly learn about Christ.

Now we come to verse twelve. But because verses 13–14 are such an integral part of verse twelve, as they are the explanation for what Paul is not permitting, I will explain verse twelve in conjunction with verses 13–14. Verses 12–14 read as, ¹²"But I do not allow a woman to teach or exercise authority over a man, but to remain quiet. ¹³For it was Adam who was first created, *and* then Eve. ¹⁴And *it was* not Adam *who* was deceived, but the woman being deceived, fell into transgression." Now before I give my rendering of verses 12–14, I would first like to say that the most common explanation that people give for verses 13–14 is based, in part or in whole, on primogeniture. They say that because God created Adam first, the man is to be the one to teach and have authority. One can even see by the rendering of the NASB that the translators have not only added several words that are not in the original Greek, but they have also translated the Greek word "plasso" (meaning "to form, mold")[9] as "created" to help fit this view. However, it is clear from Genesis 1:26–28 that God gave both the man and woman equal dominion over the earth and the animals. And nowhere is it seen in Scripture that God gave the man either dominion over the woman or any type of leadership over her because he was created first.

Furthermore, the 1 Corinthians 11:3–16 passage is clear proof that the theory of primogeniture is false because Paul's teaching in that passage is in direct opposition to primogeniture. If Paul had agreed with primogeniture, then he would have made a different case in that passage altogether; a case perhaps stating that the woman should be veiled and under the authority of a man because the man was created first and was superior. However, Paul did not make this case (as some people think). Instead, Paul stated that just as a man ought not to veil his head, Jesus Christ, because He is the image and glory of God, so also the man ought not to veil the woman because she is his glory. He then went on to remind the men that the woman came from the man because she was created for his sake, and (that her being created for his sake) is the reason why the woman ought to have authority over the man. So the 1 Corinthians 11:3–16 passage is a clear warrant against men making a claim of primogeniture, which shows us that Paul is not making an argument of primogeniture in verses 13–14. Not only are verses 13–14 not an argument for primogeniture, but there is not a single scenario in which verses 13–14 make sense with the given rendering of verse twelve. Hence, what I believe Paul is actually saying in verses 13–14 is this, [13]"For Adam was first formed [in God's command by God], then Eve [was formed in God's command by Adam]. [14]And [as a result] Adam was not deceived, but the woman being deceived fell into transgression." So Paul is not speaking of physical formation in verse thirteen, but instead, he is speaking of spiritual formation. Paul is telling us that Adam was formed in God's Word by God Himself and that Eve was formed in God's Word by Adam. And because of it, Adam was not deceived, but the woman being deceived fell into transgression. Therefore, Paul is telling us that Adam taught Eve God's Word incorrectly, which caused her to be deceived.

Therefore, I believe that verses 12–14 should be translated as follows:

> [12]"But I do not permit the man to teach his wife, nor to exercise his own jurisdiction but to be in peacefulness. [13]For Adam was first formed, then Eve. [14]And Adam was not deceived, but the woman being deceived fell into transgression."

Here, we can see that Paul is not permitting the man to teach his wife, nor is he permitting him to exercise his own jurisdiction apart from God because he is trying to prevent a repeat of what happened in the Garden of Eden. If we remember back to the first chapter, it was Adam's incorrect teaching of God's Word (or command) in conjunction with the fact that he exercised his own jurisdiction apart from God that caused Eve to be deceived and fall into transgression. So I believe that Paul mentions Adam and Eve because this man, like Adam, was not teaching by the Word of God, nor living by the Word of God. Not only was he teaching his wife God's Word differently, but he was also exercising his own jurisdiction (or authority) apart from God and was living according to his own desires. And if I surmise correctly, one of the myths that this man was teaching was the "myth of submission." I fully believe that this man was teaching his wife that submission was according to God's Word. Therefore, Paul well understood that since this man was not living by God's Word, as his life was full of pride and anger and arguments (this is evident by the fact that Paul wants him to be in peacefulness), he clearly would have asked his wife for immoral things. And if she submitted to him as he was teaching her, then she too would have been disobedient to God's Word. Hence, since Paul does not want a repeat of what happened in the garden, he does not permit the man to teach his wife, nor does he permit him to exercise his own jurisdiction apart from God.

And in case it is not already obvious, I believe that the man referenced in verse twelve is one of the believers mentioned in verses 3–4 of chapter one. He is a Jewish man who had placed his faith in Jesus Christ; however, he was teaching God's Word differently because he was paying attention to the myths and endless genealogies that were being promoted by some unsaved Jewish men. Likewise, the woman in verse twelve is one of the unsaved persons mentioned in verse four of chapter one. She is an unsaved Gentile woman who was actively searching for the truth in regard to Jesus Christ, yet she was being separated away from the truth by the false teachings of her husband. Not only did she not understand that Jesus Christ was the mediator between God and people and that He gave Himself as a ransom for all, but she also was being given information that could cause her to fall into transgression.

Before I give my explanation of why I rendered verse twelve as such, there are a few things that I would like to explain about the Greek language for those who are not familiar with Greek. The first thing that one needs to know about the Greek language is that it is a highly inflected language. This means that Greek words change form (the Greek spelling) in order to indicate the role each word plays in the sentence. So, in the Greek, it is not the word order that determines the grammatical function of a sentence, but rather the case endings attached to the stem of the noun. Therefore, in Greek, there are five main cases, or types of relationship, that the noun can have to other words in a sentence.[10] They are:

Nominative Case: The subject of a sentence or verb.
Who? What? (He)

Genitive Case: Expresses possession.
Whose? (His)

Dative Case: The indirect object of a verb.
To whom? To what? (Him)

Accusative Case: The direct object of a verb.
Whom? What? (Him)

Vocative Case: Direct address.[11]

Furthermore, because case endings determine the grammatical function of a sentence, Greek has free word order. This free word order allows the author of Greek to write a sentence in many different ways as opposed to the rigid and limiting word order of the English. It also allows the author to emphasize certain elements to convey the meaning of the sentence more fully. As a result, emphasis in Greek is often shown by words occurring out of their standard order in relation to other words in the sentence. In addition to this, the more to the left a word appears in a sentence, the more prominent it is.[12]

And finally, it is also essential to know that although the accusative case is the most commonly used case for the direct object, the genitive and dative cases are also used. In fact, some verbs specifically take a genitive or dative direct object. This is because one of the characteristics of Greek verbs is that their direct object must be of a particular case or cases.[13] (Note: Some Greek verbs take an accusative direct object; some take a genitive direct object; some take a dative direct object; some take both an accusative and genitive direct object; some take both an accusative and dative direct object. However, no verb takes both a genitive and dative direct object.)[14]

I would like to begin my explanation of verse twelve, starting with my translation of the word "authentein." And as you may have already noticed, I translated the word "authentein" with an intransitive meaning. This is because I believe that its true meaning is "to exercise one's own jurisdiction." And I believe this for two reasons. First, I believe that this is its true meaning because the word "authenteo" comes from the Greek word "autos." And "autos" means "himself, herself, itself, themselves, the same one."[15] Therefore, it has to do with "oneself" or "one's own." However, the main reason that I believe this is its true meaning is because of the context. As I stated previously, Adam exercised his own jurisdiction, or authority, apart from God, by purposefully eating from the tree which God had commanded him not to eat. In doing so, he did not correct the misinformation that he had given Eve in order to allow her to make her own decision about the fruit, but instead, took it upon himself to decide for her what she should do. So it was Adam's incorrect teaching in conjunction with the fact that he exercised his own jurisdiction apart from God that caused Eve to be deceived and fall into transgression. Therefore, I will now go over the meanings of "authenteo."

The word "authenteo" has long been debated because it is what is called a hapax legomenon, meaning it is used only once in the New Testament. Therefore, scholars have had to turn to extra-Biblical writings in the ancient Greek world to find out its possible meanings.[16] For the different meanings of the word "authenteo," I will turn to a book titled "Women in the Church." The author of the second chapter, Henry Scott Baldwin, reviews the different meanings of the word "authenteo" that scholars have found in ancient Greek writings. On page 45, Mr. Baldwin has listed the meanings of this word, which I have printed for you below. There are four definitions with seven subsets.[17]

THE MEANINGS OF AUTHENTEO:

1. To rule, to reign sovereignly

2. To control, to dominate

    a. to compel, to influence someone/something

b. middle voice: to be in effect, to have legal standing

c. hyperbolically: to domineer/play the tyrant

d. to grant authorization

3. To act independently

a. to assume authority over

b. to exercise one's own jurisdiction

c. to flout the authority of

4. To be primarily responsible for, to do or to instigate something

It is quite interesting to note in Mr. Baldwin's review of the different meanings of the verb "authenteo" that many of the meanings are intransitive. For instance, all thirteen uses of "to rule, to reign sovereignly" are intransitive (simply, "I rule"). He also notes that the meaning of "to control, to dominate" can be used either transitively or intransitively. Furthermore, the meaning of "to domineer/play the tyrant" is intransitive. The meaning of "to act independently" is intransitive. (Mr. Baldwin notes that "to act independently" carries the idea of being one's own authority.) And finally, the meaning of "to exercise one's own jurisdiction" is intransitive.[18] In addition to this, Mr. Baldwin also lists the meanings of the verb "authenteo," as defined in several modern lexicons. And it is interesting to note that the lexicographer, Lampe, gives a definition of "assume authority," which is intransitive, as opposed to the definition Mr. Baldwin has listed in 3a of "to assume authority over," which is transitive. Moreover, the lexicographer Lampe also lists other intransitive meanings, such as "act on one's own authority", "hold sovereign authority," and "act with authority." In addition, the lexicographer Sophocles lists a definition of "to be in power," BDAG[c] lists the definition of "to assume a stance of independent authority," and the lexicographers Preisigke and Mayser each list the definition of "to be master" all of which are intransitive.[19] So the bottom line is there are many intransitive meanings of the verb "authenteo," all of which point to one who wants to be their own authority or exercise their own jurisdiction apart from God.

Now, the reason why it is essential to understand that many of the meanings of "authenteo" are intransitive is that an intransitive verb cannot take a direct object. And in verse twelve, it is taught that the woman (gynaiki—dative case) is the direct object of the negated finite verb "ouk epitrepo" (not I permit) and the man (andros—genitive case) is the direct object of the infinitives "didaskein" (to teach) and "authentein" (to exercise authority over). Now it is true that the verb "epitrepo" takes a dative direct object and that verbs of ruling take a genitive direct object, which would account for the current translation of verse twelve (at least with regard to the man being the direct object of the infinitive "authentein"). However, if the meaning of "authentein" is intransitive, then the man would not be able to be the direct object of the word "authentein." This is important to understand because many scholars acknowledge the fact that the word "didaskein" cannot take a genitive direct object; it can only take an accusative or dative direct object.[20] This would mean that because the man is in the genitive case, he cannot be the direct object of the infinitive "didaskein," and because the word "authentein" is intransitive, the man likewise cannot be the direct object of the infinitive "authentein." See below for the Greek of verse twelve.

> [12]"didaskein de gynaiki ouk epitrepo oude
> authentein andros all einai en hesychia."

(Note: The words "didaskein" and "authentein" are infinitives. The infinitive is a non-finite verbal noun. As such, it has qualities of both a noun and a verb. As a noun, it may stand as the subject or object of another verb. As a verb, it has a subject which is expressed or implied, and it may have an object.)[21]

The reason why Paul had to make it unmistakably clear that the man was not the direct object of either infinitive is that the main verb "epitrepo" takes a dative direct object. (Remember, the dative is the case of the indirect object.) Hence, because the verb "epitrepo" takes a dative direct object, one would not be able to determine who was the direct and indirect object because both the direct and indirect objects are people, and both would be in the dative case. So because there was no distinction between the cases relating to the main verb, Paul had to make it absolutely clear that the man was not the direct object of the infinitives.

166

In verse twelve, because I believe that the man is not the direct object of either infinitive, I believe that Paul has used each case in its most common way. I believe that Paul has put the woman in the dative case (case of the indirect object) to show that she is the indirect object of the negated finite verb and that Paul has put the man in the genitive case (possessive case) to show that it is the man's own jurisdiction or authority that he is not permitting. This would mean that the woman is the indirect object of the negated finite verb "ouk epitrepo" and that the man is the implied subject of the infinitive "didaskein" and the expressed subject of the infinitive "authentein." (Note: When the word in the genitive case indicates possession, it usually follows the word it modifies.)[22]

Furthermore, it is also important to know that Greek should be read from left to right, just as one would hear the words. And if we read verse twelve from left to right, the natural understanding that we get from it is that the woman is the indirect object of the negated finite verb "ouk epitrepo" and that the man is the implied subject of the infinitive "didaskein" and the expressed subject of the infinitive "authentein." See below.

[12]"didaskein[1] de[2] gynaiki[3] ouk[4] epitrepo[5] oude[6] authentein[7] andros[8] all[9] einai[10] en[11] hesychia[12]."

[12]"to teach[1] but[2] to the woman[3] not[4] I permit[5] nor[6] to exercise his own jurisdiction[7] the man[8] but[9] to be[10] in[11] peacefulness[12]."

Furthermore, the fact that the words "didaskein de gynaiki" are placed to the front of the sentence shows us that Paul is greatly emphasizing these words. Just as the main reason that Eve fell into transgression was that Adam taught her God's command incorrectly, so also the main reason that this woman would fall into transgression would be due to the false teachings of her husband. In other words, if Eve had known the truth, she could have chosen not to eat, even if Adam did. Likewise, if this woman knew the truth, she could take a stand for righteousness even if her husband did not. Therefore, the incorrect forming in God's Word is Paul's main concern. Another thing to note is that the standard placement for the direct object is immediately following the finite or main verb. Therefore, there would not have been a need for Paul to veer from this norm by placing the woman before the finite verb if she was the direct object. Furthermore, the fact that the word "andros" is closest to the words "all einai en hesychia" shows us that it is the man who is to be in peacefulness.

We must understand that Paul had to compose this sentence in a way in which there would be no confusion as to who was the direct and indirect object of the main verb. He also had to show that one infinitive is transitive while the other is intransitive. And this is what Paul clearly did. Paul used not only clear cases but also a clear word order to convey his message. Now some people will argue that the man cannot be the subject of the infinitives because the subject of an infinitive is always in the accusative case. However, this is not true because the subject of the infinitive is in the genitive case twenty-three times in the New Testament when it is used as the genitive of possession.[23] Furthermore, the general rule is that the subject of an infinitive is in the accusative case, and the direct object of an infinitive is in the accusative. One can only tell by context, which is which. But as we can see, this general rule is not being followed here because neither the man nor the woman is in the accusative case. And this was intentional on Paul's part because Paul would not leave it to context to determine who was the subject of the infinitives or the direct object of the infinitives, especially when there was no distinction relating to the main verb. Again, Paul purposefully put the man in the genitive case so that he could not be the direct object of the infinitive "didaskein." If Paul had put the man in the accusative case, then people would have been able to make the argument that the man is the direct object of the infinitive "didaskein."

Now we come to the last verse in this passage, verse fifteen. And as we will see, this verse will confirm that this woman was one of the "unsaved persons" who was searching and seeking for the truth (1 Tim. 1:4). It will also confirm that her husband was one of the "certain ones" who was teaching God's Word differently because he was paying attention to myths and endless genealogies (1 Tim. 1:3–4). Verse fifteen states, [15]"But *women* will be preserved through the bearing of children if they continue in faith and love and sanctity with self-restraint." However, before I give my rendering of verse fifteen, I would like to say that this rendering should be a red flag to any believer who reads it. For it is plainly evident that women are not preserved through the bearing of children. It is also plainly evident that women are not physically saved, kept safe, or made whole through the bearing of children. And certainly, women will not "experience eschatological salvation by adhering to their proper role, which is exemplified in giving birth to children," as Thomas Schreiner ridiculously purports on page 120 of "Women in the Church."[24] In fact, no matter how the word "sothesetai" (she will be saved) is translated or interpreted, it will never fit with the typical rendering of "teknogonias" (bearing of children/childbearing) because the typical rendering of "teknogonias" is an out and out misfit. Therefore, I am utterly amazed that something that is so obviously false and contrary to God's Word would continuously be forced on God's flock as though it were the truth.

The fact of the matter is that it is plainly evident from the beginning of Paul's letter, up until verse fifteen, that his whole concern is for the salvation of the unsaved. As I previously stated, the very reason Paul wanted Timothy to remain on at Ephesus was that he was concerned about the salvation of the unsaved. Paul was so concerned that he not only urged Timothy to stay when he departed for Macedonia, but he also wrote to him to reiterate his concern. Furthermore, Paul's continued focus throughout his letter is on the salvation of the unsaved. For Paul makes clear in 1 Timothy 1:15–16 that Christ Jesus came into the world to save sinners and that it is only through belief in Jesus Christ that one gains eternal life. Furthermore, we can also see that the very first instructions that Paul gives to the believers in Ephesus are to make earnest requests for the unsaved through prayer because God desires all people to be saved and to come to the knowledge of the truth. Paul even emphasizes the fact that there is one God, and one mediator also between God and people, the man Christ Jesus, who gave Himself as a ransom for all, to remind the believers in Ephesus what the plan of God is. We can even see that the very last words that Paul states before he addresses the believing men and women in Ephesus are that he was appointed to teach the Gentiles in faith and truth about Jesus Christ. So it is utterly ridiculous for any believer to think that Paul would veer from this message and announce to all believing women that there is another way they will be saved. It is also equally ridiculous to think that Paul would contradict himself and declare that this singular unsaved woman would be saved through the bearing of children. Without a doubt, Paul would only declare that one is saved through Jesus Christ, as he has repeatedly stated throughout his letter to Timothy.

Therefore, I believe that verse fifteen should be translated as follows:

> [15]"But she will be saved through the Son of this generation if they continue in faith and love and holiness with discretion."

I would like to begin my explanation of verse fifteen, starting with the verb "sothesetai." The reason why I translated the verb "sothesetai" as "she will be saved" is because the verb "sothesetai" is the future tense, indicative mood, passive voice, 3rd person singular form of the verb "sozo."[25] And the future tense is a verb form that indicates the event described by the verb has not yet happened. The indicative mood is a statement of fact from the writer's or speaker's perspective.[26] The passive voice means that the subject receives the action of the verb.[27] And the 3rd person singular can only refer to either "he, she, or it."[28] Furthermore, as far as the meaning of the verb "sothesetai" is concerned, there is no justification for the NASB translators to give it the meaning of "preserved." Paul uses the word "sozo" twenty-eight other times in his epistles, and in every one of those occurrences, he uses the word "sozo" to refer to spiritual salvation. In addition, the clues that are given to us in this passage all point to Paul speaking of spiritual salvation here as well. So the bottom line is the translation of the word "sothesetai" as "*women* will be preserved" is incorrect, while the translation of "she will be saved" is correct.

Now, the reason why I translated the word "teknogonias" (N-GFS, Noun – Genitive, Feminine, Singular) as "Son of this generation" is that I believe the word "teknogonia" comes from the nouns "teknon" meaning "child, son, daughter, offspring, descendant" and "genea" meaning "generation, one's own kind or race, descendant; fig., age, period of time (as in "to all generations")."[29] I do not believe it comes from the verbs "tikto" meaning "to give birth to; bear, produce" and "ginomai" meaning "to be, become, happen; to come into existence, be born" as is listed in the Strongest NIV Exhaustive Concordance.[30] (Note: The Strongest NIV Exhaustive Concordance lists the noun "teknon" as coming from the verb "tikto" and the noun "genea" as coming from the verb "ginomai.")

The reason why I believe the word "teknogonia" comes from the nouns "teknon" and "genea" is because Jerome of the Latin Vulgate translated the word "teknogonias" as "filiorum generationem."[31] The word "filiorum" is the genitive plural form of the noun "filius," which means "son, child,"[32] and the word "generationem" is the accusative singular form of the noun "generatio" which means "generation."[33] So Jerome's translation of the word "teknogonias" clearly shows us that he believed the word "teknogonia" came from the nouns "teknon" and "genea." Now, although I believe that Jerome correctly identified the roots of the word "teknogonias," I believe that he translated it inaccurately. To explain why I will briefly explain the way that Greek synthetic compounds work. (Note: Synthetic compounds are compounds where the two parts are set together and are not separable.)[34]

In synthetic compounds, the former word, a noun or a verb, loses all inflection (meaning only the stem is used), while the latter word often takes a form that it could not have had out of composition.[35] So with the word "teknogonias," the former word "teknon" has lost its inflection (tekno), and the latter word "genea" has taken a form that it could not have had out of composition (gonias). However, also with synthetic compounds, the latter word generally has the leading significance and is described or modified by the former word.[36] Because the latter word generally has the leading significance, Jerome gave the latter word the leading significance by putting it in the accusative case and giving it a verbal connotation. Furthermore, he put the former word in the genitive plural to modify the latter word, even though the word "teknogonias" is in the genitive singular. Thus, his translation was "generation/generating of children."

filiorum	generationem
of children	generation/generating

However, because women are not saved through the generation or generating of children, I believe that the former word "teknon" has the leading significance and is modified or limited by the latter word "genea." Hence, I believe that the Greek word "teknogonias" means "Son of this generation." (Note: The Greek word "teknogonias" is a hapax legomenon.")

tekno	gonias
Son	of this generation

Furthermore, there is also a definite article "tes" (the) right before the word "teknogonias" in the Greek. Many translations leave this out, such as the NIV. However, it is necessary to include the definite article in English because it is showing us that Paul is referring to something specific. If Paul were referring to childbearing in general, he would not have included the article before the word "teknogonias." (Note: In Greek, a noun cannot be indefinite when it has the article.)[37] So the fact that Paul used the article before the word "teknogonias" shows us that he was referring to something specific. And indeed, Paul was specifically referring to

Jesus Christ, the Son of that generation, who came to save those from all generations. See below for the Greek of verse fifteen.

[15]"sothesetai[1] de[2] dia[3] tes[4] teknogonias[5] ean[6] meinosin[7] en[8] pistei[9] kai[10] agape[11] kai[12] hagiasmo[13] meta[14] sophrosynes[15]."

[15]"she will be saved[1] but[2] through[3] the[4] Son of this generation[5] if[6] they continue[7] in[8] faith[9] and[10] love[11] and[12] holiness[13] with[14] discretion[15]."

Before I move on, I would like to say that I believe the reason that Paul chose to use the word "teknogonias" (teknon + **genea**) is that the husband was paying more attention to "endless **genea**logies" than he was to the fact that his wife was unsaved. For as we recall, Paul stated in verses 3–4 of chapter one that he did not want certain believers to pay attention to endless genealogies because it did not further the administration of God, which is (that people come to God) by faith (in Jesus Christ). And since genealogies are nothing more than "generations of people," I believe that Paul chose this word to make the point to the husband that talking about endless generations of people are useless in helping people come to know Christ. Therefore, Paul wants the husband to focus on the "Son of this generation" so that he can help his wife come to know Christ.

Also, before I move on, I want to point out one more thing. Some people assert that verses 11–15 in chapter two are not connected to verses 3–4 in chapter one. However, verse fifteen does, in fact, connect this passage back to verses 3–4 in chapter one. This is because the verb "sothesetai" is the future tense, indicative mood, passive voice, 3rd person singular form of the verb "sozo." Indeed, because the verb "sozo" is future tense, we know that this woman is currently unsaved. Furthermore, the fact that Paul has put the verb "sozo" in the indicative mood shows us that this woman is actively searching and seeking for the truth in regard to Jesus Christ. For Paul would not have confidently asserted (as a statement of fact) that "she will be saved" if she was not actively searching and seeking for the truth. So this woman is one of the unsaved persons spoken of in verse four of chapter one. And if she is connected back to one of the unsaved persons who was searching for the truth but was being separated away from the truth, then it connects her husband back to one of the certain ones who was teaching God's Word differently. So all of the clues in Paul's letter point to the man teaching his wife God's Word incorrectly, which would confirm to us that Paul is not permitting the man to teach his wife in verse twelve.

And finally, we come to the word "meinosin," which means "they continue." Now because people maintain that Paul is speaking about all Christian women throughout this whole passage (1 Tim. 2:9–15), they are always a bit perplexed as to why Paul would switch from plural to singular to plural. However, if Paul were referring to all Christian women throughout this whole passage, then there would not have been the need for him to switch from plural to singular to plural. But the reason that Paul does switch from the plural to singular to plural is as follows:

1) In verses 9–10, Paul is referring to all of the believing women in Ephesus. (He was also referring to all of the believing men in Ephesus in verse eight.) – **P**

2) In verses 11, 12, 15a, he is referring to the unsaved woman. – **S**

3) And in verse 15b, he is referring to all of the believers in Ephesus. – **P**

Thus, we can see why Paul needed to switch from plural to singular to plural. So, in verse fifteen, the unsaved woman is the subject of "sothesetai," and all of the believers in Ephesus are the subject of "meinosin."

To break this down even further, we know that Paul has asked all of the believers in Ephesus to do two things for those who are unsaved in his letter. They are as follows:

1) Pray for their salvation (vv. 1–6).

2) Be examples to them by acting in a way that is honoring to God, with holiness and discretion (vv. 8–10).

Therefore, these two things are what Paul wants the believers to "continue" to do when he states that [15]"...she will be saved if *they continue* in faith and love and holiness with discretion."

1) Faith and love

2) Holiness with discretion

"Faith and love" (1) refer back to praying for her salvation (1), and "holiness with discretion" (2) refers back to being godly examples to her (2).

So, this passage is not speaking about all Christian women, but rather, it is speaking about an unsaved Gentile woman who is searching and seeking for the truth. And since God appointed Paul as a proclaimer and messenger to the Gentiles (v. 7), he asks the believers in Ephesus to pray for her salvation (vv. 1–6) and to be godly examples to her (vv. 8–10). He then asks Timothy to ensure that this unsaved woman has an atmosphere that is conducive to learning where she can readily and willingly learn about Christ (v. 11). And although Paul wants this woman to learn, he wants to make absolutely certain that her believing Jewish husband is not the one who teaches her (v. 12). He also wants to ensure that this man does not continue to exercise his own jurisdiction apart from God (v. 12). For Paul does not want this woman to be deceived and fall into transgression as with happened with Eve (vv. 13–14). But because Paul can see that this woman is striving to obtain the truth, he is confident that she will be saved if the believers in Ephesus continue to do their part (v. 15).

In ending this chapter, I would like to say that the reason why many women feel called by God to teach is because God is calling them to teach. Jesus has entrusted God's Word to all believers. Women are part of God's royal priesthood. Yet this passage of Scripture has been so mangled and distorted that it has stopped more than half the body of Christ from teaching His Word. Men have become so fixated on power that they have ignored clear Scripture and the most basic Greek rules when translating passages that involve women. We have a world that is darkened, and the light within it has been greatly diminished because of these lies. But women are indeed the light of the world. They are to proclaim the excellencies of Him who called us out of darkness into His marvelous light. God's Word is clear that women can teach both unbelievers and believers. And women are not limited as to where they can teach. Truly, a royal priest teaches wherever God sends her.

1 TIMOTHY 2:12
(A clear contradiction of Scripture)

¹²"But I do not allow a woman to teach or
exercise authority over a man...."

Teaching:

⁴"For just as we have many members in one body and all the members do not have the same function,⁵so we, who are many, are one body in Christ, and individually members one of another. ⁶Since we have gifts that differ according to the grace given to us, *each of us is to exercise them accordingly*: if prophecy, according to the proportion of the faith; ⁷if service, in the serving; or **the one teaching, in the teaching**..." (Rom. 12:4–7).

²⁶"What is *the outcome* then, brethren? When you assemble, each one has a psalm, **has a teaching**, has a revelation, has a tongue, has an interpretation. Let all things be done for edification" (1 Cor. 14:26).

¹⁶"Let the word of Christ richly dwell within you, with all wisdom **teaching** and admonishing one another with psalms and hymns and spiritual songs, singing with thankfulness in your hearts to God" (Col. 3:16).

¹"You therefore, my son, be strong in the grace that is in Christ Jesus. ²The things which you have heard from me in the presence of many witnesses, entrust these to faithful people who will be able **to teach** others also" (2 Tim. 2:1–2).

Exercising Authority:

"⁷...but the woman is the glory of man. ⁸For man is not of woman, but woman of man; ⁹for indeed, man was not created because of the woman, but woman because of the man. ¹⁰For this reason, **the woman ought to have authority over her head** [the man]..." (1 Cor. 11:7–10).

[3]"But I want you to understand that Christ is the head [source] of every man, and the man is the head [source] of a woman, and God is the head [source] of Christ" (1 Cor. 11:3).

1 TIMOTHY 1 & 2

1 Paul, a messenger of Christ Jesus according to the commandment of God our Savior, and of Christ Jesus, our hope.

²To Timothy, my true child in the faith: Grace, mercy, and peace from God the Father and Christ Jesus our Lord.

Instructions to Certain Believers Not to Teach God's Word Differently and Warnings Against False Teachers of the Law

³As I urged you upon my departure for Macedonia, remain on at Ephesus so that you may instruct certain ones not to teach differently, ⁴nor to pay attention to myths and endless genealogies, because it causes those who are searching for the truth to be separated away from the truth rather than *furthering* the administration of God which is by faith. ⁵But the goal of our instruction is love from a pure heart and a good conscience and a sincere faith. ⁶For some, missing the mark of these things, have turned to fruitless discussion, ⁷wanting to be teachers of the Law, even though they do not understand either what they are saying or the matters about which they make confident assertions.

⁸But we know that the Law is good, if one uses it lawfully, ⁹realizing the fact that law is not made for a righteous person, but for those who are lawless and rebellious, for the ungodly and sinners, for the unholy and profane, for those who kill their fathers or mothers, for murderers ¹⁰and immoral people and homosexuals and kidnappers and liars and perjurers, and whatever else is contrary to sound teaching, ¹¹according to the glorious gospel of the blessed God, with which I have been entrusted.

¹²I thank Christ Jesus our Lord, who has strengthened me, because He considered me faithful, putting me into service, ¹³even though I was formerly a blasphemer and a persecutor and a violent aggressor. Yet I was shown mercy because I acted ignorantly in unbelief; ¹⁴and the grace of our Lord was more than abundant, with the faith and love which are in Christ Jesus. ¹⁵It is a trustworthy statement, deserving full acceptance, that Christ Jesus came into the world to save sinners, among whom I am foremost. ¹⁶Yet for this reason I found mercy, so that in me as the foremost, Jesus Christ

might demonstrate His perfect patience as an example for those who would believe in Him for eternal life. [17]Now to the King eternal, immortal, invisible, the only God, be honor and glory forever and ever. Amen.

[18]This command I entrust to you, Timothy, my son, in accordance with the prophecies previously made concerning you, that by them you fight the good fight, [19]keeping faith and a good conscience, which some have rejected and suffered shipwreck in regard to their faith. [20]Among these are Hymenaeus and Alexander, whom I have handed over to Satan, so that they will be taught not to blaspheme.

Instructions to All of the Believers in Ephesus

2 First of all, then, I urge that requests, prayers, intercessions, and thanksgivings be made on behalf of all people; [2]for kings and all who are in authority, so that we may lead a tranquil and quiet life in all godliness and dignity. [3]For this is good and acceptable in the sight of God our Savior, [4]who desires all people to be saved and to come to the knowledge of the truth. [5]For there is one God, and one mediator also between God and people, the man Christ Jesus, [6]who gave Himself as a ransom for all, the testimony given at the proper time. [7]For this I was appointed a proclaimer and a messenger (I am telling the truth, I am not lying) as a teacher of the Gentiles in faith and truth. [8]Therefore, I want the men in every place to pray, lifting up holy hands without anger and disputing. [9]Likewise, I want the women to adorn themselves with an honorable appearance, *one* with holiness and discretion, not with braided hair and gold or pearls or costly garments, [10]but rather with what suits women who profess to worship God by means of good works.

Instructions Concerning the Unsaved Gentile Woman and Her Believing Jewish Husband

[11]Let the woman learn in a peaceful atmosphere with all willingness. [12]But I do not permit the man to teach his wife, nor to exercise his own jurisdiction but to be in peacefulness. [13]For Adam was first formed, then Eve. [14]And Adam was not deceived, but the woman being deceived fell into transgression. [15]But she will be saved through the Son of this generation if they [the believers in Ephesus] continue in faith and love and holiness with discretion.

9

OVERSEERS, DEACONS, AND ELDERS

For centuries now, we have been taught that the office of overseers, deacons, and elders are positions for men only—offices to which women cannot attain. However, I do not believe that these are offices or positions of authority. I believe that they became such due to the belief that women could not attain to them. In this chapter, I will show evidence that an "episkopos" (overseer) is a "visitor," a believer who goes to the home of another believer to render aid, service, or care. A "diakonos" (deacon) is a "servant," a believer who serves other believers within the church. And a "presbyteros" (elder) is an "older believer" who is chosen for more difficult matters because they are spiritually mature.

Episkopos	Diakonos	Presbyteros
Visitor	Servant	Older believer

Before I begin, I would like to say that in Matthew 23:8–10, Jesus said, [8]"But do not be called Rabbi; for One is your Teacher, and you are all brothers [brethren]. [9]Do not call *anyone* on earth your father; for One is your Father, He who is in heaven. [10]Do not be called leaders; for One is your Leader, *that is*, Christ." Therefore, it is clear by these words that Jesus does not want any one of us to be called by titles. We are all brethren—brothers and sisters. We are all equals, one in the body of Christ. We are fellow laborers, fellow workers, and servants of our Lord and Savior. No one is over another, and no one is to claim a title for themselves.

In 1 Timothy 3:1–7, we supposedly see Paul talking about the office of overseer. Verse one says, [1]"It is a trustworthy statement: if any man aspires to the office of overseer [episkopes], it is a fine work he desires *to do*." Now I would like to begin here by saying that the rendering of "if any **man** aspires" is incorrect. This is because the actual Greek word that is used is "tis." "Tis" means "one, anyone, anything; some, someone, something."[1] It is a word that refers to both genders and people in general. It is the same word that is used in salvation passages such as John 6:51, which states, [51]"I am the living bread that came down out of heaven; if **anyone** [tis] eats of this bread, he will live forever." So clearly, the word "tis" refers to "anyone," not just men. Furthermore, the rendering of the Greek word "epithymei" as "he desires" is also incorrect because it gives the false impression that Paul is speaking only to men. For just as the word "zesei" (translated as "he will live" in John 6:51) is 3rd person singular and refers to "he/she/it," so also the word "epithymei" is 3rd person singular and refers to "he/she/it."[2] Therefore, the singular "they" should be used in the English language to ensure that one understands that all believers are included.

Now we come to the Greek word "episkopes," which is translated as "the office of overseer." The word "episkope" is used four times in the New Testament. Therefore, to get an understanding of the true meaning of this word, let us take a look at how this word is rendered in each of the other three passages that it is used.

> Luke 19:43–44 — [43]"For the days will come upon you when your enemies will throw up a barricade against you, and surround you and hem you in on every side, [44]and they will level you to the ground and your children within you, and they will not leave in you one stone upon another, because you did not recognize the time of your **visitation** [episkopes]."

> 1 Peter 2:12 — [12]"Keep your behavior excellent among the Gentiles, so that in the thing in which they slander you as evildoers, they may because of your good deeds, as they observe *them*, glorify God in the day of **visitation** [episkopes]."

These two times, the translators have translated the word "episkope" as "visitation." The third passage is:

> Acts 1:20 — [20]"For it is written in the book of Psalms, 'LET HIS HOMESTEAD BE MADE DESOLATE, AND LET NO ONE

DWELL IN IT' [Ps. 69:25]; and 'LET ANOTHER MAN TAKE HIS **OFFICE** [episkopen] [Ps. 109:8].'"

(Note: The word that is translated as "office" in Psalm 109:8 is "pequdda" in Hebrew. "Pequdda" means "appointment, charge, visitation.")[3]

Here, the translators have translated the word "episkope" as "office." However, I believe that it should also be translated as "visitation." There is nothing in the passage that would justify the rendering of "office." Indeed, if one reads the rest of the passage, Acts 1:21–26, they will find that Peter wanted one of the men who had accompanied them all the time, whom the Lord Jesus went in and out among, beginning with the baptism of John until the day that He was taken up from them, **to become a witness** with them of His resurrection (vv. 21–22). So Matthias was not being chosen for a stationary position in a church, but rather, he was chosen to go out with them to testify of Christ and of His resurrection. Indeed, Peter and the other apostles did not stay in one place. They visited many places continually throughout their lives. Therefore, they chose someone to occupy this "service" (of visitation) and "being sent out as a messenger" from which Judas had turned aside (v. 25). Matthias was not chosen to "oversee" others in a church, but instead, he was chosen for "visitation" as a messenger, to give testimony about Christ.

Thus, I believe that verse one should be translated as,

> [1]"It is a trustworthy statement: If anyone sets their heart on visitation [episkopes], it is an excellent work they desire."

The question is, "What is meant in verse one by visitation?" Does "visitation" here mean visiting different places to testify to unbelievers about Christ as it did in Acts 1:20? No, because 1 Timothy 3:5 tells us that this work is to the church of God, those in the body of Christ. This "visitation" is to fellow believers. Moreover, in verse five, we have a clue as to what this "visitation" involves. Verse five says, [5]"...(but if a man does not know how to manage his own household, how will he **take care of** the church of God?)" Or, if accurately rendered, it would read as, [5]"For if one does not know how to be devoted to their own family, how will they take care of the people of God?" Now to digress for a moment, why did I render verse five as such? I translated verse five as such because, once again, the word that the translators translate as "man" is "tis" in Greek and means "one,

181

anyone, anything; some, someone, something." Also, the word that the translators translate as "manage" is "proistemi" in Greek and means either "to manage, direct, lead" or "to devote oneself, busy oneself to."[4] When the translators use it of men, they use words such as "manage" or "lead," but when they use it of people in general, they use the word "engage" (the NIV uses the word "devote"), which I believe is its accurate meaning. Indeed, one does not manage their family, for restaurants get managed. One should be engaged (busy or occupied) with or devoted to their family. Now returning, in verse five, the word that is translated as "take care of" is "epimeleomai" in Greek. "Epimeleomai" means "to take care of; look after."[5] It is used only three times in the New Testament, once here, and two times in Luke 10:34–35 in the story about the Good Samaritan. Now the story goes that a man was going down from Jerusalem to Jericho and fell among robbers, and they stripped him and beat him, and went away leaving him half dead. Now a priest and a Levite saw him and passed by on the other side of the road. But a Samaritan came upon him and had compassion on him. Luke 10:33–35 says, [33]"But a Samaritan, who was on a journey, came upon him; and when he saw him, he felt compassion, [34]and came to him and bandaged up his wounds, pouring oil and wine on *them*; and he put him on his own beast, and brought him to an inn and **took care** of him. [35]On the next day he took out two denarii and gave them to the innkeeper and said, '**Take care** of him; and whatever more you spend, when I return I will repay you.'"

So here, we can see the word "epimeleomai" being used for caring for another person in need. It is showing deep concern for another. It is helping a person in their affliction and their distress. It is the type of care that is at the very heart of God and is shown to us by Christ Himself. It is the type of care that Christ wants us to give to others. It is loving care, selfless care, and compassionate care. The word "epimeleomai" is used twice in this story of the man who was beaten and left for dead. Notice the Samaritan compassionately cares for him, selflessly giving of himself and his money and possessions. And the only other time this word is used in the Bible is right here in verse five. So I believe that this is the nature of the "visitation" to those in the body of Christ that Paul is talking about. It is about visiting a fellow believer in need, in order to "take care of" or "epimeleomai" them. It is visiting them, seeing what their needs are, and providing for their needs.

Next, verse two says, ²"An overseer [episkopon], then, must be above reproach, the husband of one wife, temperate, prudent, respectable, hospitable, able to teach...." Now I believe this verse is translated accurately except for the word "overseer." Clearly, if "episkope" refers to "visitation," then "episkopos" refers to the "visitor." (Note: "Episkope" (v. 1) is a noun and refers to the "service or act" as opposed to "episkopos" (v. 2) which refers to the "person.") Therefore, I believe that verse two should read as,

> ²"The visitor [episkopon], then, must be above reproach, the husband of one wife, temperate, prudent, respectable, hospitable, able to teach...."

Also, it is easy to see why Paul wants "visitors" to have these characteristics. The main job of a "visitor" was to take care of sick, injured, elderly, or bedridden believers who could not care for themselves. Therefore, since they were entering the homes of believers who were in a weakened state, they must be above reproach; otherwise, they could easily take advantage of the person they were serving. Now, many take the next requirement, the husband of one wife, to mean that only men were eligible to be an "episkopos." However, it certainly does not mean this. Paul has already stated in verse one that "episkope" was open to "anyone." Hence, verses 2–7 are showing the requirements that must be met by a believer to be an "episkopos." And so, because only men were polygamists, this requirement is addressed solely to men. Paul wants any visitors who are male to have only one wife because one cannot be a godly example to others if they are sinning themselves by practicing polygamy. Furthermore, Paul also wants those who visit others to be temperate—mild or restrained in their behavior or attitude. He wants them to be prudent—to use good judgment. He wants them to be respectable—well thought of by others. He wants them to be hospitable—warm, friendly, cordial. And he also wants them to be able to teach. The reason why it was important for a visitor to be able to teach was that many of the people they would visit would be unable to get to a church. Therefore, since these people could not get to a church to hear the Word of God, Paul wanted believers to bring the Word of God to these people. There were no audio recordings or televised sermons in that day, and people did not have their own copy of the Bible to read as we have today. The only way these people could hear the Word of God was if someone came to them to teach them.

Moving along to verse three, we can also see that Paul wants to ensure that visitors are not addicted to wine or pugnacious (violent), but gentle, peaceable, and free from the love of money so that they would not be tempted to steal. Furthermore, in verse four (my rendering), visitors must also be rightly devoted (physically, emotionally, spiritually) to their own family, having children who are willing (hypotage—see "Hypotasso, Part I and II" for review) with all gravity. The reason why Paul wants children to be "willing" is that he knows that children who are forced to accompany their parents against their will would likely be impatient and unruly. Therefore, Paul wants children who are consenting, who will give of themselves readily and cheerfully, and who will not make the sick or elderly person feel like they are an inconvenience. He also wants children to be able to grasp the seriousness of the situation so that they will act appropriately. Furthermore, Paul does not want the visitor to be a new convert so that they will not become conceited (because they are teaching) and fall into the judgment incurred by the devil. And finally, visitors must have a good reputation with those outside the church. This requirement is so that no one will think that improper things are happening inside the home. If unbelievers see believers entering into the private homes of others, they might have reason to accuse them of ulterior motives if they are not of sound character and good reputation.

So I believe that an "episkopos" is a "visitor," not an "overseer" with a stationary position in a church. And for further proof of this, let us now turn to Titus, chapter one. Indeed, the first chapter of Titus makes no sense if an "episkopos" (v. 7) is an "overseer" with a stationary position in a church. However, if an "episkopos" is a "visitor," it makes perfect sense. Let us take a look.

In the first chapter of Titus, we can see that Paul wants Titus to appoint older believers in every city of Crete (v. 5) so that they can do two things. (Notice here that Paul does not want Titus to appoint older believers in every "church" of Crete, but rather in every "city.")

    1) Exhort in sound doctrine (v. 9).

    2) Refute those who contradict (v. 9).

The reason why Paul wants Titus to do this is because of what we read in verses 10–11. Verses 10–11 read as, [10]"For there are many rebellious men, empty talkers and deceivers, especially those of the circumcision, [11]who must be silenced because they are upsetting whole families, teaching things they should not *teach* for the sake of sordid gain." Now, to get a better understanding of what was happening here, we need to understand several things. First, the word that is translated as "upsetting" in verse eleven is "anatrepo" in Greek." "Anatrepo" comes from two Greek words, "ana" and "trope." "Ana" means "each, in turn, among" and "trope" means "shifting, turning, variation, change."[6] So what was happening here was that these men were literally causing a doctrinal shift to occur in the faith of whole families, and they were doing so one family at a time. The second thing that we need to understand is that these men were going door to door to do this. And the third thing that we need to understand is that these men were wolves in sheep's clothing. They were unbelievers who were claiming the name of Christ so that they could enter into a home. Then, once inside, they were unleashing their foul and depraved teachings when the whole family had gathered around. For confirmation of this, let us look at the words of Paul.

> 1) [12]"One of themselves, a prophet of their own, said 'Cretans are always liars, evil beasts, lazy gluttons.' [13]This testimony is true. For this reason reprove them severely so that they may be sound in the faith, [14]not paying attention to Jewish myths and commandments of men who turn away from [reject] the truth" (Titus 1:12–14).

> 2) [15]"To the pure, all things are pure; but to those who are defiled and unbelieving, nothing is pure, but both their mind and their conscience are defiled" (Titus 1:15).

> 3) [16]"They profess to know God, but by *their* deeds they deny *Him*, being detestable and disobedient and worthless for any good deed" (Titus 1:16).

We can see by the words of Paul that these men were unbelievers. We know this by the fact that Paul calls one of them a prophet of THEIR OWN (v. 12). We can also see that these men were professing to know God (obviously through Jesus Christ), but by their deeds (the things they were doing and saying) they were denying Him (v. 16). In fact, these unbelieving men were so defiled that nothing was pure (v. 15). For they did not even wince when they claimed the name of Christ and then taught what was contrary to sound doctrine (v. 16) because both their mind and their conscience were defiled (v. 15). As a result, Paul wanted these men, who were listening to men who rejected Christ outright (v. 14), to be reproved severely so that they would be sound in the faith that they were claiming for themselves (v. 13).

So again, the scenario was that predominantly Jewish men were going door to door around the city of Crete and entering into homes on the pretense that they believed Christ to be the Messiah. Then, once they were inside and the family was gathered, they would teach what their crooked hearts desired for the sake of sordid gain. Thus, the families, thinking these men were believers, started to have a shift in their faith. They started to believe things that were not in accordance with the teaching. Consequently, Paul wanted Titus to stay in Crete and appoint older believers in every city so that they could go door to door and both exhort in sound doctrine and refute those who contradict. So the "episkopos" (v. 7) was a "visitor," not an "overseer" with a stationary position in a church. Indeed, the reason these men were shifting "whole families" is because they were going door to door and spreading their lies. Therefore, Paul now wants older believers to hold fast the faithful Word, which is in accordance with the teaching (v. 9) and go door to door to teach the truth.

I would also like to point out that some of the character requirements mentioned in Titus 1:5–9 are identical to the ones stated in 1 Timothy 3:2–7, while some of them are different. The reason that some of them are different is that the task is different. In 1 Timothy chapter three, the task was for believers to visit the homes of other believers to take care of their needs and teach them the Word of God. The task here, however, was to go door to door to exhort in sound doctrine and refute those who contradict. As a result, some of the homes that they would visit would be to those of the perpetrators of the false teachings. This is why Paul wants the visitors in this situation to be "older." He wants wiser, more mature believers for this task because it was more difficult and potentially more volatile. Furthermore, the potentially volatile and unpredictable nature of this task was also likely why it was not mentioned for the children of these visitors to be "willing." Paul likely did not want young people to accompany their parents on this particular task.

Furthermore, I would like to say that the reason we do not see Paul giving a job description but only character requirements is because the type of work will vary (for a visitor) depending on the need of the person or the given situation. If "episkope" referred to an "office," then certainly Paul would have given a description of the duties to be carried out because the duties would be fixed.

So, I believe that 1 Timothy 3:1–7 should be translated as follows:

> [1]"It is a trustworthy statement: If anyone sets their heart on visitation, it is an excellent work they desire. [2]The visitor, then, must be above reproach, the husband of one wife, temperate, prudent, respectable, hospitable, able to teach, [3]not an excessive drinker, not violent but gentle, peaceable, free from the love of money, [4]one who is rightly devoted to their own family, having children that are willing with all gravity. [5]For if one does not know how to be devoted to their own family, how will they take care of the people of God? [6]And not a new convert so that they will not become conceited and fall into judgment incurred by the devil. [7]They must also have a good reputation with those outside so that they will not fall into disgrace and the snare of the devil."

Today's definition of an "episkopos" is an "overseer." In this position, a few select men preside over church affairs. Yet who oversees them? Are they more knowledgeable in the ways of God than those they are overseeing? Are not all believers to exhort one another in the ways of God; or only a select few? There is no doubt that over time an "episkopos" became a position of authority due to the belief that women could not attain this position. For if women could not attain this position, then surely an "episkopos" could not be a "visitor" who serves the sick, elderly and disabled. For that is woman's work. But I must ask, "Do those who currently hold this lofty position and title still want it if its true definition is a 'visitor'?" Would they still want it with the lack of recognition and the toil and monotony of the work involved?" The fact is that most of the world's "episkopos" have been and are women. Women are the ones who go to visit others to relieve their distress and take care of their needs. But today, even women lack in this area. We are told that nursing homes and the government do these jobs now, all the while many fellow believers sit in their homes alone, wasting away. No church body acknowledges them. They sit in a dirty house, isolated, with no one to help. I believe the true meaning of "episkope" no longer exists in today's church. It has been lost, changed from its real meaning. But if there is a physical need to be met outside the church for another believer, women are always the first ones to step forth. I believe that many men will be surprised to learn when they get to heaven that they were not an "episkopos" at all and that many of the women that they excluded were the actual ones. Remember Jesus' words, "Whoever exalts himself shall be humbled; and whoever humbles himself shall be exalted" (Matt. 23:12).

So again, I believe the word "episkope" means "visitation," and "episkopos" refers to the believer who actually goes out and visits other believers to take care of their needs. It is not an office to aspire to, but rather, it is a work of service to others. And all in the body of Christ who have this heart's desire may participate as long as they meet the requirements as set forth by Paul.

Now we come to the so-called position of "deacon," which is "diakonos" in Greek. In 1 Timothy 3:1–7, Paul has just gone over the requirements that are needed for believers who desire to **"visit"** other believers **outside** of a church body in order to serve them and care for their needs. Now, in verses 8–13, Paul is talking to believers who desire to **"serve"** other believers **within** a church body. Nowhere is this more clearly seen than in Romans 16:1–2. It says, ¹"I commend to you our sister Phoebe, who is a servant [diakonon] of the church which is at Cenchrea; ²that you receive her in the Lord in a manner worthy of the saints, and that you help her in whatever matter she may have need of you; for she herself has also been a helper of many, and of myself as well." So here, we can see that Phoebe is a "servant" or "diakonos" of the church or body of believers who gather at Cenchrea. She serves those "within" the church body.

Another thing that we can see from this passage is that since Phoebe is referred to as a "diakonos," we know that women are included when Paul speaks in reference to "diakonoi." This shows us that, in verse eleven, Paul is not giving requirements for "wives of deacons," as many men have claimed, but rather that Paul is giving requirements for women who desire to serve other believers within the church just as he did the men in verses 8–10. Indeed, Paul would not have given instructions to "wives of diakonoi" but then failed to provide instructions for women who were the actual "diakonoi" such as Phoebe. Therefore, it is clear that Paul is speaking to women who want to serve other believers within the church body. Sadly, even with this explicit reference to Phoebe as "diakonos," men try to justify that Phoebe was a different kind of servant than were the men. However, the instructions for "diakonoi" are given solely here in

1 Timothy 3:8–13, and nowhere in these verses does Paul state that men and women have different functions or roles.

Still, the question remains, "Why does Paul address the men and women separately?" The men and women are given almost identical characteristics to have if they want to be "servants" of the church. Men and women are both to be "semnos," which means "worthy of respect"[7] or "dignified." Men are not to be double-tongued, and women are not to be slanderers. Men are not to be addicted to much wine, and women are to be temperate (in the use of alcohol). Men are not to pursue dishonest gain, and women are to be faithful in all things. So both men and women have nearly identical requirements. However, the reason that I believe Paul addresses the men and women separately is because Paul gives the men in this particular congregation an additional requirement. And that is, Paul wants these men to first be "tested" (v. 10). The question is, "Why would only the men need to be tested?" I believe it is because the men were angrily disputing. If we remember, in chapter two, verse eight, Paul wanted the men to pray, lifting up holy hands without wrath and dissention. Therefore, it is clear that these men were not meeting the qualifications as set forth by Paul, which is likely the reason why Paul also tells the men that they are to hold to the mystery of the faith with a "clear conscience" (v. 9). Consequently, Paul wanted these men to exhibit godly behavior before they served within this particular congregation. Then, once they demonstrated that they were beyond reproach, Timothy was to let them serve. (Note: In 1 Timothy 3:10, 13, the words "as deacons" are added by the translators.)

The bottom line is women are undeniably included as "diakonoi." Again, it is a complete impossibility that Paul would have addressed "wives of diakonoi" but then failed to address "female diakonoi" such as Phoebe. The reason the women are addressed separately from the men is that the men had shown themselves to be quarrelsome and angry. The women, on the other hand, are not shown to be quarrelsome and angry. They were acting in a dignified manner. As a result, the women did not need to be tested.

I would also like to point out that the requirement for husbands to have only one wife is likewise given for men who want to be a "diakonos" (v. 12), just as it was for men who wanted to be an "episkopos" (v. 2). Therefore, since Phoebe is a "diakonos," this is further proof that this

189

requisite is not excluding women from being an "episkopos" but rather is simply giving male believers an additional requirement. As Paul said, "episkope" is open to "anyone."

The next point that I would like to make is that, in Romans 16:1, the NASB translators have correctly translated the word "diakonos" as "servant." They have incorrectly rendered the word "diakonoi" as "deacons" in 1 Timothy 3:8, 12 (also Philippians 1:1). This is because the true meaning of this word is "servant." For further proof of this, let us look at the following Scripture.

> [25]"But Jesus called them to Himself and said, 'You know that the rulers of the Gentiles lord it over them, and *their* great men exercise authority over them. [26]It is not this way among you, but whoever wishes to become great among you shall be your **servant** [diakonos]...'" (Matt. 20:25–26).

> [13]"Then the king said **to the servants** [diakonois], 'Bind him hand and foot, and throw him into the outer darkness...'" (Matt. 22:13).

> [8]"But do not be called Rabbi; for One is your Teacher, and you are all brothers. [9]Do not call *anyone* on earth your father; for One is your Father, He who is in heaven. [10]Do not be called leaders; for One is your Leader, *that is*, Christ. [11]But the greatest among you shall be your **servant** [diakonos]" (Matt. 23:8–11).

> [35]"Sitting down, He called the twelve and said to them, 'If anyone wants to be first, he shall be last of all and **servant** [diakonos] of all'" (Mark 9:35).

> [42]"Calling them to Himself, Jesus said to them, 'You know that those who are recognized as rulers of the Gentiles lord it over them; and their great men exercise authority over them. [43]But it is not this way among you, but whoever wishes to become great among you shall be your **servant** [diakonos]...'" (Mark 10:42–43).

> [5]"His mother said **to the servants** [diakonois], 'Whatever He says to you, do it'" (John 2:5).

[9]"When the headwaiter tasted the water which had become wine, and did not know where it came from (but the **servants** [diakonoi] who had drawn the water knew), the headwaiter called the bridegroom, [10]and said to him, 'Every man serves the good wine first, and when *the people* have drunk freely, *then he serves* the poorer *wine*; but you have kept the good wine until now'" (John 2:9–10).

[26]"If anyone serves Me, he must follow Me; and where I am, there My **servant** [diakonos] will be also; if anyone serves Me, the Father will honor him" (John 12:26).

[8]"For I say that Christ has become a **servant** [diakonon] to the circumcision on behalf of the truth of God to confirm the promises *given* to the fathers..." (Rom. 15:8).

[5]"What is Apollos? And what is Paul? **Servants** [diakonoi] through whom you believed, even as the Lord gave *opportunity* to each one" (1 Cor. 3:5).

[5]"Not that we are adequate in ourselves to consider anything as *coming* from ourselves, but our adequacy is from God, [6]who also made us adequate *as* **servants** [diakonous] of a new covenant, not of the letter but of the Spirit; for the letter kills, but the Spirit gives life" (2 Cor. 3:5–6).

[4]"...but in everything commending ourselves as **servants** [diakonoi] of God, in much endurance, in afflictions, in hardships, in distresses..." (2 Cor. 6:4).

[15]"Therefore it is not surprising if his **servants** [diakonoi] also disguise themselves as **servants** [diakonoi] of righteousness, whose end will be according to their deeds" (2 Cor. 11:15).

[23]"Are they **servants** [diakonoi] of Christ?—I speak as if insane—I more so; in far more labors, in far more imprisonments, beaten times without number, often in danger of death" (2 Cor. 11:23).

[7]"...just as you learned *it* from Epaphras, our beloved fellow bond-servant, who is a faithful **servant** [diakonos] of Christ on our behalf..." (Col. 1:7).

[7]"As to all my affairs, Tychicus, *our* beloved brother and faithful **servant** [diakonos] and fellow bond-servant in the Lord, will bring you information" (Col. 4:7).

[6]"In pointing out these things to the brethren, you will be a good **servant** [diakonos] of Christ Jesus, *constantly* nourished on the words of the faith and of the sound doctrine which you have been following" (1 Tim. 4:6).

So again, the true meaning of the word "diakonos" is "servant." This becomes even more evident when we see that, in most of these verses, the translators could not get away with translating the word "diakonos" as "deacon." If they did, then their error would be obvious. For example, consider the following:

[25]"But Jesus called them to Himself and said, 'You know that the rulers of the Gentiles lord it over them, and *their* great men exercise authority over them. [26]It is not this way among you, but whoever wishes to become great among you shall be your **deacon** [diakonos]...'" (Matt. 20:25–26).

[35]"Sitting down, He called the twelve and said to them, 'If anyone wants to be first, he shall be last of all and **deacon** [diakonos] of all'" (Mark 9:35).

[26]"If anyone serves Me, he must follow Me; and where I am, there My **deacon** [diakonos] will be also; if anyone serves Me, the Father will honor him" (John 12:26).

Furthermore, the NASB translators have also taken the liberty of translating the word "diakonos" as "minister" seven times, such as we find in Ephesians 3:7 and Colossians 1:23, 25. In these verses, Paul supposedly calls himself a "minister." However, Paul is not calling himself a "minister." Instead, he is with humility and contentedness, calling himself a "servant." Consider the following verses again:

[25]"But Jesus called them to Himself and said, 'You know that the rulers of the Gentiles lord it over them, and *their* great men exercise authority over them. [26]It is not this way among you, but whoever

192

wishes to become great among you shall be your **minister** [diakonos]…'" (Matt. 20:25–26).

[35]"Sitting down, He called the twelve and said to them, 'If anyone wants to be first, he shall be last of all and **minister** [diakonos] of all'" (Mark 9:35).

[26]"If anyone serves Me, he must follow Me; and where I am, there My **minister** [diakonos] will be also; if anyone serves Me, the Father will honor him" (John 12:26).

So the translators have taken the liberty of translating the word "diakonos" as "deacon" or "minister" only when the context does not point out their error. However, the reason that the translation of "deacon" or "minister" does not fit with most verses is that the word "diakonos" refers to a person of low stature who serves another. A "deacon" or "minister," on the other hand, has an elevated status. Therefore, it does not reflect the true meaning of the word "diakonos." Consequently, the translators have no justification for translating the word "diakonos" as either "deacon" or "minister." Indeed, the true meaning of the word "diakonos" is "servant." Therefore, it should always and without exception, be translated as "servant."

Thus, I would translate 1 Timothy 3:8–13 as follows:

[8]"Menservants, likewise, are to be dignified, not double-tongued, nor indulging in much wine, nor pursuing dishonest gain, [9]but holding to the mystery of the faith with a clear conscience. [10]And also these, let first be tested; then let them serve if they are beyond reproach. [11]Women, likewise, are to be dignified, not slanderers, but temperate, faithful in all things. [12]Let servants be husbands of one wife, rightly devoted to their children and their own families. [13]For those who have served well obtain for themselves a good standing and great confidence in the faith that is in Christ Jesus."

Now we come to the so-called position of "elder," which is "presbyteros" in Greek. Now, in beginning, I would like to say that there are no qualifications given anywhere in the New Testament for a "presbyteros" as there is for an "episkopos" and "diakonos." This is a little odd if "presbyteros" refers to "a ruling class of elders." One would think that a ruling class of elders would have to meet certain requirements as well. But the reason that there are no qualifications given is that the word "presbyteros" is an adjective, not a noun. Therefore, it simply describes someone who is "older." For example, the following verse is translated correctly by the NASB translators.

> [25]"Now his **older** [presbyteros] son was in the field, and when he came and approached the house, he heard music and dancing" (Luke 15:25).

So, in this sentence, the adjective "presbyteros" (older) is modifying the noun "huios" (son). Therefore, it is speaking of his older son, not his son, who was an elder. It is also essential to know that a Greek adjective can be used alone (with or without the article) as a noun. This is called a substantive adjective. In this situation, if the adjective is masculine, it is referring to "man/men, people (both men and women), or ones." If the adjective is feminine, it is referring to "woman/women." And if the adjective is neuter, it is referring to a "class or things."[8] So in cases such as this, again, if the adjective is functioning as a noun, it would be appropriate for the translators to add the word "man/men, woman/women, people or ones." For example, the NASB translators have correctly rendered the following:

> [9]"When they heard it, they *began* to go out one by one, beginning with the **older ones** [presbyteron], and He was left alone, and the woman, where she was, in the center *of the court*" (John 8:9).

> [1]"Do not sharply rebuke an **older man** [presbytero], but *rather* appeal to *him* as a father, *to* the younger men as brothers, [2]the **older women** [presbyteras] as mothers, *and* the younger women as sisters, in all purity" (1 Tim. 5:1–2).

Again, the word "presbyteros" is an adjective, not a noun. Therefore, below I have given some examples of how the word "presbyteros" should be rendered, both when it modifies a noun and also when it stands alone and functions as a noun. I have also first given the rendering of the NASB for comparison.

> [3]"Then the chief priest and the **elders** [presbyteroi] of the people were gathered together in the court of the high priest, named Caiaphas; [4]and they plotted together to seize Jesus by stealth and kill Him" (Matt. 26:3–4).

³"Then the chief priest and the **older** [presbyteroi] people were gathered together in the court of the high priest, named Caiaphas; ⁴and they plotted together to seize Jesus by stealth and kill Him" (Matt. 26:3–4).

²⁰"But the chief priests and the **elders** [presbyteroi] persuaded the crowds to ask for Barabbas and to put Jesus to death" (Matt. 27:20).

²⁰"But the chief priests and the **older people** [presbyteroi] persuaded the crowds to ask for Barabbas and to put Jesus to death" (Matt. 27:20).

³"When he heard about Jesus, he sent some Jewish **elders** [presbyterous] asking Him to come and save the life of his slave" (Luke 7:3).

³"When he heard about Jesus, he sent **older** [presbyterous] Jews asking Him to come and save the life of his slave" (Luke 7:3).

¹⁷"'AND IT SHALL BE IN THE LAST DAYS,' God says, 'THAT I WILL POUR FORTH OF MY SPIRIT ON ALL MANKIND; AND YOUR SONS AND YOUR DAUGHTERS SHALL PROPHESY, AND YOUR YOUNG MEN SHALL SEE VISIONS, AND YOUR **OLD MEN** [presbyteroi] SHALL DREAM DREAMS...'" (Acts 2:17).

¹⁷"'AND IT SHALL BE IN THE LAST DAYS,' God says, 'THAT I WILL POUR OUT MY SPIRIT ON ALL FLESH; AND YOUR SONS AND YOUR DAUGHTERS WILL PROPHESY, AND YOUR YOUNG WILL SEE VISIONS, AND YOUR **OLD** [presbyteroi] WILL DREAM DREAMS...'" (Acts 2:17).

¹⁷"The **elders** [presbyteroi] who rule well are to be considered worthy of double honor, especially those who work hard at preaching and teaching" (1 Tim. 5:17).

¹⁷"The rightly devoted **older people** [presbyteroi] are to be considered worthy of double honor, especially those laboring in speech and teaching" (1 Tim. 5:17).

[19]"Do not receive an accusation against an **elder** [presbyterou] except on the basis of two or three witnesses" (1 Tim. 5:19).

[19]"Do not receive an accusation against an **older person** [presbyterou] except on the basis of two or three witnesses" (1 Tim. 5:19).

[5]"For this reason I left you in Crete, that you would set in order what remains and appoint **elders** [presbyterous] in every city as I directed you..." (Titus 1:5).

[5]"For this reason I left you in Crete, that you would set in order what remains and appoint **older people** [presbyterous] in every city as I directed you..." (Titus 1:5).

In these verses, we see the proper way to translate the adjective "presbyteros" both when it modifies a noun and also when it stands alone and functions as a noun. It does not refer to an elected group of officials or a ruling class of elders. It refers to older people, both in the community and in the church. Indeed, ALL older believers who rightly devote themselves are to be considered worthy of double honor, not just a select few.

In ending this chapter, I would like to say that men today try to say that the reason women were not present at the last supper was that only men were to be sent out as apostles. However, I believe the reason only men were present was that they had not yet learned what the women learned. They had not yet learned "servanthood." Throughout the New Testament, we can see women serving Jesus and the disciples. And throughout the New Testament, we can see the men bickering over which one of them would be greatest in the kingdom of heaven. Because of this bickering, Jesus repeatedly told them the following:

> [25]"You know that the rulers of the Gentiles lord it over them, and *their* great men exercise authority over them. [26]It is not this way among you, but whoever wishes to become great among you shall be your servant, [27]and whoever wishes to be first among you shall be your slave; [28]just as the Son of Man did not come to be served, but to serve, and to give His life a ransom for many" (Matt. 20:25–28).

So, Jesus repeatedly told the disciples that they were to be servants to one another, yet the disciples were resistant to His teaching. For even at the last supper, hours before Jesus was to be crucified, we can still see that the disciples were bickering over which one of them was the greatest (Luke 22:24). Therefore, I believe that only men were present at the last supper because only they needed a remedial session. They needed to learn what the women had already learned. At the last supper, Jesus got down on His knees so that He could wash the feet of His disciples (John 13:4–17). He gave them a hands-on, visual remedial session to show His disciples what servanthood looked like. The women had already learned this. They had already learned servanthood and were ready to go out for Christ. As a result, they were the first ones that Christ appeared to after His resurrection and were the first ones that were sent out as messengers. The women were happy with their title role of "servant," happy to wash the feet of their fellow brethren.

But just as Jesus' male disciples were resistant to this teaching of servant-hood, so also men today are resistant. Despite Christ's clear and simple words, men seek to gain dominion over those in the body of Christ; men seek to exercise authority over those in the body of Christ. They forget that Christ said, **"IT IS NOT THIS WAY AMONG YOU!"** (Mark 10:43).

Some will always insist that Paul set up a church government. But I say that there is no government in the body of Christ—only a family of believers who use their gifts given to them by God in order to serve one another. Jesus, our example, came not to be served but to serve. Indeed, Jesus is King of kings and Lord of lords and creator of all people, yet He chose to serve us. So are we to be anything more? There should be no thought in any believer's mind in wanting to gain authority over another. No believer should strive to advance in the ranks. There are no hierarchies. We are all on equal footing. We are servants who get on our knees to wash one another's feet. We must always remember that Jesus has NOT called us to servant leadership because One is our Leader, Christ. Truly, He has called us to servanthood.

1 TIMOTHY 3:1-7

¹"It is a trustworthy statement: If anyone sets their heart on visitation, it is an excellent work they desire. ²The visitor, then, must be above reproach, the husband of one wife, temperate, prudent, respectable, hospitable, able to teach, ³not an excessive drinker, not violent but gentle, peaceable, free from the love of money, ⁴one who is rightly devoted to their own family, having children that are willing with all gravity. ⁵For if one does not know how to be devoted to their own family, how will they take care of the people of God? ⁶And not a new convert so that they will not become conceited and fall into judgment incurred by the devil. ⁷They must also have a good reputation with those outside so that they will not fall into disgrace and the snare of the devil."

1 TIMOTHY 3:8-13

⁸"Menservants, likewise, are to be dignified, not double-tongued, nor indulging in much wine, nor pursuing dishonest gain, ⁹but holding to the mystery of the faith with a clear conscience. ¹⁰And also these, let first be tested; then let them serve if they are beyond reproach. ¹¹Women, likewise, are to be dignified, not slanderers, but temperate, faithful in all things. ¹²Let servants be husbands of one wife, rightly devoted to their children and their own families. ¹³For those who have served well obtain for themselves a good standing and great confidence in the faith that is in Christ Jesus."

1 TIMOTHY 5:17

¹⁷"The rightly devoted older people are to be considered worthy of double honor, especially those laboring in speech and teaching."

TITUS 1

1 Paul, a bond-servant of God and a messenger of Jesus Christ, for the faith of those chosen of God and the knowledge of the truth which is according to godliness, ²in the hope of eternal life, which God, who cannot lie, promised long ages ago, ³but at the proper time manifested His Word in the proclamation with which I was entrusted according to the commandment of God our Savior.

⁴To Titus, my true child in a common faith: Grace and peace from God the Father and Christ Jesus our Savior.

⁵For this reason I left you in Crete, that you would set in order what remains and appoint older people in every city as I directed you, ⁶*namely*, if anyone is above reproach, the husband of one wife, having children who believe, not accused of dissipation or rebellion. ⁷For the visitor must be above reproach as God's steward, not self-willed, not quick-tempered, not an excessive drinker, not violent, not fond of sordid gain, ⁸but hospitable, loving what is good, sensible, just, devout, self-controlled, ⁹holding fast the faithful Word which is in accordance with the teaching, so that they will be able both to exhort in sound doctrine and refute those who contradict.

¹⁰For there are many rebellious men, empty talkers and deceivers, especially those of the circumcision, ¹¹who must be silenced because they are shifting whole families, teaching things they should not *teach* for the sake of sordid gain. ¹²One of them, a prophet of their own, said, "Cretans are always liars, evil beasts, lazy gluttons." ¹³This testimony is true. For this reason, reprove them severely so that they may be sound in the faith, ¹⁴not paying attention to Jewish myths and commandments of men who reject the truth. ¹⁵To the pure, all things are pure; but to those who are defiled and unbelieving, nothing is pure, but both their mind and their conscience are defiled. ¹⁶They profess to know God, but by *their* deeds they deny *Him*, being detestable and disobedient and worthless for any good deed.

SCRIPTURE TRANSLATIONS

GENESIS 3:16

¹⁶"To the woman He said, 'A snare has increased your sorrow and your sighing. In sorrow you will bring forth children. You will turn to your husband, and he will rule over you.'"

1 Corinthians 11:3–16

Paul's Model:

[3]"But I want you to understand that Christ is the head **(F)** of every man, and the man is the head **(F)** of a woman, and God is the head **(F)** of Christ."

Paul Quotes a Faction of Men from Corinth Who Wrote Him:

[4]*"Every man who has anything down over his head (L) while praying or prophesying disgraces his head (L). [5]But every woman who has her head (L) unveiled while praying or prophesying disgraces her head (L), for it is one and the same thing as having been shaved. [6]For if a woman is not veiled, let her also have her hair cut off; but if it is disgraceful for a woman to have her hair cut off or to be shaved, let her be veiled."*

Paul's Rebuttal and Reference Back to His Model:

[7]"For a man indeed ought not to veil his head **(F)**, since He is the image and glory of God, but the woman is the glory of man. [8]For man is not of woman, but woman of man; [9]for indeed, man was not created because of the woman, but woman because of the man. [10]For this reason, the woman ought to have authority over her head **(F)**, because of our Messengers. [11]However, in the Lord, neither is woman without man, nor is man without woman. [12]For as the woman is from the man, so also the man through the woman, and all things from God. [13]Judge for yourselves that it is proper for a woman to pray to God unveiled. [14]For not even nature itself teaches you that if a man has long hair, it is a dishonor to him, [15]but if a woman has long hair, it is a glory to her because the long hair has been given instead of a covering. [16]But if one is inclined to be contentious, we have no such practice, nor have the people of God."

(F) – Figurative (source/origin)

(L) – Literal

1 CORINTHIANS 11:3-16
[with added words]

Paul's Model:

[3]"But I want you to understand that Christ is the head [source] of every man, and the man is the head [source] of a woman, and God is the head [source] of Christ [incarnate]."

Paul Quotes a Faction of Men from Corinth Who Wrote Him:

[4]*"Every man who has anything down over his head while praying or prophesying disgraces his [own] head. [5]But every woman who has her head unveiled while praying or prophesying disgraces her [own] head, for it is one and the same thing as having been shaved. [6]For if a woman is not veiled, let her also have her hair cut off; but if it is disgraceful for a woman to have her hair cut off or to be shaved, let her be veiled."*

Paul's Rebuttal and Reference Back to His Model:

[7]"For a man indeed ought not to veil his head [Christ], since He is the image and glory of God, but the woman is the glory of man [so she ought not to be veiled either]. [8]For man is not of woman, but woman of man; [9]for indeed, man was not created because of the woman, but woman because of the man [because of his need for her]. [10]For this reason, the woman ought to have authority over her head [the man], because of our Messengers [Elohim; plural of majesty]. [11]However, in the Lord, [we do not rule over one another because] neither is woman without man, nor is man without woman. [12]For as the woman is from the man, so also the man through the woman, and all things from God [so give Him the glory and let neither one boast]. [13]Judge for yourselves that it is proper for a woman to pray to God unveiled. [14]For not even nature itself teaches you that if a man has long hair, it is a dishonor to him, [15]but if a woman has long hair, it is a glory to her because the long hair has been given [to us all] instead of a covering. [16]But if one is inclined to be contentious, we have no such practice [of requiring women to veil their heads], nor have the people of God."

1 CORINTHIANS 14

Paul's View and the Lord's Commandment:

[1]"Pursue love, yet desire earnestly spiritual *gifts*, but especially that you may prophesy." [3]"But one who prophesies speaks to people for edification and exhortation and consolation." [4]"One who speaks in a tongue edifies themself; but one who prophesies edifies the church." [5]"Now I wish that you all spoke in tongues, but *even* more that you would prophesy...." [12]"So also you, since you are zealous of spiritual *gifts*, seek to abound for the edification of the church." [22]"So then tongues are for a sign, not to those who believe but to unbelievers; but prophecy *is for a sign*, not to unbelievers but to those who believe." [26]"What is *the outcome* then, brethren? When you assemble, each one has a psalm, has a teaching, has a revelation, has a tongue, has an interpretation. Let all things be done for edification." [29]"Let two or three prophets speak, and let the others pass judgment." [31]"For you can all prophesy one by one, so that all may learn and all may be exhorted."

Paul Quotes the Faction of Men from Corinth Who Wrote Him:

[34]*"The women are to keep silent among the people; for they are not permitted to speak, but are to be set as also the Law says. [35]If they desire to learn anything, let them ask their own husbands at home; for it is shameful for a woman to speak among the people."*

Paul Rebukes the Men from Corinth:

[36]"Was it from you that the Word of God *first* went forth? Or has it come to you only? [37]If anyone thinks he is a prophet or spiritual, let him fully know that the things which I write to you are the Lord's commandment. [38]But if anyone does not recognize *this*, he is not recognized."

Paul Sums Up His Previously Stated Views,
Which Are Also the Lord's Commandment:

[39]"Therefore, my brethren, desire earnestly to prophesy, and do not forbid to speak in tongues. [40]But all things must be done properly and in an orderly manner."

HEAD—SOURCE/ORIGIN/ FIRST/BEGINNING

11"He is the STONE WHICH WAS REJECTED by you, THE BUILDERS, but WHICH BECAME THE HEAD [FIRST] CORNER."

(Acts 4:11)

22"And He placed all things under His feet, and gave Him as head [source] for all things to believers, 23which is His body, the fullness of Him who fills all in all."

(Ephesians 1:22–23)

15"He is the image of the invisible God, the firstborn [first in chronological order and arrangement] of all creation. 16For by Him all things were created, *both* in the heavens and on earth, visible and invisible, whether thrones or dominions or rulers or authorities—all things have been created through Him and for Him. 17He is before all things, and in Him all things hold together. 18He is also head [source/origin/ first/beginning] of the body, the church; and He is the beginning, the firstborn [first in chronological order and arrangement] from the dead, so that He Himself will come to have first place in everything."

(Colossians 1:15–18)

19"…and not holding fast to the head [source], from whom the entire body, by means of the joints and ligaments being supplied and held together, grows with a growth which is from God."

(Colossians 2:19)

PSALM 8:4-6

(Prophecy given through King David)

[4]"What is man [enos] that You take thought of him, and the Son of Man [adam] that You care for Him? [5]Yet You have made Him for a little while lower than God, and You crown Him with glory and majesty! [6]You make Him to rule over the works of Your hands; You have put all things under His feet."

1 CORINTHIANS 15:20-28

(Paul expounds upon King David's prophecy)

[20]"But now Christ has been raised from the dead, the first fruits of those who are asleep. [21]For since by a man *came* death, by a man also *came* the resurrection of the dead. [22]For as in Adam all die, so also in Christ all will be made alive. [23]But each in his own order: Christ, the first fruits, after that those who are Christ's at His coming, [24]then *comes* the end, when the God and Father hands over the sovereign rule, as soon as He [Father] abolishes all rule and all authority and power. [25]For He [Father] must reign until He [Father] has put all His [Christ's] enemies under His [Christ's] feet. [26]The last enemy that will be abolished is death. [27]'For HE [Father] HAS PLACED ALL THINGS UNDER HIS [Christ's] FEET.' But when He says, 'All things are placed,' it is clear that it is apart from the One [Father] who placed all things to Him [Christ]. [28]But as soon as all things are willed to Him [Christ], then also the Son Himself will be appointed by the will of the One [Father] who placed all things to Him [Christ], so that God may be all in all."

HEBREWS 2:5-9

(Author of Hebrew's expounds upon King David's prophecy)

[5]"For He did not place to angels the world to come, concerning which we are speaking. [6]But one has testified somewhere, saying, 'WHAT IS MAN, THAT YOU REMEMBER HIM? OR THE SON OF MAN, THAT

YOU CARE FOR HIM? [7]YOU HAVE MADE HIM FOR A LITTLE WHILE LOWER THAN GOD; YOU HAVE CROWNED HIM WITH GLORY AND HONOR, AND HAVE APPOINTED HIM OVER THE WORKS OF YOUR HANDS; [8]YOU HAVE PLACED ALL THINGS UNDER HIS FEET.' For in placing all things to Him, He left nothing to Him that is disobedient. But at this present time, we do not yet see all things willed to Him. [9]But we do see Jesus, the One having been made for a little while lower than God, now crowned with glory and honor because of the suffering of death, so that by the grace of God on behalf of everyone He might taste death."

HYPOTASSO/HYPOTAGE (42)

Hypotasso (28) — Word of placement – To place, to put, to set; to be set in this way.

Hypotage (14) — Will, willed, appointed by the will of, willing, willingness, etc.

Luke 2:41–52 (1)

[41]"Now His parents went to Jerusalem every year at the Feast of the Passover. [42]And when He became twelve, they went up there according to the custom of the Feast; [43]and as they were returning, after spending the full number of days, the boy Jesus stood firmly in Jerusalem. But His parents were unaware of it, [44]and thought Him to be in the company of travelers and went a day's journey; and they began looking for Him among their relatives and acquaintances. [45]When they did not find Him, they returned to Jerusalem looking for Him. [46]Then, after three days, they found Him in the temple, sitting in the midst of the teachers, both listening to them and asking them questions. [47]And all who heard Him were astonished at His understanding and His answers. [48]Also seeing Him, they were amazed. Then His mother said to Him, 'Son, why have You treated us this way? Behold, Your father and I have continued in agony looking for You.' [49]And He said to them, 'Why is it that you were looking for Me? Did you not know that I had to be doing that of My Father's?' [50]But they did not understand the statement which He had spoke to them. [51]And He went down with them and came to Nazareth, and He **continued to be set in this way** [hypotassomenos] to them; and His mother treasured all His words in her heart. [52]And Jesus kept increasing in wisdom and stature and favor with God and people."

[17]"The seventy returned with joy saying, 'Lord, even the demons **are placed** [hypotassetai] to us in Your name.' [18]And He said to them, 'I was watching Satan fall from heaven like lightning. [19]Behold, I have given you authority to tread on serpents and scorpions, and over all the power of the enemy, and nothing will injure you. [20]Nevertheless do not rejoice in this, that the spirits **are placed** [hypotassetai] to you, but rejoice that your names are recorded in heaven.'"

Romans 8:6–8 (1)

[6]"For the mind set on the flesh is death, but the mind set on the Spirit is life and peace, [7]because the mind set on the flesh is hostile toward God; for **it is** not **set** [hypotassetai] to the law of God, neither indeed can it, [8]and those in the flesh cannot please God."

Romans 8:20–21 (2)

[20]"For the creation **was willed** [hypetage] to futility, not by their own choice, but by the One who **placed** [hypotaxanta] it, in hope [21]that the creation itself then will be set free from its slavery to corruption into the freedom of the glory of the children of God."

Romans 10:1–3 (1)

[1]"Brethren, my heart's desire and my prayer to God for them is for *their* salvation. [2]For I testify about them that they have a zeal for God, but not in accordance with knowledge. [3]For not knowing about God's righteousness and seeking to establish their own, **they did** not **will** [hypetagesan] the righteousness of God."

Romans 13:1–7 (2)

[1]"Every mind **is to be set** [hypotassestho] on transcending the authorities. For it is not authority if *it is* not by God, and those which are by God are ordained. [2]Therefore, the one who continues to establish against the authority of God's ordinance has opposed, and those having opposed will receive condemnation on themselves. [3]For the rulers *set by God* are not a cause of fear for good work, but for evil. And if you do not want to fear

their authority, then do what is good and you will have praise from them. [4]For God's servant is to you for the good. But if one does evil, then be afraid. For it is not for nothing the sword they bear. For God's servant is an avenger for wrath to the one practicing evil. [5]Therefore, it is necessary **to be set in this way** [doing what is good] [hypotassesthai], not only because of wrath but also because of conscience. [6]For because of this [being set righteously] you also pay taxes, for *believers are* ministers of God *who* are constantly devoting themselves for this [righteousness]. [7]Render to all what is due them; to the tax the tax; to the tribute the tribute; to the respect the respect; to the honor the honor."

1 Corinthians 14:31–33 (1)

[31]"For you can all prophesy one by one, so that all may learn and all may be exhorted; [32]and the spirits of prophets **are set** [hypotassetai] *in order* for prophets; [33]for God is not of disorder but of peace, as among all the people that are holy."

1 Corinthians 14:34–35 (1)

[34]"*'The women are to keep silent among the people; for they are not permitted to speak, but **are to be set** [hypotassesthosan] as also the Law says. [35]If they desire to learn anything, let them ask their own husbands at home; for it is shameful for a woman to speak among the people.'*"

1 Corinthians 15:27–28 (6)

[27]"For HE **HAS PLACED** [hypetaxen] ALL THINGS UNDER HIS FEET.' But when He says, 'All things **are placed** [hypotetaktai],' it is clear that it is apart from the One who **placed** [hypotaxantos] all things to Him. [28]But as soon as all things **are willed** [hypotage] to Him, then also the Son Himself **will be appointed by the will** [hypotagesetai] of the One who **placed** [hypotaxanti] all things to Him, so that God may be all in all."

1 Corinthians 16:15–18 (1)

[15]"Now I urge you, brethren, *for* you know the household of Stephanas, that they were the first fruits of Achaia and that they have devoted themselves for service to the saints, [16]that you also **be set in this way** [hypotassesthe] to such ones and to everyone who helps in the work and labors. [17]I rejoice

over the coming of Stephanas and Fortunatus and Achaicus, because they have supplied what was lacking on your part. [18]For they have refreshed my spirit and yours. Therefore, acknowledge such ones."

2 Corinthians 9:13–14 (1)

[13]"Because of the proof given by this service, they will glorify God over the **willingness** [hypotage] of your commitment to the gospel of Christ and for the liberality of your contribution to them and to all [14]while they also, by prayer on your behalf, yearn for you because of the surpassing grace of God in you."

Galatians 2:4–5 (1)

[4]"But *it was* because of the false brethren secretly brought in, who had sneaked in to spy out our liberty which we have in Christ Jesus, in order to bring us into bondage. [5]But we did not yield to their **will** [hypotage] for even an hour, so that the truth of the gospel would remain with you."

Ephesians 1:22–23 (1)

[22]"And He **placed** [hypetaxen] all things under His feet, and gave Him as head [source] for all things to believers, [23]which is His body, the fullness of Him who fills all in all."

Ephesians 5:18–21 (1)

[18]"And do not get drunk with wine, for that is dissipation, but be filled with the Spirit, [19]speaking to one another with psalms and hymns and spiritual songs, singing with songs of praise in your heart to the Lord, [20]always giving thanks for all things in the name of our Lord Jesus Christ to the God and Father, [21]and be **continuously set in this way** [hypotassomenoi] toward one another out of reverence for Christ."

Ephesians 5:22–33 (1)

[22]"The wives to their own husbands, as to the Lord. [23]For the man is the head [source] of the woman, as Christ also is the head [source] of the church, He Himself *being* the Savior of the body. [24]So as the church **is set** [hypotassetai] to Christ, so also the wives to their husbands in everything.

213

²⁵You husbands love your wives just as Christ also loved the church and gave Himself up for her, ²⁶so that He might sanctify her, having cleansed her by the washing of water with the Word, ²⁷so that He might present to Himself the church in all her glory, having no spot or wrinkle or any such thing; but that she would be holy and blameless. ²⁸So husbands ought also to love their own wives as their own bodies. He who loves his own wife loves himself; ²⁹for no one ever hated his own flesh, but nourishes and cherishes it, just as Christ also *does* the church, ³⁰because we are members of His body. ³¹'FOR THIS REASON A MAN SHALL LEAVE HIS FATHER AND MOTHER AND SHALL HOLD FAST TO HIS WIFE AND THE TWO SHALL BECOME ONE FLESH.' ³²This mystery is great; but I am speaking with reference to Christ and the church. ³³Nevertheless, each one of you also is to love his own wife as himself, and the wife will then have a deep respect for her husband."

Philippians 3:20–21 (1)

²⁰"For our citizenship is in heaven, from where also we eagerly wait for a Savior, the Lord Jesus Christ; ²¹who will transform the body of our low state into conformity with the body of His glory, according to the power that He has even **to place** [hypotaxai] all things to Himself."

Colossians 3:18 (1)

¹⁸"Wives, **be set** [hypotassesthe] to your husband's **in a way** that is fitting in the Lord."

1 Timothy 2:8–15 (1)

⁸"Therefore, I want the men in every place to pray, lifting up holy hands without anger and disputing. ⁹Likewise, I want the women to adorn themselves with an honorable appearance, *one* with holiness and discretion, not with braided hair and gold or pearls or costly garments, ¹⁰but rather with what suits women who profess to worship God by means of good works. ¹¹Let the woman learn in a peaceful atmosphere with all **willingness** [hypotage]. ¹²But I do not permit the man to teach his wife, nor to exercise his own jurisdiction but to be in peacefulness. ¹³For Adam was first formed, then Eve. ¹⁴And Adam was not deceived, but the woman being deceived fell into transgression. ¹⁵But she will be saved through the

Son of this generation if they [the believers in Ephesus] continue in faith and love and holiness with discretion."

1 Timothy 3:1–7 (1)

[1]"It is a trustworthy statement: If anyone sets their heart on visitation, it is an excellent work they desire. [2]The visitor, then, must be above reproach, the husband of one wife, temperate, prudent, respectable, hospitable, able to teach, [3]not an excessive drinker, not violent but gentle, peaceable, free from the love of money, [4]one who is rightly devoted to their own family, having children that are **willing** [hypotage] with all gravity. [5]For if one does not know how to be devoted to their own family, how will they take care of the people of God? [6]And not a new convert so that they will not become conceited and fall into judgment incurred by the devil. [7]They must also have a good reputation with those outside so that they will not fall into disgrace and the snare of the devil."

Titus 2:3–5 (1)

[3]"Older women, likewise, are to be with behavior appropriate to holiness, not false accusers, nor enslaved by much wine, *being* teachers of what is good, [4]so that they may encourage the young women to love their husbands, love their children, [5]to exercise sound judgment, to be pure, diligent at home, kind, **being set in this way** [hypotassomenas] to their own husbands so that the Word of God will not be dishonored."

Titus 2:9–10 (1)

[9]"Bond slaves to their own masters, in all things, **are to be set in a way** [hypotassesthai] that is well-pleasing, not argumentative, [10]not pilfering, but showing all good faith so that the teaching of God our Savior will be made attractive in all things."

Titus 3:1–2 (1)

[1]"Remind them **to be set** [hypotassesthai] to rulers and authorities **in a way** that they are ready to be obedient to every good work, [2]to malign no one, to be peaceable, gentle, showing every consideration for all people."

Hebrews 2:5–9 (4)

[5]"For He did not **place** [hypetaxen] to angels the world to come, concerning which we are speaking. [6]But one has testified somewhere, saying, 'WHAT IS MAN, THAT YOU REMEMBER HIM? OR THE SON OF MAN, THAT YOU CARE FOR HIM? [7]YOU HAVE MADE HIM FOR A LITTLE WHILE LOWER THAN GOD; YOU HAVE CROWNED HIM WITH GLORY AND HONOR, AND HAVE APPOINTED HIM OVER THE WORKS OF YOUR HANDS; [8]YOU **HAVE PLACED** [hypetaxas] ALL THINGS UNDER HIS FEET.' For in **placing** [hypotaxai] all things to Him, He left nothing to Him that is disobedient. But at this present time, we do not yet see all things **willed** [hypotetagmena] to Him. [9]But we do see Jesus, the One having been made for a little while lower than God, now crowned with glory and honor because of the suffering of death, so that by the grace of God on behalf of everyone He might taste death."

Hebrews 12:4–11 (1)

[4]"You have not yet resisted to the point of shedding blood in your struggle against sin; [5]and you have forgotten the exhortation which is addressed to you as children, 'MY CHILD, DO NOT DESPISE THE CORRECTION OF THE LORD, NOR LOSE HEART WHEN YOU ARE REPROVED BY HIM; [6]FOR THOSE WHOM THE LORD LOVES HE CORRECTS, AND HE SCOURGES EVERY CHILD WHOM HE RECEIVES.' [7]God deals with you as with children, so endure correction for this reason. For what child is there whom their father does not correct? [8]But if you are without correction, of which you all have taken part in, then you are illegitimate and not children. [9]Furthermore, we had fathers of our flesh to correct us, and we respected them. Shall we not, even more than, also live **to do the will** [hypotagesometha] of the Father of our spirits? [10]For they corrected us for a short time according to what seemed best to them, but He for our benefit so that we can share in His holiness. [11]All correction at the moment seems not to be pleasant, but sorrowful; yet to those who have been trained by it, afterwards it yields the peaceful fruit of righteousness."

James 4:7 (1)

[7]"**Do the will** [hypotagete], then, of God. Resist the devil and he will flee from you. [8]Draw near to God and He will draw near to you."

216

1 Peter 2:13–17 (1)

[13]"**Be willing** [hypotagete] *to do good* toward every human institution because of the Lord, whether to a king as the one in authority, [14]or to governors as sent by him, so that punishment will come on those who do evil and praise will come on those who do good. [15]For such is the will of God that by doing good, you may silence the ignorance of foolish people. [16]Act as free people, and do not use your freedom as a covering for evil, but use it as bondslaves of God. [17]Honor all people, love fellow believers, fear God, show proper respect to the king."

1 Peter 2:18–20 (1)

[18]"Servants, **be set** [hypotassomenoi] to your masters with all respect, not only to those who are good and gentle but also to those who are corrupt. [19]For this *finds* favor if, for the sake of conscience toward God, a person bears up under sorrows when suffering unjustly. [20]For what honor is there if, when you sin, you endure harsh treatment *for it*? But if when you do what is right and endure suffering *for it*, this *finds* favor with God."

1 Peter 2:20–25; 3:1–6 (2)

[2:20]"…But if when you do what is right and endure suffering *for it*, this *finds* favor with God. [21]For you have been called for this purpose, since Christ also suffered for you, leaving an example for you to follow in His steps, [22]WHO COMMITTED NO SIN, NOR WAS ANY DECEIT FOUND IN HIS MOUTH; [23]and while being reviled, He did not revile in return; while suffering, He uttered no threats, but kept entrusting Himself to Him who judges righteously; [24]and He Himself bore our sins in His body on the cross, so that we might die to sin and live to righteousness; for by His wounds you were healed. [25]For you were continually straying like sheep, but now you have returned to the Shepherd and the One who cares for your souls. [3:1]So in the same way *that Christ was set*, you wives, *also* **be set** [hypotassomenai] to your own husbands, so that even if any of them are disobedient to the Word, they may be won over without a word by the behavior of their wives, [2]by observing the reverent and pure way you live your lives. [3]Let it not be the outward appearance—braiding the hair and wearing gold jewelry or putting on worldly clothing, [4]but let it be the hidden person of the heart, with the imperishable quality of a gentle and peaceful spirit, which is of great worth in the sight of God.

217

⁵For in this way in former times the holy women also, who hoped in God, used to make themselves beautiful by **being set** [hypotassomenai] to their own husbands; ⁶just as Sarah answered Abraham, calling him her dear husband, and you have become her children if you do what is right without giving way to fear."

1 Peter 3:21–22 (1)

²¹"And this *water even* symbolizes now that you are saved. *For* baptism does not *represent* the putting away of the filth of the flesh, but *rather* a request to God for a morally good conscience through the resurrection of Jesus Christ, ²²who is at the right hand of God, having gone into heaven, **having willed** [hypotagenton] to Him angels and authorities and powers."

1 Peter 5:1–5 (1)

¹"Therefore, I exhort the older ones among you, as someone who is also older and a witness of the sufferings of Christ and a partaker also of the glory that is to be revealed, ²take care of the flock of God among you, not under compulsion, but voluntarily, according to God; and not for sordid gain, but eagerly; ³nor yet as lording it over those who share the inheritance but being examples to the flock. ⁴And when the Chief Shepherd appears, you will receive the unfading crown of glory. ⁵Likewise, you younger ones **be willing** [hypotagete] toward the older ones; and all of you clothe yourselves with humility toward one another, for GOD IS OPPOSED TO THE PROUD, BUT GIVES GRACE TO THE HUMBLE."

HYPAKOUO (21)

(To answer)

1) ^{27}"The men were amazed, and said, 'What kind of a man is this, that even the winds and the sea **answer** [hypakouousin] Him?'" (Matt. 8:27).

2) ^{27}"They were all amazed, so that they debated among themselves, saying, 'What is this? A new teaching with authority! He commands even the unclean spirits, and they **answer** [hypakouousin] Him'" (Mark 1:27).

3) ^{41}"They became very much afraid and said to one another, 'Who then is this that even the wind and the sea **answer** [hypakouei] Him?'" (Mark 4:41).

4) ^{25}"And He said to them, 'Where is your faith?' They were fearful and amazed, saying to one another, 'Who then is this that He commands even the winds and the water, and they **answer** [hypakouousin] Him?'" (Luke 8:25).

5) ^{6}"And the Lord said, 'If you had faith like a mustard seed, you would say to this mulberry tree, 'Be uprooted and be planted in the sea'; and it would **answer** [hypekousen] you'" (Luke 17:6).

6) ^{7}"The Word of God kept on spreading; and the number of the disciples continued to increase greatly in Jerusalem, and a great many of the priests **were answering** [hypekouon] the faith" (Acts 6:7).

7) ^{13}"When he knocked at the entryway door, a servant-girl named Rhoda came **to answer** [hypakousai]" (Acts 12:13).

8) ^{12}"Therefore, do not let sin reign in your mortal body so that you **answer** [hypakouein] its lusts…" (Rom. 6:12).

9) [16]"Do you not know that when you present yourselves to someone *as* slaves for obedience, you are slaves of the one to whom you **answer** [hypakouete], either of sin resulting in death, or of obedience resulting in righteousness?" (Rom. 6:16).

10) [17]"But thanks be to God that though you were slaves of sin, you **answered** [hypekousate] from the heart to that form of teaching to which you were committed, [18]and having been freed from sin, you became slaves of righteousness" (Rom. 6:17–18).

11) [16]"However, they did not all **answer** [hypekousan] the good news; for Isaiah says, 'LORD, WHO HAS BELIEVED OUR MESSAGE?'" (Rom. 10:16).

12) [1]"Children, **answer** [hypakouete] your parents in the Lord, for this is right. [2]HONOR YOUR FATHER AND MOTHER (which is the first commandment with a promise), [3]SO THAT IT MAY BE WELL WITH YOU, AND THAT YOU MAY LIVE LONG ON THE EARTH" (Eph. 6:1–3).

13) [5]"Slaves, **answer** [hypakouete] those who are your masters according to the flesh, with respect and fear, in the sincerity of your heart, as to Christ; [6]not by way of eyeservice, as men-pleasers, but as slaves of Christ, doing the will of God from the heart" (Eph. 6:5–6).

14) [12]"So then, my beloved, just as you have always **answered** [hypekousate], not as in my presence only, but now much more in my absence, with respect and fear, accomplish much with your salvation; [13]for it is God who is at work in you, both to will and to work for *His* good pleasure" (Phil. 2:12–13).

15) [20]"Children, **answer** [hypakouete] your parents in all things, for this is well-pleasing to the Lord" (Col. 3:20).

16) [22]"Slaves, in all things **answer** [hypakouete] those who are your masters on earth, not with eyeservice, as those who *merely* please men, but with sincerity of heart, fearing the Lord" (Col. 3:22).

17) [6]"For after all it is *only* just for God to repay with affliction those who afflict you, [7]and *to give* relief to you who are afflicted and to us as well

when the Lord Jesus will be revealed from heaven with His mighty angels in flaming fire, ⁸dealing out retribution to those who do not know God and to those who do not **answer** [hypakouousin] the gospel of our Lord Jesus" (2 Thess. 1:6–8).

18) ¹⁴"If anyone does not **answer** [hypakouei] our instruction in this letter, take special note of that person and do not associate with him, so that he will be put to shame" (2 Thess. 3:14).

19) ⁹"And having been made perfect, He became to all those who **answer** [hypakouousin] Him the source of eternal salvation, ¹⁰being designated by God as a high priest according to the order of Melchizedek" (Heb. 5:9–10).

20) ⁸"By faith Abraham, when he was called, **answered** [hypekousen] by going out to a place which he was to receive for an inheritance; and he went out, not knowing where he was going" (Heb. 11:8).

21) ⁴"…but let *it* be the hidden person of the heart, with the imperishable quality of a gentle and peaceful spirit, which is of great worth in the sight of God. ⁵For in this way in former times the holy women also, who hoped in God, used to make themselves beautiful by being set to their own husbands; ⁶just as Sarah **answered** [hypekousen] Abraham, calling him her dear husband, and you have become her children if you do what is right without giving way to fear" (1 Pet. 3:4–6).

1 TIMOTHY 1 & 2

1 Paul, a messenger of Christ Jesus according to the commandment of God our Savior, and of Christ Jesus, our hope.

[2]To Timothy, my true child in the faith: Grace, mercy, and peace from God the Father and Christ Jesus our Lord.

Instructions to Certain Believers Not to Teach God's Word Differently and Warnings Against False Teachers of the Law

[3]As I urged you upon my departure for Macedonia, remain on at Ephesus so that you may instruct certain ones not to teach differently, [4]nor to pay attention to myths and endless genealogies, because it causes those who are searching for the truth to be separated away from the truth rather than *furthering* the administration of God which is by faith. [5]But the goal of our instruction is love from a pure heart and a good conscience and a sincere faith. [6]For some, missing the mark of these things, have turned to fruitless discussion, [7]wanting to be teachers of the Law, even though they do not understand either what they are saying or the matters about which they make confident assertions.

[8]But we know that the Law is good, if one uses it lawfully, [9]realizing the fact that law is not made for a righteous person, but for those who are lawless and rebellious, for the ungodly and sinners, for the unholy and profane, for those who kill their fathers or mothers, for murderers [10]and immoral people and homosexuals and kidnappers and liars and perjurers, and whatever else is contrary to sound teaching, [11]according to the glorious gospel of the blessed God, with which I have been entrusted.

[12]I thank Christ Jesus our Lord, who has strengthened me, because He considered me faithful, putting me into service, [13]even though I was formerly a blasphemer and a persecutor and a violent aggressor. Yet I was shown mercy because I acted ignorantly in unbelief; [14]and the grace of our Lord was more than abundant, with the faith and love which are in Christ Jesus. [15]It is a trustworthy statement, deserving full acceptance, that Christ Jesus came into the world to save sinners, among whom I am foremost. [16]Yet

for this reason I found mercy, so that in me as the foremost, Jesus Christ might demonstrate His perfect patience as an example for those who would believe in Him for eternal life. [17]Now to the King eternal, immortal, invisible, the only God, be honor and glory forever and ever. Amen.

[18]This command I entrust to you, Timothy, my son, in accordance with the prophecies previously made concerning you, that by them you fight the good fight, [19]keeping faith and a good conscience, which some have rejected and suffered shipwreck in regard to their faith. [20]Among these are Hymenaeus and Alexander, whom I have handed over to Satan, so that they will be taught not to blaspheme.

Instructions to All of the Believers in Ephesus

2 First of all, then, I urge that requests, prayers, intercessions and thanksgivings be made on behalf of all people; [2]for kings and all who are in authority, so that we may lead a tranquil and quiet life in all godliness and dignity. [3]For this is good and acceptable in the sight of God our Savior, [4]who desires all people to be saved and to come to the knowledge of the truth. [5]For there is one God, and one mediator also between God and people, the man Christ Jesus, [6]who gave Himself as a ransom for all, the testimony given at the proper time. [7]For this I was appointed a proclaimer and a messenger (I am telling the truth, I am not lying) as a teacher of the Gentiles in faith and truth. [8]Therefore, I want the men in every place to pray, lifting up holy hands without anger and disputing. [9]Likewise, I want the women to adorn themselves with an honorable appearance, *one* with holiness and discretion, not with braided hair and gold or pearls or costly garments, [10]but rather with what suits women who profess to worship God by means of good works.

Instructions Concerning the Unsaved Gentile Woman and Her Believing Jewish Husband

[11]Let the woman learn in a peaceful atmosphere with all willingness. [12]But I do not permit the man to teach his wife, nor to exercise his own jurisdiction but to be in peacefulness. [13]For Adam was first formed, then Eve. [14]And Adam was not deceived, but the woman being deceived fell into transgression. [15]But she will be saved through the Son of this generation if they [the believers in Ephesus] continue in faith and love and holiness with discretion.

1 TIMOTHY 3:1-7

[1]"It is a trustworthy statement: If anyone sets their heart on visitation, it is an excellent work they desire. [2]The visitor, then, must be above reproach, the husband of one wife, temperate, prudent, respectable, hospitable, able to teach, [3]not an excessive drinker, not violent but gentle, peaceable, free from the love of money, [4]one who is rightly devoted to their own family, having children that are willing with all gravity. [5]For if one does not know how to be devoted to their own family, how will they take care of the people of God? [6]And not a new convert so that they will not become conceited and fall into judgment incurred by the devil. [7]They must also have a good reputation with those outside so that they will not fall into disgrace and the snare of the devil."

1 TIMOTHY 3:8-13

[8]"Menservants, likewise, are to be dignified, not double-tongued, nor indulging in much wine, nor pursuing dishonest gain, [9]but holding to the mystery of the faith with a clear conscience. [10]And also these, let first be tested; then let them serve if they are beyond reproach. [11]Women, likewise, are to be dignified, not slanderers, but temperate, faithful in all things. [12]Let servants be husbands of one wife, rightly devoted to their children and their own families. [13]For those who have served well obtain for themselves a good standing and great confidence in the faith that is in Christ Jesus."

1 TIMOTHY 5:17

[17]"The rightly devoted older people are to be considered worthy of double honor, especially those laboring in speech and teaching."

TITUS 1

1 Paul, a bond-servant of God and a messenger of Jesus Christ, for the faith of those chosen of God and the knowledge of the truth which is according to godliness, ²in the hope of eternal life, which God, who cannot lie, promised long ages ago, ³but at the proper time manifested His Word in the proclamation with which I was entrusted according to the commandment of God our Savior.

⁴To Titus, my true child in a common faith: Grace and peace from God the Father and Christ Jesus our Savior.

⁵For this reason I left you in Crete, that you would set in order what remains and appoint older people in every city as I directed you, ⁶*namely*, if anyone is above reproach, the husband of one wife, having children who believe, not accused of dissipation or rebellion. ⁷For the visitor must be above reproach as God's steward, not self-willed, not quick-tempered, not an excessive drinker, not violent, not fond of sordid gain, ⁸but hospitable, loving what is good, sensible, just, devout, self-controlled, ⁹holding fast the faithful Word which is in accordance with the teaching, so that they will be able both to exhort in sound doctrine and refute those who contradict.

¹⁰For there are many rebellious men, empty talkers and deceivers, especially those of the circumcision, ¹¹who must be silenced because they are shifting whole families, teaching things they should not *teach* for the sake of sordid gain. ¹²One of them, a prophet of their own, said, "Cretans are always liars, evil beasts, lazy gluttons." ¹³This testimony is true. For this reason, reprove them severely so that they may be sound in the faith, ¹⁴not paying attention to Jewish myths and commandments of men who reject the truth. ¹⁵To the pure, all things are pure; but to those who are defiled and unbelieving, nothing is pure, but both their mind and their conscience are defiled. ¹⁶They profess to know God, but by *their* deeds they deny *Him*, being detestable and disobedient and worthless for any good deed.

NOTES

Chapter 1: Who Sinned First—Adam or Eve?

1. Goodrick and Kohlenberger, *NIV Exhaustive Concordance*, 1361.

Chapter 2: Genesis 3:16

1. Bushnell, *God's Word to Women*, 45, 50.
2. Bushnell, *God's Word to Women*, back cover.
3. Bushnell, *God's Word to Women*, 3–4.
4. Bushnell, *God's Word to Women*, 55–66.
5. Bushnell, *God's Word to Women*, 55–66.
6. Bushnell, *God's Word to Women*, 54–55. Katharine Bushnell gave the rendering of the first and third sentences in her book. However, she did not give a rendering of the second sentence but says on page sixty-one of her book that the word "sorrow" in this verse does not refer to labor pains because the same word is used of Adam in the very next verse. Ms. Bushnell also says on page fifty-four that the Septuagint gives the rendering of "thy sighing."
7. Bushnell, *God's Word to Women*, 51 (see footnote).
8. Bushnell, *God's Word to Women*, 55.
9. Bushnell, *God's Word to Women*, 28–31.
10. Bushnell, *God's Word to Women*, 29–36.
11. Bushnell, *God's Word to Women*, 61.
12. Bushnell, *God's Word to Women*, 36.
13. Bushnell, *God's Word to Women*, 34.
14. Bushnell, *God's Word to Women*, 43.
15. Bushnell, *God's Word to Women*, 34.
16. Bushnell, *God's Word to Women*, 42.
17. Bushnell, *God's Word to Women*, 62.
18. Bushnell, *God's Word to Women*, 58.
19. Bushnell, *God's Word to Women*, 54–55.

20. Bushnell, *God's Word to Women*, 36. There is no present tense in Hebrew, only past and future tense. Therefore, I used the future tense "will turn" instead of the present tense "turning."

21. Bushnell, *God's Word to Women*, 68–69.

Chapter 3: 1 Corinthians 11:3–16

1. Ramey, *Sights and Sounds*, 17–22.
2. Goodrick and Kohlenberger, *NIV Exhaustive Concordance*, 1550.
3. Goodrick and Kohlenberger, *NIV Exhaustive Concordance*, 1561.
4. Goodrick and Kohlenberger, NIV Exhaustive Concordance, 1528–1529.
5. Goodrick and Kohlenberger, *NIV Exhaustive Concordance*, 1564.
6. Goodrick and Kohlenberger, *NIV Exhaustive Concordance*, 1486.
7. Goodrick and Kohlenberger, *NIV Exhaustive Concordance*, 1479.
8. Goodrick and Kohlenberger, *NIV Exhaustive Concordance*, 1598.
9. Goodrick and Kohlenberger, *NIV Exhaustive Concordance*, 1463.
10. Freedman, *Woman, A Power Equal to Man*, 56–58.
11. Goodrick and Kohlenberger, *NIV Exhaustive Concordance*, 1421, 1449.
12. Goodrick and Kohlenberger, *NIV Exhaustive Concordance*, 1540, 1578.
13. Goodrick and Kohlenberger, *NIV Exhaustive Concordance*, 1550–1551.
14. Goodrick and Kohlenberger, *NIV Exhaustive Concordance*, 1558.
15. Goodrick and Kohlenberger, *NIV Exhaustive Concordance*, 1366.
16. Bushnell, *God's Word to Women*, 116.
17. Bushnell, *God's Word to Women*, 116.
18. Goodrick and Kohlenberger, *NIV Exhaustive Concordance*, 1522, 1556 (Greek G/K number 2445).
19. Goodrick and Kohlenberger, *NIV Exhaustive Concordance*, 1529.
20. Marlowe, *The Woman's Headcovering*, (see Text-critical notes).
21. Goodrich and Kohlenberger, *NIV Exhaustive Concordance*, 1597.

Chapter 4: 1 Corinthians 14:34–35

1. Bushnell, *God's Word to Women*, 91–95 (see Lesson 27). This faction of men was likely Jewish due to their reference to the Law.
2. Goodrick and Kohlenberger, *NIV Exhaustive Concordance*, 1525.
3. Bushnell, *God's Word to Women*, 91.

4. Goodrick and Kohlenberger, *NIV Exhaustive Concordance*, 1568.
5. Goodrick and Kohlenberger, *NIV Exhaustive Concordance*, 1446.
6. Agnes, *Webster's Dictionary*, 4th ed., "edify, exhort, console."

Chapter 5: Head—Source or Leader?

1. Goodrick and Kohlenberger, *NIV Exhaustive Concordance*, 1564.
2. Wikipedia, *Cornerstone*.
3. Agnes, *Webster's Dictionary*, 4th ed., "water tower."

Chapter 6: Hypotasso (Part I)

1. Goodrick and Kohlenberger, *NIV Exhaustive Concordance*, 1600.
2. Goodrick and Kohlenberger, *NIV Exhaustive Concordance*, 1499.
3. Goodrick and Kohlenberger, *NIV Exhaustive Concordance*, 1535.
4. Goodrick and Kohlenberger, *NIV Exhaustive Concordance*, 1535.
5. Goodrick and Kohlenberger, *NIV Exhaustive Concordance*, 1535.
6. Goodrick and Kohlenberger, *NIV Exhaustive Concordance*, 1368.
7. Goodrick and Kohlenberger, *NIV Exhaustive Concordance*, 1360.
8. Goodrick and Kohlenberger, *NIV Exhaustive Concordance*, 1442.
9. Goodrick and Kohlenberger, *NIV Exhaustive Concordance*, 1529.

Chapter 7: Hypotasso (Part II)

1. Martin, *Tasso*.
2. Goodrick and Kohlenberger, *NIV Exhaustive Concordance*, 1596.
3. Goodrick and Kohlenberger, *NIV Exhaustive Concordance*, 1599.
4. Goodrick and Kohlenberger, *NIV Exhaustive Concordance*, 1570.
5. Goodrick and Kohlenberger, *NIV Exhaustive Concordance*, 1599.
6. Goodrick and Kohlenberger, *NIV Exhaustive Concordance*, 1604.
7. Goodrick and Kohlenberger, *NIV Exhaustive Concordance*, 1599.
8. Goodrick and Kohlenberger, *NIV Exhaustive Concordance*, 1529.
9. Goodrick and Kohlenberger, *NIV Exhaustive Concordance*, 1540.
10. Goodrick and Kohlenberger, *NIV Exhaustive Concordance*, 1567.
11. Goodrick and Kohlenberger, *NIV Exhaustive Concordance*, 1567.
12. Goodrick and Kohlenberger, *NIV Exhaustive Concordance*, 1559.
13. Bible Hub, *1 Peter 2:18*.
14. Goodrick and Kohlenberger, *NIV Exhaustive Concordance*, 1591.
15. Goodrick and Kohlenberger, *NIV Exhaustive Concordance*, 1566.

Chapter 8: 1 Timothy 2:11–15

1. Goodrick and Kohlenberger, *NIV Exhaustive Concordance*, 1597.
2. Goodrick and Kohlenberger, *NIV Exhaustive Concordance*, 1533.
3. Goodrick and Kohlenberger, *NIV Exhaustive Concordance*, 1523, 1579.
4. Goodrick and Kohlenberger, *NIV Exhaustive Concordance*, 1545–1546, 1556.
5. Goodrick and Kohlenberger, *NIV Exhaustive Concordance*, 1563.
6. Goodrick and Kohlenberger, *NIV Exhaustive Concordance*, 1565.
7. Zodhiates, *Complete Word Study Dictionary*, "aidos."
8. Goodrick and Kohlenberger, *NIV Exhaustive Concordance*, 1556.
9. Goodrick and Kohlenberger, *NIV Exhaustive Concordance*, 1583.
10. Mounce, *Basics of Biblical Greek*.
11. Mounce, *Basics of Biblical Greek*.
12. Larsen, *Word Order*.
13. Newberry, *Divine Pattern*, 93.
14. Appendix J, *Teaching Over a Man*.
15. Goodrick and Kohlenberger, *NIV Exhaustive Concordance*, 1534. The word "authentein" could also be translated as "to exercise his own authority" in verse twelve. However, I prefer the translation of "to exercise his own jurisdiction" because it is the stronger translation. Only God has jurisdiction over His Word.
16. Baldwin et al., *Women in the Church*, 39–40.
17. Baldwin et al., *Women in the Church*, 45.
18. Baldwin et al., *Women in the Church*, 46–51.
19. Baldwin et al., *Women in the Church*, 41.
20. Newberry, *Divine Pattern*, 93. The scholars who acknowledge the fact that the word "didaskein" cannot take a genitive direct object most commonly say that it means that a woman cannot teach anyone, that is, publicly (see pp. 90–95).
21. Nunn, *Key to the Elements*.
22. Mounce, *Basics of Biblical Greek*.
23. Boyer, *Classification of Infinitives*, 22.
24. Baldwin et al., *Women in the Church*, 120.
25. Bible Hub, *1 Timothy 2:15*.
26. Keating, *Greek Verbs*.
27. Mounce, *Basics of Biblical Greek*.
28. Mounce, *Basics of Biblical Greek*.

29. Goodrick and Kohlenberger, *NIV Exhaustive Concordance*, 1537, 1596.

30. Goodrick and Kohlenberger, *NIV Exhaustive Concordance*, 1537, 1597.

31. Bible Study Tools, *1 Timothy 2:15*.

32. Wiktionary, *Filius*.

33. Harper, *Online Etymology Dictionary*.

34. Green, *Grammar of Greek Testament*, 150.

35. Green, *Grammar of Greek Testament*, 150.

36. Green, *Grammar of Greek Testament*, 153.

37. Cook, *He Kaine Diatheke*, 97.

Chapter 9: Overseers, Deacons, and Elders

1. Goodrick and Kohlenberger, *NIV Exhaustive Concordance*, 1597.

2. Bible Hub, *1 Timothy 3:1*.

3. Goodrick and Kohlenberger, *NIV Exhaustive Concordance*, 1475.

4. Goodrick and Kohlenberger, *NIV Exhaustive Concordance*, 1586.

5. Goodrick and Kohlenberger, *NIV Exhaustive Concordance*, 1552.

6. Goodrick and Kohlenberger, *NIV Exhaustive Concordance*, 1527, 1598.

7. Goodrick and Kohlenberger, *NIV Exhaustive Concordance*, 1590.

8. Palmer, *Masculine and Neuter Adjectives*.

BIBLIOGRAPHY

Agnes, Michael, ed. *Webster's New World College Dictionary*. 4th ed. Cleveland, OH: Wiley Publishing, Inc., 2006.

Appendix J. *Is the Prohibition, of 1 Tim. 2:12, Only Prohibiting a Woman "Teaching Over a Man?"* n.d. Accessed April 12, 2013. http://five-publishing.com/appendixj.pdf.

Baldwin, Henry, S. M. Baugh, Andreas Kostenberger, ed., Dorothy Patterson, Thomas Schreiner, ed., and Robert Yarbrough. *Women in the Church*. 2nd ed. Grand Rapids, MI: Baker Academic, 2005.

Bible Hub. *1 Peter 2:18*. 2004–2020. https://biblehub.com/1_peter/2-18.htm.

Bible Hub. *1 Timothy 2:15*. 2004–2020. https://biblehub.com/text/1_timothy/2-15.htm.

Bible Hub. *1 Timothy 3:1*. 2004–2020. https://biblehub.com/text/1_timothy/3-1.htm.

Bible Study Tools. *1 Timothy 2:15 (The Latin Vulgate w/ Apocrypha)*. 2013. http://www.biblestudytools.com/vula/1-timothy/2-15.html.

Boyer, James L. *The Classification of Infinitives: A Statistical Study*. Grace Theological Journal 6.1, 1985. http://www.biblicalstudies.org.uk/pdf/gtj/06-1_003.pdf.

Bushnell, Katharine C. *God's Word to Women*. Minneapolis, MN: Christians for Biblical Equality, [1921] 2003.

Cook, Terry. *Notes for the Study of He Kaine Diatheke*. n.d. http://www.scrollandscreen.com/files/Greek%20Notes.TerryCook.pdf.

Freedman, R. David. *Woman, a Power Equal to Man*. In Biblical Archaeology Review 9, 1983.

Goodrick, Edward W., and John R. Kohlenberger III. *The Strongest NIV Exhaustive Concordance*. Grand Rapids, MI: Zondervan, 1999.

Green, Samuel Gosnell. *Handbook to the Grammar of the Greek Testament*. n.d. http://books.google.com/books?id=R1FFAAAAYA AJ&pg=PR24&lpg=PR24dq=exam.

Harper, D. In *Online Etymology Dictionary*. 2013. Accessed March 2, 2013. http://www.etymonline.com/index.php?term=generation.

Keating, Cory. *Greek Verbs*. n.d. http://ntgreek.org/learn_nt_greek/ verbs1.htm.

Larsen, Iver. *Word Order and Relative Prominence in New Testament Greek*. 2001. http://www.academia.edu/749499/ Word_order_and_relative_prominence_in_New_Tes.

Marlowe, Michael. *The Woman's Headcovering*. 2008. Accessed March 15, 2010. http://www.bible-researcher.com/headcoverings.html.

Martin, Charlie. *Tasso – Appointed or Ordained*. 2011. Accessed August 27, 2012. http://acharlie.tripod.com/doct/elect30.html.

Mounce, William D. *Basics of Biblical Greek*. 2000. http://www.teknia.com/ public/pdf/Summary.pdf.

Nunn, Henry Preston. *Key to the Elements of New Testament Greek*. Cambridge: University Press, 1915.

Ramey, William. *Sights and Sounds of Greek Words*. 1996. Accessed November 1, 2011. http://www.inthebeginning.org/ntgreek/lesson3/ lesson3.pdf.

Newberry, Alfred L. *The Divine Pattern Advocate*. n.d. http://docplayer. net/145677651-The-divine-pattern-advocate.html.

234

Palmer, Michael W. *Lesson 5: Masculine and Neuter Adjectives.* 2009. http://greek-language.com/grammar/05.html.

Wikipedia. *Cornerstone.* n.d. Accessed July 1, 2011. http://en.wikipedia.org/wiki/Cornerstone.

Wiktionary. *Filius.* 2013. Accessed February 26, 1013. http://www.en.wiktionary.org/wiki/filiorum.

Zodhiates, Spiros. *The Complete Word Study Dictionary.* Chattanooga, TN: AMG Publishers, 1992.

CPSIA information can be obtained
at www.ICGtesting.com
Printed in the USA
BVHW080046070521
606650BV00003B/327